Fugitive Modernities

Fugitive Modernities

Kisama

AND THE POLITICS OF FREEDOM

———

JESSICA A. KRUG

DUKE UNIVERSITY PRESS *Durham & London* 2018

© 2018 Duke University Press
All rights reserved
Printed in the United States of America on acid-free paper ∞
Designed by by Matthew Tauch
Typeset in Garamond Premier Pro by Westchester

Library of Congress Cataloguing-in-Publication Data
Names: Krug, Jessica A., [date] author.
Title: Fugitive modernities : Kisama and the politics of
freedom / Jessica A. Krug.
Description: Durham : Duke University Press, 2018. |
Includes bibliographical references and index.
Identifiers: LCCN 2018016917 (print) |
LCCN 2018019866 (ebook)
ISBN 9781478002628 (ebook)
ISBN 9781478001195 (hardcover : alk. paper)
ISBN 9781478001546 (pbk. : alk. paper)
Subjects: LCSH: Sama (Angolan people) | Fugitive
slaves—Angola. | Fugitive slaves—Colombia. | Fugitive
slaves—Brazil.
Classification: LCC DT1308.S34 (ebook) | LCC DT1308.S34
K78 2018 (print) | DDC 305.896/36—dc23
LC record available at https://lccn.loc.gov/2018016917

Cover art: Francisco McCurry, *We Are Here: 3076*. Mixed
media on paper, 9 in. × 12 in. Courtesy of the artist.

I HAVE LONG BELIEVED that love is not possible in translation, and yet, inevitably, I find myself interpreting ways of seeing the world, of being, of knowing, from one context to another, daily. It goes far deeper than language.

This is a book about the political imagination and intellectual labor of fugitives. It is about people who didn't write, by choice. And yet, it is a book. A textual artifact created by someone who learned to tell stories and ask questions from those who never read or wrote, but who loves the written word. It is an act of translation. It is a love letter.

It is an inadequate and perhaps unintelligible love letter to and for those who do not read. My grandparents, who gave me the best parts of themselves, music and movement and storytelling, the inclination to ask and the soul to listen. My ancestors, unknown, unnamed, who bled life into a future they had no reason to believe could or should exist. My brother, the fastest, the smartest, the most charming of us all. Those whose names I cannot say for their own safety, whether in my barrio, in Angola, or in Brazil.

It is a love letter for all of those who have been murdered fighting for freedom, and all of those who stay dying because we have not yet achieved it. It is a love letter for my siblings in solitary, from Rikers to San Quentin, for my cousins being held on gang charges, for my femmes turning tricks. For those who will never be cloaked in the protective veil of innocence woven from five centuries of theft and dismemberment.

It is a love letter for the youth in Angola who find new languages to articulate their unwillingness to smilingly comply with their own murder at the hands of those who claim the right to rule over the sunken-eyed corpse of hollow revolutionary slogans.

It is a love letter for all of us who have no choice but to dream an entirely different way forward.

I wouldn't be here, writing this love letter, if I myself were not formed from the love of all I've named and all I can't name.

———

CONTENTS

═══════

ACKNOWLEDGMENTS

For years, I told everyone who knew I was writing a book that my entire acknowledgments section would be cribbed from Biggie: "This book is dedicated to all the teachers who told me I'd never amount to nothing . . ." And while there is no small part of me that is still tempted to leave it there, to stunt on every institution and person who has ever stood in my way, by framing my work or Biggie's like this, we reinforce the pernicious idea that amounting to something can be measured by the metrics that I inherently reject.

I don't know if I've amounted to anything or not, but I know that the love and labor of a worldwide community of people has made this book possible.

But those who know already know, and listing them here is superfluous. Community is not built through an economy of gratitude.

And so I won't name individuals here, because there are other, better ways of telling you how essential you are, how critical we are.

Institutions and funders operate under different logics, however. Here, I acknowledge the substantial financial and institutional support for this project, from its inception, from the University of Wisconsin–Madison, the SSRC, Fulbright-Hayes, the Department of Education, George Washington University, the Schomburg Center for Research in Black Culture, and the National Endowment for the Humanities.

NOTE ON CARTOGRAPHY

Visually depicting space and power—cartography—is a political act in every sense. Maps represent things not as they are, but rather as we need or want them to be for particular purposes. The conventions of mapmaking to which we are accustomed today are rooted in the very violent histories with which I grapple in this book. It is impossible to separate a north-up map or the typical centering of the Atlantic Ocean from the relationships of power that brought millions of Africans across this ocean in chains.

Thus, the maps in this book depart from convention. They do not center the Atlantic Ocean. They do not orient north.

In each case, these maps attempt to represent the political orientation of the historical actors in whom I am interested: fugitives. They did not face the ocean nor assume that power was ever northward. Reorienting these maps is an important part of this book's intervention, a critical element of reconceiving narratives of modernity.

LIST OF ARCHIVES AND ABBREVIATIONS

AGI   *Archivo General de Indias, Seville, Spain*

AHM   *Arquivo Histórico Militar, Lisbon, Portugal*

AHNA   *Arquivo Histórico Nacional de Angola, Luanda, Angola*

AHU   *Arquivo Histórico Ultramarino, Lisbon, Portugal*

BdA   *Biblioteca da Ajuda, Lisbon, Portugal*

IHGB   *Instituto Histórico e Geográfico Brasileiro, Rio de Janeiro, Brazil*

MMA   *Monumenta Missionária Africana*

Fugitive Modernities

Chronotope, Epistemology, and Subjectivity

In 1632, seven Portuguese captains ventured north from Rio de Janeiro into a region of Brazil to which Europeans had not yet directly brought their violence. There, they encountered a group of indigenous people and among them, one Black (*preto*) man. Because this meeting took place at a great distance from any established towns or plantations, the Portuguese captains were "perplexed" and asked the man "who he was and how he came to be" in the area. When he responded that he was an emancipated slave, the Portuguese asked him if he was Brazilian-born. He replied that he was not, but was rather "of the nation of Quissamã."[1] After noting that they did not see the man afterward, and surmising that he had fled from his master and was wary of their queries, the Portuguese captains named the location after him. It bears the name Quissamã to this day.[2] The same year, the former governor of the Portuguese colony of Angola, Fernão de Sousa, wrote from the colonial capital of Luanda of the fragility of the Portuguese military, slave raiding and trading, and plantation enterprises in the region that they had occupied for more than a half century, complaining that the "souas on whom we border are many and powerful, and warlike; in the province of Quissama . . . [they are] all non-Christians and our enemies."[3]

While the maroon in Brazil identifies Kisama as a nation and de Sousa casts it as a place, both drew on the same set of globally circulating signifiers that I refer to as "the Kisama meme." By the 1630s, the nonstate, nonliterate, and largely fugitive adults and children who fashioned the Kisama meme—a construction of Kisama as synonymous with a particularly belligerent, obdurate form of resistance to all outside authority or state power, African and European alike—had not only forged a political praxis that would shape action, discourse, and archives until the present, but had also ensnared diffuse people far from the ocean and mobile, merchant capital into a dynamic reputational geography. This is a study of the people who crafted and contested the changing ideologies concerning political legitimacy and the relationship of violence to community that bubbled beneath the seemingly still surface of the Kisama meme in West Central Africa and the Americas. This is a story of conflict *through* violence and conflict *about* violence in an era marked by unprecedented forms and scale of aggression against individuals and communities. The Kisama meme, and the reputational geography it engendered, not only drew fugitives from a broad swath of West Central Africa but also pulsed through the Americas, informing the intellectual repertoires and political technologies of fugitives from the seventeenth century forward. Narrating the history of political ideas of those who never wrote a word requires new methods, and creative application of older ones; tracing a five-century history of people whose existence was largely predicated upon and defined by their eschewing the very practices through which identities normally gain salience and political thought enters the archives necessitates new kinds of questions.

West Central Africans in the late sixteenth and seventeenth centuries experienced violence of unprecedented forms and catastrophic scale. While the Portuguese established regular diplomatic relationships with the expansionist Kingdom of Kongo beginning in the late fifteenth century, Portuguese merchants quickly expanded their trade in captive people to the south. As the Portuguese, and later the Dutch, moved along the coast and into the interior following the formal establishment of the colony in Luanda (1575), compelling the states like Kongo and Ndongo with whom they allied, fought, and traded to procure an ever-increasing number of captives for sale, these states directed their forces toward their neighbors. For the vast majority of those in the region, who did not live under the suzerainty of any powerful state, everyday life was fraught with peril. More than three and a half million West Central Africans were eventually bound in chains on board slave ships and transported to the Americas, most from Luanda and Benguela; at least twice that number were killed in the wars instigated by this trade. Countless more were up-rooted, alienated from family, community, and home, and cast into alien lands where they attempted to reconstitute viable communities. It is within this world that thousands of fugitives created and contested the meaning of Kisama as a political signifier, within this context of totaliz-ing terror that Africans and their descendants in the Americas drew from diverse repertoires of nonstate fugitive political ideologies to make a life in the endless echoes of death. Within this context, what did these geo-graphically and sociopolitically disparate seventeenth-century men mean when they identified "Kisama," either as a nation of origin or as the center of anti-Portuguese resistance? What did the fugitive in Brazil intend to convey when he spoke of himself as part of a "nation" which—even by seventeenth-century standards—without centralized authority, common political institutions, or shared and distinctive linguistic practices, hardly qualified? To gloss Kisama as a simple toponym referring to the arid lands between Angola's Kwanza and Longa Rivers is to miss the cross-regional, trans-Atlantic political processes through which thousands of the most individually weak and vulnerable people in sixteenth- and seventeenth-century Angola collectively fashioned dynamic political identities ori-ented around renouncing state formations, martial idioms for social organization, and resisting slavery, the slave trade, and imbrication in mar-ket economies. To grasp the meanings with which these fugitives imbued Kisama, too, requires embedding ourselves in a different epistemological framework, or system of ideas, that, in turn, fosters new chronotopes, or visions of time, and notions of subjectivity, or views of personhood.

We know this unnamed figure in Brazil through a Portuguese-ascribed racial designation ("preto") and, more importantly, through a political af-filiation he himself claimed ("of the nation of Quissamã"). We can also discern his social silhouette through the political discourse evinced by his fugitivity that preceded this encounter with the Portuguese, and his sub-sequent decision to flee yet again, after. This otherwise anonymous man in Brazil is the first person whom I have located in archival records who identified *himself* as Kisama, and it is no coincidence that he, as a fugi-tive, claimed membership in a "nation" that, by the 1630s, was renowned throughout Angola and the broader world as the home of resisters and runaways. While this archival Polaroid can only leave us guessing as to the political or social capital such an assertion would have carried for an Af-rican man seemingly alone in a community of indigenous Brazilians, the

Brazilian maroon expected his Portuguese interlocutors to understand his description of origins as a claim concerning political orientation. Kisama meant something to him, something that transcended the matter of origins that fascinated his Portuguese interlocutors then as much as it preoccupies scholars now, and he expected it to mean something, to convey something resonant about politics and space, even in this alien and alienating land. And it did. The synchronicity of these moments in Angola and Brazil, too, hints at a hidden history of revolutionary ideology circulating through Africa and the Americas in the early seventeenth century—a history silenced both as it was happening and as it was later narrated.[4]

Fugitive Modernities is the story of the political actions and intellectual labor that constituted the terrain of meaning and signification upon which these actors and others evoked Kisama in the sixteenth and seventeenth centuries until the present, from West Central Africa to the New Kingdom of Grenada (modern-day Colombia, Venezuela, Ecuador, and Panamá), Brazil, and beyond. At its root, it is the history of thousands of individually vulnerable fugitives from unprecedented violence and social and political rupture who constituted new communities that were collectively viable. Rather than embracing ideologies of centralization and hierarchy, however, these fugitives forged an ethos centered on the horizontal integration of newcomers. In both a material and symbolic sense, their very survival was predicated on martial skill and on projecting a reputation for military success; however, unlike other novel political entities of the period, those who evoked Kisama identities systemically rejected a martial idiom for social organization. As war became an integral part of life in West Central Africa throughout the seventeenth century and beyond, both older political entities and new formations placed warriors and warrior identities at the center of their schematic maps of social and political life. Warfare was essential, and in many societies, warriors, warrior masculinities, and the practices associated with warfare became the guiding paradigm for social and political life. Not so for those who constituted Kisama. And while those who became and made Kisama rejected centralized political authority and unification, to the frustration and disgruntlement of both African and European state leaders from the sixteenth to the twentieth centuries, much of what it meant to be Kisama derived from the reputation of one Kisama soba, Kafuxi Ambari.

Time Is Illmatic: Jita Kwatakwata, Archives, and the Multicontinental, Multicentury Life of Kafuxi Ambari

A history of Kisama requires a comprehensive reimagining of the terrain upon which we tell stories. Time, personhood, space: none of these are universal or apolitical categories.[5] Power imposes limitations on our imaginations, and this is nowhere more apparent than in this, an effort to tell the history of radical political ideas and practices that relies on sources and disciplinary practices fundamentally and inescapably rooted not only in different epistemes, or ways of knowing, but in ways of knowing that emerged as part of centuries of systemic murder, torture, rape, commodification, and bondage of the people whose lives and ideas are meant to sit at the center of this story. It is not enough to excavate evidence of existence, of political being, from an archive of terror. Rather, it is essential to employ the epistemes through which those who created Kisama made political and moral sense of the bloody milieu within which they lived, loved, and made new worlds.

In many important ways, this is a five-century, multicontinental biography of Kafuxi Ambari that challenges how we conceive of biography, life history, and subjectivities. As Clifton Crais and Pamela Scully note in their efforts to write the life history of Sara Baartman, "Biography... emerged at a particular time and place in Europe's imagining of the self.... It emerged along with the idea of the possessive individual, the person who has agency, autonomy, a vision of self. This idea of the person, of the self, is not so easily transferred to anytime and anyplace and to worlds where there is no clearly possessive subject, no 'me,' 'myself.'"[6]

So what are the possibilities for narrating life stories that emerge from alternate epistemes of self and subject? If the fundamental unit of being is not the liberal subject—the atomic individual with rights and obligations ensured by the legal apparatus of state—but rather a collective self, fashioned through the instrumental deployment of historical memory and rituo-political choreography, then, unsurprisingly, biography *must* function differently.[7] It cannot be bound by the limits of an individual life span or chained to the teloi or chronotopes of state. Instead, it must take seriously the ways of conceiving time and being that derive from and foster other political logics. To render Kisama's history through Kafuxi Ambari's biography and the reputational geographies he helped engender, I draw from archival sources intermeshed in their own generation with oral sources, and oral sources recurring to archival records—an effort to discern the oblique contours of complex political, intellectual, and social histories through the life of a single, rather atypical figure—with all of the caveats that microhistories inevitably entail.[8]

Here, it is useful to situate Kafuxi Ambari's nonstate subjectivity and the history of time, personhood, and ideology that I am endeavoring to tell in the context of a broader historical idiom, employed by Kimbundu speakers both in geographical Kisama and north of the Kwanza River: the Jita Kwatakwata.[9] "Jita Kwatakwata" translates directly as "War of Acquisition." The reduplication of the term *kwata* to *kwatakwata* serves to emphasize the unitary focus on acquisition, to the exclusion of the social reciprocity that normally governed political and economic relationships in the region. When Kimbundu speakers refer to the Jita Kwatakwata, they collapse a period beginning with the commencement of intensive slave raiding in the late fifteenth century all the way to the extractive economies of forced plantation agriculture in the twentieth century. More ruling party inflected versions of the chronotope end the Jita Kwatakwata with the uprising among cotton cultivators in the Baixa de Kasanje in 1961; living in the twentieth century doesn't change the materiality of slavery. Others, more wary of the ongoing topographies of extraction and exploitation in Angola, explain that the offshore petroleum comes from the bones of the enslaved whom the Portuguese tossed off of ships, and only when the oil is exhausted will the Jita Kwatakwata truly end. By framing history in this way, Kimbundu speakers make an argument about change over time that connects moral community to capital and politics—an idiom and argument far more effective than any provincially European chronotope.

Time is always an argument about power and morality. Epochs like "the Enlightenment" and "the Age of Revolution" posit a Whiggishness—a belief in progress over time—that surely crushes the bones of those on whom that progress for a few is built. This is a history set in the Jita Kwatakwata, and the choices and practices of the people whose story I tell—those who fled made Kisama, or some other fugitive modernity in Angola, those who rewove fugitive fabrics of community anew in the Americas—were conditioned by the bloody topographies of time and being within which they lived. But they could and did create other worlds, and using notions of subjectivity and time grounded in the political and moral epistemology of Kisama can help us access those worlds.

Telling Kisama's history in part as a biography of Kafuxi Ambari involves adopting a concept of personhood unfamiliar to many readers. When people within geographical Kisama refer to Kafuxi Ambari, they do so as if they are speaking of an individual. Specific elements of these histories, however, can be linked through external epistemologies—colonial archives—to events over a number of centuries in the written record. Scholars traditionally refer to this practice as positional succession, or "the notion that social roles or positions termed 'names' . . . with permanently defined rights and obligations exist independently of actual living persons."[10] However, this notion of positional succession serves more as a strategy of translation and less as an explanation of a radically different episteme. Positional succession as a construct assumes a contractual, statist notion of community and political and social order, and imposes it on contexts, like Kisama, where it does not belong.

Kafuxi Ambari was not a title, like "king" or "pope," but rather a living embodiment of the essence of an enduring subjectivity. In this sense, then, "Kafuxi Ambari" and names of other sobas referred to a particular structural relationship with both the ancestors and the living, a specific social contour of power and legitimacy.[11] Far from being easily synonymous with political titles, this widely dispersed practice in Africa points to notions of selfhood and identity centered on the incorporation of sedimented pasts into an embodied present—a nonlinear construct of time and being. Kafuxi Ambari was not a position to which any and all could aspire. In the late sixteenth and early seventeenth centuries, European and African conceptions of chronology and leadership were often far closer than a twenty-first-century person would imagine. Just as Kisama-based narrators speak of Kafuxi Ambari as a singular entity across the centuries, so too do records generated by the colonial officials and priests who were present in Angola from the sixteenth to the twentieth centuries refer to Kafuxi Ambari as one individual.[12]

This fortuitous archival silence compelled me to look for ways of understanding Kisama history that had more to do with how those who created Kisama in the seventeenth century understood time, being, and the world, and how their descendants, living in the brutal twenty-first-century machinations of the Jita Kwatakwata, comprehend the relationship of time, being, and narrative, and less to do with the imperatives of a liberal academic habitus. Because a conception of Kafuxi Ambari as a being who transcends the time of discrete, liberal selves is essential to understanding the emergence and contestation of the fugitive politics of Kisama, I refer to Kafuxi Ambari in the same terms and using the same pronouns as my sources: as a single person. What follows is thus the fractal biography of one man over centuries and continents, and the permutations of his reputation and evocation in disparate political and social spaces, toward remarkably consistent ends.

This is, of course, an act of narrative and conceptual imagination on my part. Narrative is *always* an act of selection, framing, editing, adjusting, silencing, and amplifying, and neither radical positivist nor constructivist pretensions alter the reality that choices regarding narrative structure always reflect and construct relations of power. While I certainly disagree with Benedict Anderson's famous notion that literacy is the basis for imagining modern political communities—this entire book may be read as a grounded rejection of Andersonian logics—there is an undeniable connection between narrative and social reality.[13] Indeed, there is something metanarrative about *Fugitive Modernities*; I am trying to tell the story of the ways in which those in Angola and the Americas, and their interlocutors globally, told the stories that made Kisama a potent tool of political conjuring.[14] Those whose political praxis and imagination created Kisama chose to eschew writing and forms of oral history and tradition that reinforce hierarchy, just as they rejected warrior identities and masculinities as the central ethos for their society. I take these choices as seriously as I do the political, aesthetic, and narrative conventions of my own indigenous language of hip hop, and use them to guide this story and the politics underpinning the ways in which I tell it.[15]

I do not pretend to offer an unmediated glimpse into the history of Kisama in this text. Communication is *always* mediated, and authenticity forever the armor of power, acknowledged or otherwise. Many of my sources will be familiar to students of West Central African and African Diaspora history. In my footnotes, you'll find the same assortment of military, colonial governmental, judicial, and missionary sources from the same colonial archives that grace the pages of all canonical works in the field. While I gesture backward in time, I principally begin my story in 1594, when Kisama first leaves its most profound imprint in the colonial archive, and indeed argue that the events of 1594 are essential to the geography of reputation at the core of Kisama's history. This is an approach to archives that, while building on the insights of Michel-Rolph Trouillot, Ann Stoler, Luise White, Nancy Rose Hunt, and others, owes much, too, to the work of Neil Kodesh and others who insist on reading archival sources through the epistemic lens of oral histories, with sensitivity to genre and setting.[16] My assertion that the history of Kisama is a biography of Kafuxi Ambari is, of course, my own narrative polemic, rooted in the voices and silences through which people in Kisama construct their own stories, and always aware and wary of the contours of power of the world in which we live.

Ten years ago, Saidiya Hartman asked, "How can a narrative of defeat enable a place for the living or envision any alternative future?"[17] Hartman's question compels us to do far more than weigh between a narrative pole of agency that obfuscates horror or one of totalizing brutality that erases being. She challenges us to accept neither the inhuman anti-Blackness of the archive nor the problematically one-note heroics as the threads linking our present to our past. Taking Hartman's query as a starting point, in *Fugitive Modernities*, I engage ways of knowing about time, being, and political imagination that come from those who built worlds outside of state hegemony in the past, and ask how these imaginations help us ask questions of our present that can open a future always already foreclosed to the children of slaves in a liberal capitalist state hegemony.

Bemoaning archival silences places the historian in the role of the slave catcher, prowling through the darkness to capture the bodies of those fleeing violence and terror to subject them to bright searchlights, interrogations, and all manner of disciplining/disciplinary brutality.[18] The absence of those in whose histories I am most interested from the archives is a reason to celebrate, not mourn. The extent to which Kisama is and has remained a blank spot on the map, materially and symbolically, represents the degree to which the fugitive politics of Kisama has been successful. Of course, not all who evade the violence through which African people and their descendants in the Americas enter the archives live and die unmarked by the viciousness of state and capital.[19] However, it is certain that none who enter the archives do.[20] *Fugitive Modernities* is not a romance, nor is it a tragedy.[21] I claim not to uncover or recover anything so much as to take seriously the intellectual work of fugitives and to ask how the epistemic, ontological, and chronotypical paradigms they devised— their ways of conceiving knowledge, categories of being, and the nature of time—compel not only a different narrative of Kisama history, or of Angolan history, but also of the history of modernity itself.

Here, I differ both methodologically and politically from the approach of other scholars like Marisa Fuentes, who powerfully critiques, "The manner in which the violent systems and structures of white supremacy produced devastating images of enslaved female personhood, and how these pervade the archive and govern what can be known about them."[22] While I share Fuentes's impetus to make clear the imperial nature of archives, to register that these archives not only record material acts of violence, but themselves engender discursive and epistemic aggression, this is not the story of archives nor of those whose regimes of power they buttressed. Archives, state power, and capitalism do not represent the only ways of knowing about the world past or present, and it is the forms, shapes, and content of the other stories possible through these other regimes of knowledge that interest me. I stand on the shoulders of those without whose important critique of archives and the practice of history this work would be impossible, but I remain committed to fugitivity as both the focus of this history and as a paradigm.

Like Aisha Finch, I too perceive the archives as a "pedagogy of state terror [that] contains a variety of teachings for those who study its history." In writing about La Escalera Rebellion in nineteenth-century Cuba, Finch problematizes both scholarly and popular views of the action and agency of enslaved and fugitive people in the Americas that efface the political and intellectual labor of those who do not enter the archives, and fixate instead on the totalizing violence of state. And so too, like Finch, here I endeavor to write a history of the rural, non-elite, nonmercantalist, nonliterate thinkers and actors who "knew those lessons [of totalizing state violence, as encoded in the archives], but defied them anyway."[23] Indeed, it is these histories of ideas and political action at the greatest distance from the institutions of power that create archives that hold the greatest potential for opening new terrain of political imagination and action.

Meaning from the Margins: Against Identity and the Black Atlantic

Located at the ground zero bull's-eye of the trans-Atlantic slave trade, between the Portuguese colonial ports of Luanda and Benguela— the first- and third-highest volume ports of the trans-Atlantic slave trade, respectively—residents and interlocutors of geographical Kisama inescapably shaped and were shaped by the features of violence, capital, and subjugation that are often bundled under problematically benign terms like "the (Black) Atlantic" or "modernity."[24] However, beginning in the late sixteenth century, the particular political, intellectual, martial, social, and cultural responses of African people to the mounting violence that accompanied the expansion of both slavery and the slave trade in the region led to the emergence of Kisama identities associated as much with resistance, military efficacy, spiritual power, political decentralization, and the harboring of fugitives as with the earlier connection to high-quality rock salt. The story of how Kisama grew to convey particular political meanings is at once intensely local and profoundly global. It requires grounding in the deep past of West Central Africa, but also in the complexities of Central American and Caribbean pirate cultures, and the labor, gender, and ideological contours of the lives of Africans and their descendants within and against the institution of American (hemispherically speaking) chattel slavery.

By any measure, geographical Kisama is a small, remote place. The territory between the Kwanza and Longa Rivers occupies roughly 8,700 square miles, or about the same area as the state of Massachusetts.[25] While it is only approximately forty miles from Luanda to the nearest part of geographical Kisama along the Atlantic coast, the social distance from the capital has long been considerably greater. Since at least the sixteenth century, the region has been relatively sparsely populated, at least in relation to the Central Plateau and the Lukala and Bengo River valleys, in no small part because of its endemic aridity.[26] Though the relationship between the natural dryness of the land and the subsistence patterns of those living on it undoubtedly changed during the sixteenth- and seventeenth-century period on which I focus here—perhaps most importantly, through the adoption of the American cultigens manioc, maize, and sweet potatoes, as I discuss in chapter 3—the regularity of drought in the region does seem to be an enduring feature.[27] While a lack of rain may have been a long-standing attribute of the region, we should read the historical descriptions of the region's depopulation through endemic disease and drought with a degree of skepticism. Beyond the highly questionable methodology (read: varying degrees of poorly informed speculation) through which these observers obtained their estimates, it is worth noting that the high mortality that early twentieth-century German soldier and ethnographer Ernst Wilhelm Mattenklodt's source attributes to sleeping sickness belies the large number of those killed and displaced in Portuguese early twentieth-century efforts to fully occupy the land and impose forced cultivation of cotton on the people living there. Later colonial accounts of population are suspect because they reinforce Portuguese arguments in favor of declaring the area first a game reserve (1938) and later a national park (1957).[28] Twentieth-century colonial, state, and conservationalist actors interested in maintaining the region as a game park and national park have instrumentally forged a national and international imagination of the region between the Kwanza and Longa Rivers as devoid of human settlement and history—a blank space on the map.[29] Indeed, despite all of the advancement of technology and outsider knowledge about the region, even today, most maps show nothing in the region save the national park and, perhaps, the colonial fort at Muxima on the banks of the Kwanza River, and Cabo Ledo, the government's fantasy aspirational tourist surf destination at the bar of the river. In the most literal sense, then, Kisama has been and remains an empty space in the imaginary within and about Angola, on the maps that define and delineate the modern nation-state as they did the imperial designs on the colony.

Some of the most prominent historians and anthropologists of Africa have long studied West Central Africa, and seventeenth-century Angola in particular, but Kisama always plays at the margins of this work. The historiography tends to focus either on the machinations of states and their considerable archival corpus, or on those who generated archives through their purchase and sale of human beings.[30] In a sea of literature about Kongo, Ndongo and Matamba, and, in recent years, the port of Benguela, there are only two works that focus on Kisama, beyond sporadic footnotes: Beatrix Heintze's 1970 article (translated in abridged form from German to English in 1972) and Aurora da Fonseca Ferreira's 2012 book.[31] Heintze treats Kisama as critical in a broader regional politics as a haven for fugitives, and Ferreira largely narrates earlier Kisama history by way of locating it in a twentieth-century ruling party narrative of resistance. But neither Heintze nor Ferreira interrogates the relationship between Kisama's strategic marginality, its absence from archives, and the means through which a particular kind of fugitive modernity emerged in Kisama.

As marginal as Kisama is in the literature of Angolan history, it is nonexistent in Diasporic texts. Kisama has not left an obvious mark in the Americas in the same way that other African ur-identities, like Yoruba

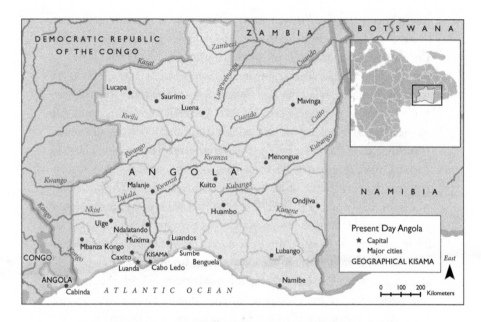

Map Intro.1 — Present Day Angola. Map by Heather Rosenfeld.

or Kongo, have. There are no practices or people in the Americas labeled Kisama who reverberate with anthropological and cultural/nationalist visions of Blackness. In terms of seemingly straightforward toponymic connections, there are only a handful of places in the Americas that are named Kisama—two towns in Brazil (including the one in Rio de Janeiro mentioned above and another in Sergipe), one in Panamá, and one in Chile. What can these toponyms tell us, however? In the case of the town in Rio de Janeiro, even the apparently obvious connection between the self-proclaimed provenance of a single seventeenth-century individual and the name of the town obscures centuries of political and social imaginations and imaginaries. There is no clear, direct link between the seventeenth century and today that does not pass through the reentrenchment of slavery in Rio and beyond in the nineteenth century, and the subsequent growth of sugar plantations around Quissamã, but stories of origins inevitably excise these bloody complexities.

Indeed, the Brazilian municipality's account of the origins of the name moves beyond relating the maroon's tale at the beginning of this book, further contending that Kisama (Quissamã) is "a word with Angolan origin which signifies 'fruit of the land that is located between the river and the sea' and gave its name to a city 80 km from Luanda, at the mouth of the Kwanza River, that was the principal origin of blacks who were sold or traded in Brasil."[32] This highly imaginative account of the lexicon, geography, historical relations, and demography of the trans-Atlantic slave trade dates to a twenty-first century visit of Angolan government officials to the area. Overlooking the tangled interrelations of politics, ideologies, identities, and economies over a global four centuries not only blurs our concept of *Kisama*'s particular histories—and Quissamã's—but it also obfuscates the very nature of history itself. If history is naught but a telos of a bounded people who were always already coherent, in possession of a self-evident identity, then—even from the perspective of storytelling—what conflicts can possibly drive the narrative? Such quests, understandably animated by a desire to salve the gaping wounds of centuries of the slave trade, slavery, and its colonial life and legacies in both the Americas and Africa, replace the burden of an unknowable history with answers that stifle a possibility of political imagination and creativity beyond moribund colonial statist anthropological views of Africans. Replacing "tribe" with "ethnicity" or "culture" doesn't render these ways of thinking of Africa any less one-dimensional, and substituting the derision of white supremacy ("Africans were primitives!") with flattened, state and state-aspirational politics ("Africans had kingdoms, too! And our ancestors brought the practices of these states with them to the Americas!") not only ignores the histories and worlds of most African people but it promises that our political imagination will remain hollow, stillborn, forever shackled to a fantasy built on the very violence we seek to address.

As James Lorand Matory keenly observed, since its inception throughout the Americas, and particularly in the United States, African Diasporic scholarship has been preoccupied by questions of identity that center geographical origins and are animated by geographic logics.[33] Though some, like Mariza de Carvalho Soares, Luis Nicolau Parés, and James Sweet, have pointed to the multiplicity and fluidity of African identities, arguing that over a lifetime and depending on context many Africans, both on the continent and in the Americas, claimed multiple identities, even for these more process-oriented scholars, identity is still, primarily, a function of geographic origin.[34] Others focus on the role that European (mis)conceptions played in assigning nation labels to African people in the Americas. Pablo Gómez, echoing scholarship by Mariana Candido and others, characterizes *naciones* (*nações* in Portuguese) as "African ethnic groups as defined by Europeans."[35] This recent focus on process, multiplicity, and the power relationships encoded in nation labels represents a more nuanced and sophisticated approach to African Diasporic nations than generations of straightforwardly geographically deterministic scholarship. However, the literature still remains engrossed with geographic origins as the primary component of identity, and with a notion of identity as a materiality, a characteristic or set of characteristics someone has or doesn't have.

However, my research in other contexts suggests that identity is less a materiality and more of a language through which people describe and orient politics, often independent from geography. In eighteenth-century Jamaica, enslaved and fugitive people from origins as diverse as Madagascar, Kongo, Calabar (modern-day southeastern Nigeria), and throughout the Americas evoked a Kromanti identity—which scholars typically identify as connoting origins in Akan-speaking parts of present-day Ghana—as a means of constructing communities of resistance. Kromanti identity was never about the fishing village whose name it shares, but rather signified a ritual practice and oath, a political idiom, that emerged after a devastating betrayal and the loss of both a head of state and the means by which to properly memorialize him. The oath, employed in both West Africa and the Americas, became a means by which those from diverse geographic origins could link acts of memory with the political practice of reconstituting viable communities bound together by oath.[36] Whether articulating an identity that cohered around a ritual idiom, like Kromanti, or a geography of reputation, like Kisama, African nation identities—so-called ethnic identities more globally—are *always* primarily political claims rather than ascriptions of location or origin.

An instructive example comes from the excellent scholarship on perhaps the most omnipresent and iconic of all African Diasporic ur-identities, the Yoruba. A semiotic view of Yoruba ritual as history combined with political economy enable us to see purity and primordialism as instrumental discourses in a broader field of political and economic power.[37] Amplifying the analysis of Stephan Palmié, Matory, and others in the case of Yoruba identities, what if we begin to ask what *identity means at all*, even in the cases where it would seem to cohere with earlier anthropological constructs, such as possession of a shared language and distinct set of cultural practices, evocation of a centralized political regime, and so on? Kisama's contingent, constructed nature should not stand as an exception in a field contoured largely through an implicit notion of the materiality of identities, particularly those associated with kingdoms legible through Eurocentric epistemologies and ontologies (e.g., Oyo, Kongo, Dahomey). Following Vincent Brown's call to move beyond the "mistaken impression that people's sole aim was to achieve a distinct cultural identity"—a preoccupation determined by the devastating culturalist obsessions of twentieth- and twenty-first-century states—I instead interrogate the political work and ideological valences that those invoking Kisama meant to do, whether in Africa or the Americas. Because the intellectual underpinnings of this labor are visible to us only through fractured archives and evidence of action, Brown describes this as "the politics of practical behavior."[38] Here, and throughout my work, "politics" refers not to the institutional relationship between state or state-sanctioned entities, but rather to the machinations and maneuverings of individuals, constituencies, and communities in relationship to power. This expansive view of politics excludes little. Its inclusiveness, however, allows us to move beyond antiquated notions of culture and identity—and equally outdated yet enduring notions of atavism and Africa—to use the seemingly marginal case of Kisama to advance new understandings of political thought outside of states, its relationship to modernity, alternate chronotopes emerging from fugitive epistemologies, and new concepts of personhood and subjectivity springing from this newly imagined space/time.

I seek to unravel the processes by which Kisama shifted from a primarily geographical referent in the lexicon of Kongo nobility ("the province of Kisama") to one with which fugitives identified politically ("the nation of Quissamã") through debates over the meaning and the contours of political legitimacy and its relationship to violence in a world characterized for most by dislocation, alienation, and deprivation.[39] In Angola, changes in local conceptions about the relationship between military prowess and leadership during the late sixteenth century, and in particular the emergence of a charismatic and particularly martially and spiritually powerful soba named Kafuxi Ambari, animated the development of an internally relevant and externally compelling Kisama meme. The Kisama meme is a remarkably abiding discourse across time (sixteenth century to the present) and space (Africa, the Americas, and Europe) in which Kisama is characterized through (1) the importance and universal desirability of the rock salt mines at Ndemba; (2) the fundamentally obdurate and martially and spiritually potent nature of its inhabitants, especially the soba Kafuxi

Ambari; and (3) the dedication with which the people of Kisama welcomed maroons and fugitives, harbored them, and fought to defend them. Those participating in this process transformed the meaning of Kisama from a territorial referent to a set of traits modeled on the exceptional qualities and practices of Kafuxi Ambari, including ferocity, commitment to autonomy, and intractable resistance. As the reputation of geographical Kisama as the locus of effective military resistance grew, it attracted thousands of runaways, including entire groups of trained soldiers from the armies of Ndongo and Portugal and large numbers of women. These fugitives in turn reconfigured the political and ideological landscape of Kisama, preserving and encouraging the association of Kisama with martial skill and spiritual aptitude while—in contrast to other groups, like the Imbangala, who also formed in response to the omnipresent violence and dislocation of the period—refusing to institutionalize martial social idioms.[40] Kisama became a society of warriors by reputation while abjuring the creation of any enduring warrior class. It is no coincidence that during this same critical period of the 1630s, Kisama-identified people first appear in sources from the Americas, almost always in conjunction with maroonage and resistance, as in the case of the Brazilian anecdote above or the several Kisama-identified men and women who appear in documents concerning a *palenque* (maroon settlement) outside of Cartagena in 1634.

A study of Kisama can therefore illuminate the complex history of Africans in Africa and the Americas during the era of the trans-Atlantic slave trade from the perspective of the vulnerable as they worked to transform themselves into the collectively inviolable. By studying Kisama, we can understand how local histories informed global historical memories for centuries, and how these global historical memories in turn dialogically shaped local practices and identities; indeed, Kisama's history compels us to move beyond the politically coded language of "local" and "global." We are further driven to reimagine time, space, and being, in order to locate Kisama and multiple Kisama-like streams of consciousness emanating from without and against states at the center of the modern world. Modernity looks different from Kisama, and Kisama is far from exceptional, globally. What we thought we knew about modernity has largely been a product of our complicity with state hegemonies.

Those who imbued Kisama with its reputations are paradigmatic examples of the sort of people James C. Scott evoked in his work to develop "a global history of populations trying to avoid, or having been extruded by, the state."[41] Scott calls for a transnational, cross-regional approach that understands "hill people" in a mutually constitutive relationship with the states in resistance to whom their identities were forged and reforged. Arguing against scholarship that tends to, unsurprisingly, replicate ontologies of state by viewing those who live outside of centralized political entities as uncivilized remnants of an earlier stage of human political development (often glossed, especially in Africanist scholarship, as "the hinterlands"), Scott asserts that fragmented, diverse, and noncentralized political regions evolved as conscious responses to the acquisitive, repressive nature of states. According to Scott, "Shatter zones are found wherever the expansion of states, empires, slave-trading, and wars, as well as natural disasters, have driven large numbers of people to seek refuge in out-of-the-way places."[42] Geographical Kisama is exactly such a place, where fugitives from kingdoms and expansionist powers in the north, south, and east had long settled, and where those fleeing Portuguese incursions from at least the early seventeenth century into the twentieth found refuge. Archaeological, linguistic, botanical, and further oral historical research is necessary to be able to say with certainty, but Kisama likely served as a haven from expanding states since the fifteenth- and early sixteenth-century conquests of Kongo and Ndongo.[43] It is Kisama's status as a shatter zone, or long-standing maroon society, that makes it an ideal place from which to reconfigure many of the most basic categories of time and space. Beyond redefining approaches to African and African Diasporic histories, and emphatically scuttling the "Atlantic" and all of its modifiers (Black, African, etc.), I seek to delineate a new intellectual terrain.[44] The putative heuristic value of "the Atlantic," however qualified by Blackness, Africanity, or any other modifier, is considerably less than its conceptual weakness and political alignment with effacing the bloody hegemonies of capital and state.

On Time and Being: Imagining History and Consciousness beyond the State

A serious study of the political ideologies underlying the formation of fugitive communities—societies that shunned centralization, the adoption of statist technologies like lineage, history, and writing, and the naturalization of idioms of violence or social identification with warriors—compels a reimagination of some of the critical concepts used by historians and so-cial scientists, not just of Africa, but of the world. If we date modernity to Columbus's voyages or to the French Revolution, to urban industrializa-tion or to the advent of nation-states as the hegemonic form of spatiopo-litical organization, do we inherently relegate the peoples of Africa, Latin America and the Caribbean, Asia, and the Pacific Islands to the exclusive role of labor and/or cultural inputs, malcontents or after-the-beat reac-tionaries?[45] And if we accept even the seemingly more radical notion of "alternate" modernities emanating from states outside of Western Europe, or from imperial subjects' interlocution with Western Europe, do we then inherently deny the histories of other political trajectories and the inter-related systems of spatiotemporal imaginations and subjectivities they fostered? If being "a people without history" is a deliberate choice rather than a developmental failure, what animates that choice, and what are its consequences? What happens when we adopt ways of organizing knowl-edge that arise from within fugitive societies as analytic categories?[46]

Since at least the mid-1990s, scholars have assailed the still-prevailing convention of dividing the history of Africa (and the rest of the world outside of Europe, for that matter) into precolonial, colonial, and postco-lonial periods.[47] The shortcomings of this schematic are clear: "It 'privi-leges as primary the role of colonialism', and implies that 'all that came before colonialism becomes its own prehistory and whatever comes after can only be lived as infinite aftermath.'"[48] From a historical perspective, this periodization flattens everything that came before the Europeans into a single, indistinct mass, attributes agency only to European actors and those Africans who were influenced by and emulated them, and im-poses the illusion of autonomy onto people who don't experience their own lives as postcolonial in any meaningful way. For example, the Con-golese soldiers who, mere days after the official declaration of indepen-dence on June 30, 1960, witnessed the Belgian commander who remained in charge of the supposedly sovereign national army write "Before Inde-pendence = After Independence" on a chalk board, would likely contest such categories.[49] Surely, no one imagines that an eleventh-century mer-chant in an urban settlement in the Niger River bend or a goatherd in the twelfth-century Sahel or a blacksmith in fourteenth-century Central Africa paused during their daily activities to wonder when colonialism would commence and their history would begin. So what categories did these goatherds and blacksmiths, farmers and fisherpeople, weavers and potters, use to imagine time? And what do we lose in understanding the worlds they occupied when we neglect to even ask this?

And, indeed, when *did* colonialism begin? Did colonialism arrive in West Central Africa in 1482 on board Diogo Cão's ships, or with Paulo Dias de Novais's formal establishment of a colony in Luanda in 1575? Were those who were forced to work growing manioc in the Lukala and Bengo River valleys of early seventeenth-century Angola colonial subjects? Were their contemporaries who lived under vassalage treaties with the Portuguese? Did a child captured deep in the interior, forcibly marched to the coast, boarded on a slave ship in chains, and then made to labor until death on a sugar plantation in Brazil transition from pre-colonial Africa to colonial Latin America? Did colonialism start only after 1808, though the British abolition of the slave trade would take another few decades to impact life in the region? Or was it the other date commonly recognized by those who divide African history curricula: the beginning of the so-called scramble for Africa in the late nineteenth century? The Portuguese did not gain full territorial control over geographical Kisama until the 1920s. Does that mean that Kisama alone was precolonial and experienced only fifty years of colonial rule, even in the shadow of the sixteenth-century Portuguese fort at Muxima? Such questions merely illustrate the indefensible teleology and Eurocentric perspective of the precolonial/colonial/postcolonial divide. Furthermore, they reinforce how, given Portuguese marginality within Europe and the conventional scholarship of empires, the common use of the nineteenth century as the dividing line only renders places like Guinea-Bissau, São Tomé, Cape Verde, Angola, and Mozambique further outside of the normative discussions about African history.

Into the twentieth century, Portuguese colonial officials still spoke of the necessity of conquering Kisama and bringing it into the colonial sphere, and yet the Portuguese built a fort on the southern banks of the Kwanza River, in geographic Kisama, in the late sixteenth century. In the early sixteenth century, the king of Kongo claimed Kisama as one of his provinces, and yet in the mid-seventeenth century, Njinga described the conquest of Kisama as something no one had yet accomplished.[50] While there is no doubt that the violence through which the Portuguese and other European powers and their allies acquired bondsmen and women for sale was on an unprecedented scale, there is no reason to assume that those who may have fled across the Kwanza River to escape Kongo and

Ndongo state power would have understood their political options in radically different terms than later fugitives from the Portuguese. Further, as in many other cases, West Central Africans likely understood their lived experiences of violence through the lens of regional political conflicts, again troubling our neat divisions between "local" and "global" categories. Only centuries of hindsight, for example, makes it possible to extend the notion of colonialism backward to include these state expansions—and characterizing resistance to it as anticolonial—but inevitably ignores the particularities of local politics in favor of adopting a concept that fails to even adequately explain practices of Europeans in the fifteenth through twentieth centuries.

The long scholarly collusion in identifying Angola—the place from which more people left the continent in chains than any other—as a *feitoria*, or trading post, rather than as a colony, silences the connections across the long centuries of Portuguese violence in Angola.[51] This was all the Jita Kwatakwata, and debates about the distinctions in European desires and intentions center agents of devastation in the history of those against whom they turned their destructive powers. The notion of precolonial, colonial, and postcolonial realities reveals less about the experiences and paradigms of most of the world and more about what those who benefited from this exploitation thought about it. They are etic categories, or ideas from outside the realities and paradigms of those whom they pretend to describe, that foreclose possibilities, political imaginations.

Because colonial time has a spatial element as well, deracinating my study of Kisama from a temporal ontology centered on colonization compels me to define a new conceptual terrain within which to locate my research, separate from—or at least distinct within—the most obvious field within which to locate a study of Kisama history: the long, dynamic body of scholarship concerning the African Diaspora and, in the last couple of decades, the newer domain of (Black) Atlantic Studies. Both of these approaches are tacitly undergirded by colonial time and undermined by their conflation of time, space, and politics. In particular, the popular notion of "creolization" and "Atlantic creoles" correlates cultural change with European contact.[52] By contrast, my study of Kisama and my notion of fugitive modernities allow us to follow the political practices and discursive strategies of those fleeing from and resisting the violence of states—in this period, violence closely associated with the trans-Atlantic slave trade—without yoking agency to actors' embeddedness within states. Those who forged Kisama politics in Angola were not the African source of a more modern African American cultural or political practice, nor the more backward kin of their neighbors in Kongo or Ndongo. Rather, their histories provide a critical perspective on intellectual and political history in sixteenth- and seventeenth-century Africa and the Americas distinct from the problematic chronotopes of earlier scholarship.

While the often depoliticized culturalist discourse underlying much of the scholarship on the African Diaspora emerged out of a desire by scholars to counter the economically determined structural literature that reduced enslaved Africans and their descendants to mere units of capital production, as Jason Young argues, it is more generative to move beyond the demography/culture dichotomy to instead view the world wrought by slavery as "more than a simple scattering of dispersed bodies ... [but rather] as a system of theoretical and intellectual engagement whereby Africans on the continent and enslaved in the Americas redressed and resisted the trauma and violence of slavery and the slave trade."[53] In other words, rather than investigating the transmission of particular cultural practices from Africa to the Americas by waves of people who left Africa from the same ports, I will be exploring the contours of debates about the meanings of community, freedom, and political legitimacy in geographical Kisama and through the lens of Kisama politics. I will ask how those who advocated particular political positions evoked these through the deployment of the Kisama meme in the context of maroonage in the Americas. I am less interested in the movements of individual bodies and more interested in the political consequences of the movement of ideologies that coalesced under an identity called Kisama.

What is necessary, then, is to begin imagining a new intellectual space, distinct from both (Black) Atlantic Studies and the African Diaspora, beyond the creolist and revisionist debates, within which to locate Kisama's dynamic, diffuse histories and the ripples of fugitive ideologies spreading both within the lands between the Kwanza and Longa Rivers and well beyond, both regionally and trans Atlantically. As appealing and prolific as the term "Atlantic" is as a heuristic, I believe that it is important to move away from the Eurocentric nature of this term, from the comforting sense of the mobile, the literate, the privileged, with which it too often paints over the histories of the majorities. It is not a term with which those in whose histories I am interested would have identified, and it does nothing to explain lives lived far from the ocean and, by political choice, as far removed from the machinations of capital as possible. The practical politics of dissent through flight and evasion of the state was a deep tradition in geographical Kisama, though of course the contours of this practice shifted in the sixteenth and seventeenth centuries, both in Angola and in the Americas. Those shaping Kisama, however, did not face the Atlantic Ocean, even in the sense in which "the Atlantic" is synecdoche for "mobile, profit-focused merchants."

Fugitive modernities encompass the political strategies, economic and subsistence adaptations, and intellectual and cultural conceits forged by those who fled from totalizing state power and all of its manifestations. Pirates, bandits, maroons, and others wove together distinct, often interacting, and at times conflicting forms of fugitive modernities in contiguous spaces. Just as James C. Scott argues for the multimillennia "anarchist history" of southeast Asia that spans several epochs of history and conventional, state-centered periodization schemes, I too contend that the practice of flight from the intolerable excesses of states in West Central Africa is a long-standing practice.[54] In other words, there is nothing particularly "modern" about the practice of flight from tyrannical states and their violence, in the sense that "modern" represents a profound rupture from a "nonmodern" antiquity. However, if we understand modernities as multiple—not only in a geographic or cultural sense, but also chronologically, rejecting the notion that there was ever a static zero point of political, cultural, intellectual, or social history—then we can begin to resolve the tensions and contradictions that Frederick Cooper details in his critique of the use of the concept.[55] While those living between the Kwanza and Longa Rivers may not have articulated their political strategies as modern, whether fleeing from an expanding and consolidating Kongo or Ndongo or from the predations of the Portuguese and their allies, these maroons certainly did perceive significant ruptures in their world.

As an emic, or internal, category, then, modernity is synonymous with political and social disjuncture; as an etic, or externally imposed, category, modernity requires qualifiers. The modernity within which this study is situated has multiple historical sources, including the broader political traditions of West Central Africa, the particular political cultures of neighboring state and nonstate people, and, perhaps most importantly, the local intellectual repertoires of resistance from which sixteenth- and seventeenth-century West Central Africans drew. Unlike Jan Vansina, I do not argue that the onslaught of colonialism—whether in the sixteenth century or the nineteenth—represented the end of political tradition in Kisama or in the region more broadly.[56] However, if we understand the tradition of Kisama as a constant adaptation to the broader regional predations of state from which people fled, then we can cease viewing modernity and tradition as diametrically opposed, and more closely approach asking what contemporary actors would have perceived as novel about their own experiences, given local historical understandings. The fugitive modernities on which I focus here evolved primarily between the Kwanza and Longa Rivers in the sixteenth and seventeenth centuries, and by the reputation and rumor about the political life in between the Kwanza and Longa Rivers throughout the broader region, likely building on older paradigms and structures of political thought and action throughout West Central Africa. However, those who evoked, constructed, and contested Kisama during this time did so as a response to the truly unprecedented scope of bloodshed and warfare that were the local experiences of the Jita Kwatakwata. The political, intellectual, and social strategies of sixteenth- and seventeenth-century Kisama are thus best understood not only from within a deeper regional history where those resisting expanding states had created other fugitive modernities, but also in a contemporary, comparative perspective with the fugitive modernities that emerged throughout the region, in Kasanze, Imbangala society, and in the Americas. Fugitive modernities allows us to consider histories that occurred entirely within Africa and among Africans within the same intellectual framework as transoceanic people. It allows us to view maroon communities in seventeenth-century Angola and in the Americas as part of an intellectually, politically, socially, and culturally contiguous space; its capaciousness also permits us to imagine a new way to periodize modernity itself.

The terrain of fugitive modernities is rich with possibilities for conceiving of new logics of historical causality and new frameworks through which to grapple with the political and social strategies of those who have long played at and against the margins of national and nationalist imaginations. While nations across the globe have adopted some form of "Out of Many, One People" as their official motto, in the past decade, it has become increasingly clear that the notion of distinct peoples seamlessly joining together to forge secular nation-states governed by the rule of law has always already been, at best, a fantasy. Fugitive modernities allows us to untangle the intellectual and political histories of nonstate identities on their own terms, as distinct from and yet always in conversation with states and each other.[57] It provides a framework for voicing counternarratives to colonial time and to the well-documented tendency since the 1960s for scholars of African history to seek to legitimate African political, cultural, and social forms by fitting them into an inherently provincial, Eurocentric/universalizing concept of modernity.[58] Fugitive modernities and state modernities were always in dialogue with each other, at times borrowing discourses, practices, and institutions in order to adapt to new circumstances. If fugitive modernities seems an inherently reactionary concept, it is—but no more so than state modernities, be they monarchical or republican.

Summary of the Chapters

Drawing from archives in Angola, Brazil, Portugal, and Spain, as well as oral histories, linguistics, and ethnographic fieldwork in various maroon communities in Pará, Brazil, and villages throughout geographical Kisama, Angola, in 2007 and 2010, I present my major arguments concerning Kisama's histories and the ways in which it fundamentally reconfigures our understandings of identity, modernity, and subjectivity in the six chapters and conclusion that follow.

Chapter 1, "Kafuxi Ambari and the People without State's History: Forging Kisama Reputations, c. 1580–1630," argues for the central role of one local leader in the emergence of the contours of Kisama politics and ideologies, even in the absence of political, cultural, or social unity within geographic Kisama. This chapter functions as the introduction to the longue durée biography of soba Kafuxi Ambari. Local epistemologies of personhood function radically differently than more familiar, corporeally bounded ones, and Kafuxi Ambari is understood locally as being an enduring, structural relationship between an embodied personhood and ancestral and local spirits. An iconic 1594 battle during which Kafuxi Ambari defeated a much larger force of Portuguese soldiers and their allies, would define the Kisama meme for centuries to come. Kafuxi Ambari's efficacy against Portuguese forces, as well as against Ndongo and Matamba, attracted thousands of fugitives to seek a haven in Kisama. By using oral histories to think about the sixteenth- and seventeenth-century forging of reputation, I interrogate how Kisama grew to a legible, coherent identity in the absence of centralization. This approach compels us to rethink the relationship between time, state, personhood, and identity.

Kafuxi Ambari's reputation was critical in drawing fugitives into many regions of geographic Kisama, and these fugitives in turn reconfigured and contested the very fabric of social and political life. Chapter 2, "'They Publicize to the Neighboring Nations that the Arms of Your Majesty Do Not Conquer': Fugitive Politics and Legitimacy, c. 1620–55," places Kisama within the broader context of violence, social rupture, and the radical political and social shifts of early seventeenth-century Angola. Geographical Kisama was not the only place to which those fleeing enslavement or seeking refuge from violence and extraction fled, and by comparing the ways in which politics was practiced by those identified as Kisama to other state- and nonstate fugitives, a more distinct picture of Kisama's ideologies emerges. By analyzing in detail a succession struggle in the lands of another Kisama soba, Langere, in the early 1630s, we gain a sharper view of the ways in which political constituencies formed and functioned in the nonstate maroon communities of seventeenth-century Kisama.

Chapter 3, "'The Husbands Having First Laid Down Their Lives in Their Defense': Gender, Food, and Politics in the War of 1655–58," details the relationship between martial practices and political ideologies, material production, the environment, and the experiences of those in geographical Kisama who endured a devastating three-year war in the mid-seventeenth century. After Njinga of Matamba and Ndongo negotiated an end to their three-decade long conflict with the Portuguese in 1655, they turned their forces on Kisama, instigating a war that physically transformed the always-arid landscape of Kisama into a land of endemic, politically produced famine. Accounts of the battles of the War of 1655–58 reveal the centrality of fugitives in weaving the political fabric of the region, and their insistence on rejecting warrior identities even as the practice of warfare grew increasingly vital, resulting in the emergence of distinct gender ideologies.

The ideologies of political practice and their broad circulation move beyond a regional story to a truly global one in chapter 4, "(Mis)Taken Identities: Kisama and the Politics of Naming in the Palenque Limón, New Kingdom of Grenada, c. 1570–1634," based on a detailed reading of a thousand pages of documents produced by the trial of several captured leaders of a maroon society outside of Cartagena in 1634. This chapter interrogates how the arrival of several Kisama-identified men in a century-old fugitive society in the Americas established primarily by those whose experiences with antistate resistance derived from the riverine societies of Guinea instigated sharp conflicts about the relationship of violence to political legitimacy. Not only do these Kisama-identified individuals trouble geographically distinct notions of social order but they also conflicted and collaborated politically with other West Central Africans whose ideologies regarding violence and social organization operated differently. These trial records constitute the greatest archival source of Kisama-identified individual people prior to the twentieth century, including in Angolan materials. This chapter does not argue for the direct transmission of people from geographical Kisama to the Americas, or for an inherent and inevitable conflict between those of different geographic origins, but rather for the global flow of reputations, memes, and ideologies and the plurality of fugitive political repertoires available to maroons in the seventeenth-century Americas.

This semiotic approach also drives chapter 5, "Fugitive Angola: Toward a New History of Palmares." Palmares's history, historiography, and historical evocation are intimately bound to the racialized formation of the Brazilian nation-state. Indeed, those who have studied maroonage in Brazil, and the famous seventeenth-century maroon society of Palmares in particular, have long searched for legible Angolan antecedents to Brazilian practice. Notably, many have observed that the term *quilombo*, used in Brazilian Portuguese only since the late seventeenth century to refer to maroon societies, derives from the Imbangala term for "war camp," and have attempted to link Palmares to Njinga and their alliance with Imbangala factions. However, rejecting the traditional scholarly search for origins, I instead employ an approach grounded in Angolan history and knowledge of the Kimbundu language. In particular, by demonstrating how a phrase that has been glossed for more than three centuries as "little Angola" actually means "*fugitive* Angola," I establish a history of Palmares rooted in the lived experiences of those who created it. Indeed, it is on the basis of this accidental testimony of the affective realities of maroons in seventeenth-century Brazil that I derive the notion of *fugitive modernities* as an emic category. From this perspective, Imbangala antisociability was hardly a political antecedent from which those who were likely captured and sold into slavery by the Imbangala would have drawn. Instead, I review the evidence for political dissent and conflict within Palmares as commentary on the multiplicity of West Central African political ideologies within the maroon society, including those informed by Kisama's reputations.

Chapter 6, "The Ashes of Revolutionary Fires Burn Hot": Brazilian and Angolan Nationalism and the 'Colonial' and 'Postcolonial' Life of the Kisama Meme, c. 1700–Present," interrogates the relationship between the radical macropolitical transformations within nineteenth-, twentieth-, and twenty-first-century Angola and Brazil and the uses and obfuscations of Kisama and the Kisama meme. Beginning with an exploration of Kisama and Kafuxi Ambari's relative absence from the eighteenth-century archives and Portuguese imputations of Kisama's connection to revolutionary ideologies spanning the Atlantic, I then trace the processes through which revolutionary Kisama has been written out of Angolan and Diasporic histories in favor of legible, literate, state-oriented interlocutors. Drawing not only from colonial archives, but also from textbooks, tourist propaganda, novels, and plays, I argue for Kisama's fundamental unthinkability within the statist ontologies of the nineteenth, twentieth, and twenty-first centuries. While Kisama's—and in particular, Kafuxi Ambari's—resistance has a certain romantic appeal both for anticolonial propagandists in Angola and for cultural nationalist scholars and activists in Brazil, fugitive modernities present an insurmountable conundrum for those aspiring to take the reins of state.

The conclusion, "Fugitive Modernities in the Neoliberal Afterlife of the Nation-State," considers the relationship of fugitive modernities to the fierce urgency of now. Given the range of coercive political forms across present-day Africa and Latin America and the Caribbean, from outright dictatorship in Angola to the extractive anti-Black neocolonies of Brazil and Colombia, I apply my concept of fugitive modernities and the alternate subjectivities it engenders to the question of political imagination in the age of neoliberalism. If sovereign nation-states are today little more than operating fictions, then what possibilities do nonstate intellectual histories offer for conceiving alternate political paths? How can fugitive modernities enable us to escape the confines of colonial ontologies and state epistemologies to envision alternate political strategies and futures?

This is a story about Angola, and the New Kingdom of Grenada, and Brazil; a story about ideas that circulated and recirculated in the minds and dreams of those who never wrote a single word; a story about those who created vibrant life in the shadow of death. It is a story about time, and space, and the violence through which we are interpolated into them and the creativity with which we can bend them, break them, shatter them, and make them anew. There are many villains, few named individuals, and even fewer who skew toward heroism. This is a story about the seventeenth century, primarily, but it is, after all, a story *for* now, for us, for all of the people drowning and barely keeping their heads above the rising tide of nation and capital, where we were never meant to belong anyway. It's not a celebration, nor a mourning of postcolonial failure, but an exploration of the threads by which we may weave a different cloth.

CHAPTER 1

Kafuxi Ambari and the People without State's History

Forging Kisama Reputations, c. 1580–1630

How much history a people have, far from indicating their low stage of evolution, is always an active choice, one that positions them vis-à-vis their powerful text-based neighbors.
— JAMES C. SCOTT, *The Art of Not Being Governed: An Anarchist History of Upland Southeast Asia*, 2009

During my field research in 2010, time and time again, when I explained to residents of geographical Kisama—old, young, male, female, literate or without access to education, from the northern boundaries along the Kwanza River to the southern limits along the Longa River—that I was interested in the past, I was asked if I knew the story of Kafuxi Ambari. It was essential, they told me repeatedly, that I know and understand his history, because too many of the young people today did not know about him. Even teenagers remarked ruefully on their concern that members of their generation or generations yet to come would fail to appreciate the importance of Kafuxi Ambari's legacy. When I asked what I needed to know about Kafuxi Ambari, the response was unequivocal: he mounted the most sustained, effective, and important campaign of resistance against the Portuguese during the time of the Jita Kwatakwata. In a context in which the elaborate lineage-based histories long favored by scholars of Africa are absent—strategically absent—Kafuxi Ambari alone occupies a critical genre of historical narrative throughout today's geographic Kisama. I found this emphatic and universal assertion interesting, given that not only had I heard personal accounts of living residents of Kisama who had themselves participated in anti-Portuguese resistance or whose parents and grandparents had, but I also knew of archival records of sobas in geographic Kisama who organized armed campaigns against Portuguese well into the twentieth century. With seemingly contradictory evidence of more recent resistance flourishing in both living memory and the archives, I was compelled to better understand the enduring impact of Kafuxi Ambari's legacy and to discern what made the resistance of Kafuxi Ambari merit its own category of historical memory in present-day geographical Kisama.[1]

Indeed, the stories about Kafuxi Ambari that I heard in Kisama—whether I actively solicited them, overheard them, or was offered them by way of responding to other questions—were unique in several respects. Not only was Kafuxi Ambari the only named leader of anti-Portuguese resistance in tales about the Jita Kwatakwata, but he was also the only named warrior. In a society whose very survival and identity were predicated for centuries on the accrual and exercise of exceptional martial skill, there is seemingly no mythology or storytelling related to warriors or warrior identities with the exception of Kafuxi Ambari. While it is always perilous to make an argument based on a perceived lack of evidence, Kafuxi Ambari's exclusive occupation of this genre of historical knowledge suggests a deliberate, politically animated connection between the very contours of silence regarding warfare and warriors in Kisama history and the ways in which the thousands of fugitives who created Kisama societies conceived of justice. The reputation increasingly associated with Kafuxi Ambari and Kisama was a rich resource on which those throughout the region and in the Americas—regardless of whether they had ever set foot in geographical Kisama—could draw.[2]

Kafuxi Ambari does not just serve as an organizing historical/narrative trope in today's Kisama, however. In 1885—a signal year that most students of global history imagine through sepia-toned images of steamships, railroads, industrial capital, and the mustaches of the Europeans in Berlin who bargained away the lives, labor, and land of millions of Africans—a Portuguese military captain in Angola, José Ignacio de Souza Andrade, was charged with imposing a particular vision of colonial modernity onto people who had actively evaded various forms of state and nonstate power since at least the sixteenth century. Andrade knew well the enduring reputation of Kisama; memories of centuries of frustrated Kongo, Ndongo, Imbangala, and Portuguese ambitions flourished in living political lexica throughout the region as well as in trans-Atlantically circulating printed sources. In his detailed report on the state of Portuguese attempts to subdue the people and territories they understood as Kisama, Andrade included not only relevant details of the campaigns in progress, but also, intriguingly, a rather lengthy transcription of an account of the iconic 1594 battle between Kafuxi Ambari's forces and the Portuguese. After transcribing the account of the battle, Andrade argued that this three-century-old tale was "well known" "to affirm his argument that, more than imprudent, [it is] mad to penetrate Quissama to make a war there, with the goal of conquering territory."[3]

While later I follow the global iterations of the Kisama meme from the time of the 1594 battle to José Ignacio de Souza Andrade's campaign to my own fieldwork in the twenty-first century, this chapter explores the ways in which the highly effective practices of Kafuxi Ambari at the turn of the seventeenth century defined the political and discursive landscapes of Kisama-ness for centuries to come. Despite the fact that Kafuxi Ambari was often in conflict with other sobas within the region between the Kwanza and Longa Rivers—or perhaps because of it—for those living in present-day geographical Kisama, he uniquely signals local authenticity. If states elevate certain figures as "father(s) of the nation," how do nonstate societies that have been at odds with each other for centuries jointly lay claim to the prestige, authority, and legacy of a single figure to give shape and structure to a politically charged identity? What is the connection between Kafuxi Ambari's praxis and the meanings with which various West Central Africans and Africans and their descendants in the Americas imbued "Kisama"?

In this political biography, by focusing on the changes in local notions of political legitimacy in the period from roughly the 1580s to the 1630s, I argue that the growing role of the lands between the Kwanza and Longa Rivers as a refuge for those fleeing the trans-Atlantic slave trade and the accompanying escalation of the scale of violence, slavery, and the slave trade within Angola necessitated the formation of new concepts about political legitimacy and the role of authority, and, in turn, new understandings of identity. For those living in this tumultuous period, rupture, disorder, and chaos were more common than stability and continuity.[4] So it should come as no surprise that West Central Africans reforged older notions of political and social practice to adapt. The ways in which Kafuxi Ambari navigated through and capitalized upon these changes cemented him in the historical consciousness of residents of Kisama to this day as "the last soba to resist the Portuguese." In fact, Kafuxi Ambari's enduring subjectivity is the very nexus of the discourses and ideologies of fugitive modernities in Kisama. He is the skeleton onto which all who claim Kisama attach themselves.

Both historians who have written about Kisama, Beatrix Heintze and Aurora da Fonseca Ferreira, discuss Kafuxi Ambari's importance as "the most powerful ruler in Kisama," and both also mention the early twentieth-century oral tradition recorded in neighboring Libolo that Kafuxi Ambari immigrated to Kisama in the wake of Portuguese incursions along the Kwanza River.[5] Of course, notions that powerful leaders come from the outside are widespread throughout African oral political cultures, and this account from Libolo may reflect either a genre convention or some deeper political imperative that we can no longer access. What is indisputable, however, and what Heintze and Ferreira both acknowledge, is Kafuxi Ambari's power and importance within Kisama—a fact that emerges starkly from seventeenth-century sources.

I go further, however, arguing that it was the actions of Kafuxi Ambari in the late sixteenth and early seventeenth centuries that made Kisama a coherent, legible trope with which to conjure political power. Kafuxi Ambari came to signal this power for those living between the Kwanza and Longa Rivers who would identify as Kisama, for those who heard rumors of the martial and spiritual aptitudes of Kafuxi Ambari and other sobas in Kisama and fled there, for those state actors, African and European alike, who strove unsuccessfully to subdue Kisama, and, ultimately, for fugitives in the Americas who evoked Kisama as a means for orienting themselves politically. However, Kafuxi Ambari's exercise of these unique powers and charisma located him on the shadowy borderlands between effective leadership and dangerous witchcraft. Therefore, there are multiple strands of oral traditions that identify him as an "outsider," and claims of Kafuxi Ambari's immigration should be read through that lens. He was at the same time the figure around which Kisama identity cohered and always and forever outside of Kisama-ness.

While Kafuxi Ambari's reputation endures into the twenty-first century, however, it is important to note that the remarkable characteristics associated with him are not the exclusive property of those who consider themselves his descendants or descendants over whom he directly ruled. In other words, people in the late sixteenth and seventeenth centuries in Angola transposed these traits from Kafuxi Ambari onto the land of geographical Kisama itself and then identified as "Kisama" rather than as personal followers or descendants of Kafuxi Ambari. While those who lived in geographical Kisama, who fled to geographical Kisama, and who drew the contours of what it meant to be Kisama relied on Kafuxi Ambari's power to help secure their freedom, a warrior identity was more of a strategic presentation to outsiders than an organizing social idiom for Kisama. This process stands in important contrast to the life and afterlife of Njinga, ruler of Ndongo and Matamba. After they died—and their personhood did not transcend a single lifetime—those who remained in their state identified as and were identified as "Njingas." This vital distinction compels us to remember that, regardless of the language through which people situate identity as primordial, and tradition as the guiding principal of social and political life, identities are *always* fungible currencies within a field of political negotiation.

I trace the emergence of Kisama's reputation in conjunction with the rising power of Kafuxi Ambari to a growing regional emphasis on military skill. In an era of unprecedented, apocalyptic violence and social rupture, the ability to protect vulnerable people from the depredations of expansionist states and lineage-eschewing bands of warriors and their Portuguese allies increasingly became a prerequisite for leadership of equal or greater importance to older notions of inherited authority. Kafuxi Ambari's military success helped the region of geographical Kisama develop into a relatively secure asylum for those fleeing Portuguese captivity by the 1620s. In turn, these refugees participated in the complicated debates around political legitimacy and the relationship of violence to both the conceptualization and practice of social justice through which Kisama gained salience as a trope and political strategy.

Narrating Kisama history through the lens of Kafuxi Ambari's political biography is something of a compromise. On the one hand, it allows us insight into the vital means through which notions of time and personhood were crafted and maintained in service of politics outside the state. On the other hand, it may reinforce problematic concepts of leadership—notions likely foreign to the praxis of Kisama. In choosing to tell Kisama's history as people in Kisama tell it, I risk silencing the voices of those who are entirely invisible in the archives, who leave no trace, not even the echoes and whispers left by Kafuxi Ambari. So I frame this as a story of Kafuxi Ambari with caveats, cautions, and every effort to speak to collective political action and agency.[6]

"A Time When Seeds Were Lost for Lack of Water"

Aridity has long been the defining natural characteristic of the land between the Kwanza and Longa Rivers. The people living between these two rivers developed complex survival strategies that largely favored low population densities, widely dispersed, small settlements, trade, extensive hunting and fishing, and subsistence practices that maximized the potential of riverine areas with intensive cultivation of beans, sorghum, and plantains as a way to survive and thrive.[7] If the rains do not come in the short rainy season between late October and March, however, local people are still highly vulnerable to drought.[8] While hunting, fishing, foraging, trade, and mobility are important ways to augment food resources, they did not and do not always provide enough food for everybody.[9]

Living along the Atlantic coast and at some distance from the more fertile inland river valleys of the Kwanza and Longa Rivers, in 1588, Kafuxi Ambari and his people suffered from drought and local crop failure. Though the Jesuit author of the 1588 account on the religious and political state of Angola does not detail the precise location of Kafuxi Ambari's lands, he does mention that he was on the sea coast, only twenty or thirty leagues (approximately 52 to 78 miles, or 83 to 125 kilometers) from a land "abundant in meats, and provisions, very cool and well-watered, all resembling a fresh garden"—a description that corresponds best to both historical and present-day conditions in the Longa River valley. While such fertile lands existed only a short distance away, Kafuxi Ambari's people suffered the deprivation of what the author described as "a time when seeds were lost for lack of water." In order to remedy the situation, Kafuxi Ambari called on one of his ritual authorities to initiate a rain-making ceremony.[10] In front of a large crowd composed of both local people and the same Portuguese soldiers who briefly served as Kafuxi Ambari's allies, the ritual authority arranged a circle of bells and other instruments around him. He used these to invoke the subjectivities who could help bring rain.[11] However, after much lightning, thunder, and gathering clouds, no rain came. According to the author, the ritual authority himself was decapitated by a bolt of lightning sent to instruct the local people about the Christian god's power.[12]

It is impossible to know how those most central to this story—those suffering from drought, who looked to Kafuxi Ambari and his ritual authority to ameliorate their plight—reacted to such a theatrically grave failure, if indeed this event was anything more than a Portuguese morality tale. The Jesuit author of the account was not preoccupied with the shifting terrain of ideologies of political legitimacy, and I have been unable to find any kind of oral histories or other sources that even obliquely refer to this particular moment. Indeed, simply because it is the first time that Kafuxi Ambari appears in a *written archive* does not mean that this moment was particularly significant, or that it even happened. Were we able to zoom out to a broader perspective, we might be able to determine if, in the longer narrative arc of Kafuxi Ambari's power and regional history, this moment was relatively insignificant, or of paramount importance. Did Kafuxi Ambari lose legitimacy locally? Did his nganga? These are important questions that we cannot now answer.

What we can know, however, is that after the failure of his ritual specialist, Kafuxi Ambari elected to make war on one of his neighbors. This was likely a long-standing strategy in times of drought, but, given the broader regional context, it also reflects the growing importance of martial aptitude for maintaining political legitimacy and authority. While the author does not specify against which "enemy" Kafuxi Ambari waged his campaign, nor speculate as to the motives for such a battle, we can reasonably infer from the context of extreme drought and deprivation that Kafuxi Ambari intended either to raid for provisions—presumably from the neighboring peoples whose land was fertile and well watered—or to raid for captives, or, most likely, both.[13] That the Portuguese were active in this campaign with Kafuxi Ambari on their trek toward Cambambe makes it even more likely that they were interested in purchasing those whom Kafuxi Ambari captured during war. The author reports that due to the drought conditions, the Portuguese "couldn't proceed for him [Kafuxi Ambari] without carrying all necessary supplies[,] water, and vessels in which to cook or eat, and all of this on the shoulders of blacks, because there are no beasts [of burden] in this land."[14] Such porterage was the domain of enslaved laborers whom their masters valued the least—newly acquired war captives who were a danger to those holding them in bondage. Kafuxi Ambari could have traded such captives to the Portuguese for food, as was apparently common throughout geographical Kisama in later centuries.[15]

Whether the Portuguese retained these captives after they arrived in Cambambe is unclear from the records. We can only speculate on the fate of these bondsmen and women, who may have lived the remainder of their lives in a variety of states of servitude in Cambambe, at Massangano, in Luanda, or even in the Americas. It is also possible that some of these prisoners from 1588 fled their Portuguese captors, recrossed the Kwanza River, and rejoined their home communities—a path traveled by many in the decades that followed. While neither oral nor written records allow us to trace the paths of these individuals, we can recognize them as among the first people from the geographical region who were projected into the broad and violent world of the trans-Atlantic slave trade and forced labor in Angola. Kisama as a geographical entity appeared to already have some salience for outsiders—for example, King Mbemba a Nzinga of the Kongo who in 1535 claimed suzerainty over Kisama as a province, likely in an effort to assert control over the salt mines of Ndemba—but Kisama as a political or social signifier seemed not yet marked by the reputation that would come to distinguish it within the sociocultural and political matrix of the region.[16]

It Is "Mad to Penetrate Quissama to Make a War There, with the Goal of Conquering Territory"

In 1593, a mere five years after Kafuxi Ambari used Portuguese soldiers in his campaign against his unnamed neighbor as a response to localized drought and crop failure, the Portuguese succeeded in briefly defeating the soba who controlled the lucrative rock salt mines of Ndemba. People throughout the region used bars of the high-quality Kisama rock salt as currency from antiquity until as late as the mid-nineteenth century. Because of the salt's regional value and circulation, from at least the sixteenth century through the nineteenth century powerful outsiders, including the king of Kongo and the Portuguese, were always intent on gaining control of its source in order to facilitate their purchase of enslaved captives.[17] Indeed, it was likely the importance of this resource that led the king of Kongo to claim suzerainty over Kisama in 1535, just as the king of Portugal specifically granted Paulo Dias de Novais rights to these salt mines in the 1571 charter that enabled him to establish the colony of Angola.[18] For centuries to come, the Portuguese would continue to dream of controlling the salt of Ndemba as a means to fund their ever-inflating administrative costs and insatiable appetite for human captives; this ambition was never realized. In 1594, the Jesuit chronicler Pero Rodrigues mentioned that "the mines of silver [in Cambambe] mean little to them, but the salt is their treasure, because it is the currency with which one can buy slaves [peças] and all types of provisions."[19] The Portuguese in fact retained control of the mines for less than a year and would never again regain it. Even today, the autonomy of this community and its enduring control over this valuable commodity remains vital to the ways in which history informs the politics of the present. Residents of geographical Kisama today assert that "no white man has ever set foot in Ndemba" and no one is permitted near the mines except on foot and with special clearance from the local soba and ritual authority.[20]

In 1593, however, the Portuguese were confident that their victory over the soba of Ndemba was enduring and the critical foothold to conquest of the entire region. Rodrigues predicted that "it was necessary to conquer a powerful Soba, by the name of Cafuche Cambare, in order to subjugate all of Kisama."[21] The Portuguese governor at the time, Jerónimo de Almeida, "march[ed] for Quissama with the intention of subjugating first Cafuxe Cambare." Kafuxi Ambari, however, did not enter into a vassalage treaty with the Portuguese, instead choosing to engage them in battle.[22] The following year, Portuguese Captain-General Baltazar de Almeida had some success against Kafuxi Ambari's forces, primarily through his use of cavalry.[23] Rodrigues writes that Kafuxi Ambari's forces "could not resist, and so gathered themselves and all of their families together, some shattered, and fled for the big forest."[24] While the majority of the armed men stayed to guard the women and children, a smaller force left to provoke the Portuguese.[25] These troops fought those whom Almeida had put under the command of a subordinate, who approached Kafuxi Ambari's forces with a barrage of musket fire from horseback. Kafuxi Ambari allowed the Portuguese to enter their camp and believe that they had won, only to attack the retreating forces and lead the cavalry into the forest, thus mitigating their advantage. By the end of this campaign, Kafuxi Ambari's forces had killed "almost all [except for] ... two captains ... with old veteran soldiers, and some sobas who fought for us [the Portuguese] with their people. The captain general fought until there was nothing left to do, no more ammunition, and the horses that he brought were broken and fell dead ... only five portuguese escaped."[26] According to another account, Kafuxi Ambari's forces killed "two hundred and six whites and a large number of our vassals ... [this account was] by one of the seven Portuguese who escaped."[27]

Though it is difficult to surmise through existing sources the precise routes that tales of Kafuxi Ambari's dramatic victory over the Portuguese and their allies traveled through the region and the ways in which his victory was articulated through locally intelligible idioms of political and ritual power, his success could only have augmented his prestige, power, and reputation. In addition to his defeat of the Portuguese forces near Cambambe, later in 1594 Kafuxi Ambari attacked the Portuguese in their fort at Ndemba, "defeat[ing] them in an ambush, and this fort, of which they say few vestiges still remain, was abandoned."[28] While the Portuguese soldiers who participated in this campaign had been promised lavish rewards, including land near Muxima and the labor of enslaved captives to work it, in the decades that followed, the surviving routed soldiers repeatedly complained that they had not been compensated in any way.[29] Indeed, Kafuxi Ambari's victory was so complete that all physical and conceptual traces of the occupation have disappeared from material and mental landscapes, from the terrain of memory.

Suggestively, an oral history in the region today, collected by Kisama historian and resident António Sondoka, recounts that the salt mines of Ndemba were first discovered by goats. After noticing that goats grazing in dense brush returned with crusted white material on their faces and bloated bellies, people alerted their soba. When the soba went to investigate, he discovered pristine, crystalline rock salt. Recognizing that he lacked the military might to retain control of this valuable resource, the soba asked a neighboring, more powerful soba who was his older brother to help him protect the mines.[30] Such foundational stories work within a different chronotope than liberal time, rendering years, decades, or even centuries of change in a single narrative moment.[31] In this case, the unnamed historical soba's awareness that he needed more powerful protection of his resources and the description of the neighboring soba as his "older brother" may record a memory of political shifts in the region that occurred in the late sixteenth and early seventeenth centuries, when Kafuxi Ambari helped the soba of Ndemba free his lands from Portuguese occupation.

It is difficult to know for certain if the relationship between Kafuxi Ambari and the soba of Ndemba was fleeting or more enduring. In an account written in 1594, Kafuxi Ambari is described as having at his command twenty-five sobas and all of their men of war.[32] Later in the seventeenth century, António de Oliveira de Cadornega, recounting the history of the period of 1600–1601, depicts Kafuxi Ambari as "the Head and ruler of this province [Kisama], and then King of it without qualification despite being the former tributary of the King of Angola [Ndongo]."[33] Contemporary written accounts and present-day oral histories universally concur that Kafuxi Ambari was the most powerful soba in the region at the time. But was he the head of some formalized regional political institution, or did he rather command the allegiance of many of the other local leaders through his own personal charisma and military skill?

Attempts to locate Kafuxi Ambari in a more readily legible, hierarchical notion of political formation—"King"—seem acts of political translation that contradict the evidence, even within the same source.[34] Belying his earlier description of Kafuxi Ambari as king, Cadornega confirms the lack of enduring political hierarchy or formally institutionalized centralization within the region, commenting on the continuous conflicts between soba Mulumba Akambolo with his neighbors Kafuxi Ambari and Katala Kasala by observing, "His Lordship [Mulumba Akambolo] is in the middle of these two Potentates [Kafuxi Ambari and Katala Kasala], if you can call them that, because they are not ruled by a King nor any Prince, but each one lives in Liberty and independence."[35] By the seventeenth century, then, the prevailing political culture of the region emphasized the autonomy of individual leaders whose power depended not on affiliation with a centralized locus of ritual authority, but rather their own ability to attract followers—which increasingly meant fugitive bondsmen and women—through ritual and military prowess. These political strategies were flexible and fluid; autonomous sobas could form alliances in moments of need, though as the oral history suggests, these political confederations were often not relationships between equals. If the oral history about Soba Ndemba and the salt does indeed reflect this period, then Kafuxi Ambari was, in this moment, the "elder brother" to Soba

Ndemba, but he was not his king, nor did this subordinate relationship persist indefinitely. This story also does not convey how the relationships between the anonymous people living on Soba Ndemba's or Kafuxi Ambari's lands viewed these relationships or mediated them. These temporary alliances allowed for the people of geographical Kisama to respond effectively to imminent threats without compromising their autonomy in the long term.

Kafuxi Ambari's commanding defeats of the Portuguese near Cambambe and within their own fortress at Ndemba alone would have greatly enhanced his prestige and reputation. However, in contrast to his relative weakness in the case of the drought in 1588, from 1593 onward Kafuxi Ambari's martial skill combined with apparent ritual aptitude—two distinct realms in present-day European and Eurocolonial epistemologies but aspects of the same power in the seventeenth-century perceptions of locals and Portuguese alike—to give him power over his adversaries. Citing contemporary documents, the anonymous compiler of the "Catalogo dos governadores de Angola" (Catalogue of the governors of Angola, 1784) affirms that João Rodrigues Coutinho was named as governor in January 1601 "but only arrived in Angola in 1602, bringing many reinforcements of men and arms and munitions, and greater powers than his antecessors . . . entering in the lands of Cafuxe who attacked him with an illness of the country that carried him off in six days."[36] While twenty-first-century historians may view Coutinho's affliction through the lens of epidemiology or coincidence, seventeenth-century residents of geographical Kisama and neighboring areas and Portuguese alike attributed Coutinho's dramatic, sudden death to Kafuxi Ambari's power.[37] As a consequence of Kafuxi Ambari's defeat of Coutinho, "all of the hopes that this Conquest would achieve the desired ends were lost."[38] Kafuxi Ambari eluded defeat and subjugation by both Portuguese and Africans through the apparent superiority of his powers, both conventionally martial and spiritual/medical.

Such formidable powers influenced not only the Portuguese colonial officials and priests who produced the documents that became archives, that became scholarly narratives, but also other residents of geographical Kisama and those in neighboring regions. In the year following Kafuxi Ambari's success at Ndemba, sobas along the southern bank of the Kwanza River—whom the Portuguese had allegedly decisively pacified in the campaigns of the 1580s that led to the establishment of the fort at Massangano by 1583—crossed the river with their people to lay siege to the Portuguese stronghold itself.[39] Inspired by Kafuxi Ambari's success at Ndemba, these neighboring people struck at the fortified citadel of Portuguese power in the region. The Portuguese were able to subdue these sobas and their followers, however momentarily, only by constructing a fort in Muxima, on the southern bank of the Kwanza River, in 1599; this "pacification" was fleeting, and many of these same people, identified through the names of their sobas, were again fighting against the Portuguese by the turn of the century.

Indeed, the ramifications of Kafuxi Ambari's victory in 1594 were international and lasted for centuries. It is perhaps unsurprising that such a dramatic event still lived strongly in the historical consciousness of those Portuguese with whom the English sailor Andrew Battell would have had contact only a few short years after 1594. Battell, who traveled across the interior of Angola in the late sixteenth and early seventeenth centuries, wrote of meeting the forces of Kafuxi Ambari in 1601, while he accompanied Kalandula's band of Imbangala. Battell wrote that Kafuxi Ambari "was a great warrior, for he had some seven years before [sic; in 1594] overthrown the Portugals camp, and killed eight hundred Portugals and forty-thousand negroes, that were on the Portugals side."[40] In the late 1790s, infantry colonel Paulo Martins Pinheiro de Lacerda wrote in his account of his own military activities that in the lands of Kafuxi Ambari, "there is a tradition, that in ancient times an Army of Portuguese were lost there in a Trap that this Barbarian set, in which all died including the leader [of the Portuguese]."[41] And, as we saw at the beginning of this chapter, as late as 1885, as the Portuguese struggled to gain control of the island of Kisanga (so-called by the Portuguese; Kisanga actually means "island" in Kimbundu) in the Kwanza River, the captain in charge of the campaign, José Ignacio de Sousa Andrade, transcribed a detailed account of 1594 in his report by way of asserting that the story of the battle was "well known [–] to affirm his argument that, more than imprudent, [it is] mad to penetrate Quissama to make a war there, with the goal of conquering territory."[42] In the immediate wake of Kafuxi Ambari's triumph, both the local political and social landscape and the terms within which those in the region and their European interlocutors viewed it shifted dramatically. These changes would reverberate throughout Angola and the Americas for centuries to come. Kafuxi Ambari's political strategies, practices, and personal characteristics would shape not only the ways in which the people between the Kwanza and Longa Rivers responded to the violence and dislocation of the trans-Atlantic slave trade, but also the intellectual terrain within which people throughout the region—and, ultimately, throughout the Americas—imagined the possibilities for (re)constructing viable communities. The late sixteenth and early seventeenth centuries were a critical juncture in shaping the contours of political imagination within and about Kisama.

Warfare, the Kisama Meme, and Reputational Geographies, c. 1600–30

Those living between the Kwanza and Longa Rivers acquired a reputation as skilled warriors and intractable resistors that would endure, and that circulated throughout three continents from the time of Kafuxi Ambari's crushing defeat of the Portuguese until the first few decades of the twentieth century and beyond. The adjectives with which European interlocutors described Kisama, too, became as static and unchanging as the reputation itself. Most frequently, those who identified as and were identified as Kisama were "bellicose" and "ferocious." These descriptors appear to date from the ur-account of Kafuxi Ambari's momentous victory, Jesuit priest Pero Rodrigues's annual report of 1594. Rodrigues wrote, "The people [of Kisama are] the most bellicose, and ferocious that there are in the Kingdom [of Angola] who will fight in the battlefield with much force and at times come and take hold of the rifles [of the Portuguese] without fear of death."[43]

Indeed, the archetype of a Kisama man fearlessly charging a better-armed European adversary in the course of battle itself became part of a subtrope within Kisama's burgeoning reputation. In the late sixteenth century, those who fought alongside Kafuxi Ambari were seizing Portuguese rifles. By the time of Cadornega's later seventeenth-century account of the campaigns in geographical Kisama in the 1610s (based, perhaps, on sources to which we no longer have access), he describes a conflict in which one particularly "valorous and reckless" Kisama man attacked a mounted Portuguese lancer with nothing but a short knife. Cadornega suggests that this man's attack was prompted not only by his bravery, but also by his desire to "offend" the cavalryman. Not only did he succeed in doing so, but he also "succeeded in not losing his life first."[44] Unwittingly, this account allows us insight into the choreographies of war through which those who made Kisama forged their remarkable and enduring reputation, as well as an intriguing window into the ways in which Kisama troubled the martial core of Portuguese, and state-centered, masculinities more broadly.[45]

The transformation of Kisama from a regional designation to a political identity was rooted in the attachment of Kafuxi Ambari's military success in the 1590s to this emerging, static trope that would come not only to represent a heterogeneous and broadly dispersed group of people in the world at large, but also to attract an ever-growing number of vulnerable in the region to *become* Kisama. The European shift from describing Kisama as a province to maligning "the Kisama"—the difference between using the term "Kisama" as a toponym and having it stand for a resonant and well-known repertoire of political practices and orientations, rather than a specific place of origin—took place over the seventeenth century. It reflected a strategic performance of identity by Kafuxi Ambari and those who followed his lead, particularly those fugitives whom he attracted, who, like those mentioned above, knew how to evoke notions of bellicosity, ferociousness, and intractability, threatening not only the material security of Portuguese imperial and slaving endeavors, but also the rhetorical security of state and masculinity. While in 1594 Rodrigues described "the people of Quissama" as ferocious and bellicose, it was Cadornega who, writing later in the seventeenth century, first spoke of "quissamas." For the next four centuries, African, American, and European outsiders continued to describe "Kisamas" through this trope. The people of geographical Kisama ensured that the land between the Kwanza and Longa Rivers would be a secure refuge for the thousands of people who fled slavery and the devastation caused by slave raids by continuing to interact with Portuguese and their allies in ways that reinforced this image. However, it is possible to more finely historicize both the process through which outsiders grew to understand those living between the Kwanza and Longa Rivers as a distinctive people characterized by their resistance to the power of neighboring states and nonstate warriors and their European allies, and their military valor and the means by which these qualities informed a locally relevant and resonant sense of identity tied to the land and yet portable beyond its borders.

By 1593, Kafuxi Ambari was close to Cambambe, and by 1601, Battell found him "within three days' journey of Massangano," representing a sizeable expansion of his lands. Not only did Kafuxi Ambari rule over more land by 1601, but he also ruled over more populous and fertile land along the Longa River—possibly the same lands whose people he had attacked in 1588.[46] This shift was crucial in the emerging politics of Kafuxi Ambari, whose name Cadornega later (erroneously) glossed as "multitude of people."[47] It also points to the complexities of political geography in Kisama in the early seventeenth century, when the boundaries of communities increasingly comprised of fugitives were in near-constant flux. Kafuxi Ambari's use of violence against his neighbors suggests that while the less powerful within geographical Kisama may have come to identify with Kafuxi Ambari, the powerful leader of the early seventeenth century did not necessarily share a sense of common identity with those who may have identified with him. Conquest expanded Kafuxi Ambari's power by increasing his pool of dependents, but it did not fundamentally alter the decentralized, nonstate form of politics that he and those who came to identify and be identified as Kisama practiced.

After the turn of the century, those outside of the legible state structures of Ndongo and Kongo often found themselves simultaneously vulnerable to the predations of these states and of Portuguese soldiers and slavers, but also highly desirable as potential allies for both these states and the Portuguese in their campaigns. Most historians acknowledge the critical role that stateless Imbangala warriors played in the Portuguese defeat of Ndongo by 1620.[48] As I will discuss later, Imbangala could often be found on all sides of every conflict in seventeenth-century Angola. However, in this pre-1620 period, the Portuguese worked with the Imbangala by necessity when their chosen ally, Kafuxi Ambari, declined to participate in their campaign. According to Cadornega, the Portuguese governor and military officials wanted to ally with Kafuxi Ambari against the king of Ndongo because "it would make his conquest the easiest; he [Kafuxi Ambari] had had many victories and [his] encounters well demonstrated his valor and the nobility who followed him showed on all occasions a great disposition, as those who well understood things of war[,] of which he was a master."[49] With his martial and ritual power well recognized and his regional prestige at an all-time high, Portuguese attempts to compel or persuade Kafuxi Ambari to ally with them against Ndongo had little chance of success.

By the early seventeenth century, Ndongo itself recognized Kafuxi Ambari's formidable authority. In 1603, the Jesuit priest Fernão Guerreiro related that "even the King of Angola [Ndongo] is afraid [of Kafuxi Ambari], because it is he who according to their laws succeeds him . . . [as king] and whom the other sobas [of Ndongo] agree to make the next king, because he is so brave, that he can defend them from the Portuguese."[50] The king of Ndongo, Mbandi Ngola Kiluanji, Njinga's father, may well have feared Kafuxi Ambari. At that time, Ndongo was embroiled in a constitutional crisis over forms of political legitimacy. The king and nobles (the "other sobas" Guerreiro mentioned) vied for control of the polity and to define the role of an increasing number of enslaved people in procuring, maintaining, and transmitting that power. The king employed these enslaved people to strengthen himself in relation to the nobles, usurping their previously held source of military powers, relative local autonomy, and perhaps their ability to influence royal succession. Rival factions within Ndongo cited historical precedent to support either a notion of strict hereditary succession or of the right of nobles to appoint a more (militarily) suitable leader.[51]

Guerreiro's report that the king of Angola feared Kafuxi Ambari because he was acclaimed for his bravery and the local nobles believed him better able to protect them from the depredations of the Portuguese reflects the growing importance of military defense and particular kinds of power in regional notions of political legitimacy. If people throughout the region supported Kafuxi Ambari as a more suitable leader than Mbandi Ngola Kiluanji because he seemed better able to defend them against the Portuguese, then at least some of the sobas of Ndongo believed that protecting citizens from foreign violence was not only an essential prerequisite for rule, but *the* defining metric of leadership, above and beyond, for example, the capacity to bring rains.[52] Within this idiom of political legitimacy alone, those in Ndongo who feared the inevitable devastation of Portuguese conquest understandably perceived Kafuxi Ambari as the best possible ruler. Kafuxi Ambari's ability to inspire such confidence in his power by the early seventeenth century contrasts sharply with the situation in 1588, when he faced a local crisis of legitimacy for his failure to bring rains. In the context of the early seventeenth century, a figure like Kafuxi Ambari, unhindered by the apparatus of state and the lineages that dictated the topographies of power within it, would have been an attractive protector for the many vulnerable people within the region.[53]

While at the turn of the seventeenth century the Portuguese imagined harnessing Kafuxi Ambari's martial skill for their conquest of Ndongo, and some of Ndongo's sobas envisioned him as the leader of a more secure, better defended state, Kafuxi Ambari ultimately played neither of these roles; the desires of those within Ndongo were not necessarily congruent with Kafuxi Ambari's interests. Instead, in 1603, he faced a concerted attack by the newly appointed Portuguese governor, Manuel Cerveira Pereira, whose goal was to open the way for the Portuguese occupation of the famed, fictitious silver mines at Cambambe. According to Guerreiro, Pereira attacked Kafuxi Ambari's forces in three major battles, in which he destroyed Kafuxi Ambari's largest town, caused "great destruction and mortality," and compelled Kafuxi Ambari himself to flee.[54] The author of the 1784 "Catalogo dos governadores de Angola" claims that Pereira subjugated Kafuxi Ambari and forced him into vassalage to the Portuguese on his way to defeating the soba of Cambambe.[55] While the Portuguese did advance to Cambambe and build a fort there, the claim that Kafuxi Ambari was subjugated in 1603 appears to be patently false.

Those sobas whom the Portuguese had decisively subjugated in this period accommodated their conquerors not only by allowing them to build forts and other outposts as in Muxima, Massangano, and Cambambe, but also through providing their own vassals as a tribute for the never-ending Portuguese appetite for enslaved laborers both to work in Angola as plantation laborers, porters, and soldiers, and to be sold in the Americas.[56] In the only known existing archival record of tribute payments in the seventeenth century, dated 1630, Kafuxi Ambari does not appear.[57] Indeed, only nine years after Pereira supposedly conquered Kafuxi Ambari, André Velho da Fonseca wrote from Luanda that the entire reason for the difficult, costly maintenance of the three Portuguese forts along the Kwanza River was to guard the enslaved for trade to

> the sugar plantations of parts of Brazil, all of which without the service of slaves that leave from these Kingdoms would be very difficult. And the reason for maintaining the fortresses, is because between this port of Luanda and the mentioned forts [Muxima, Massangano, and Cambambe] there are very powerful enemies with vast territories, like in part of the province of Quiçama, Capacassa, Cafuche[,] Langere and many others, who do not trade with the black merchants . . . who must come through many enemy lands . . . to arrive at this port of Luanda, neither will the white merchants send their black pombeiros [itinerant African merchants who worked as dependents of the

Portuguese[58]] through this wilderness to trade, because they will rob and kill the pombeiros and even some whites that enter the wilderness, as happened many times during the time of Paullos Dias de Nouaes [sic], when there were no forts.[59]

Rather than a vanquished vassal of the Portuguese, here Kafuxi Ambari and other sobas, including Kapakasa and Langere, appear as the single greatest threat to the lucrative commerce in enslaved Africans to fuel the powerful and growing Brazilian sugar industry of the early seventeenth century. While Fonseca and his contemporaries often used "kingdom" as a generic term without reference to specific political forms, what we can gather from the economic geography of his account is that those lands outside of the control of the major kingdoms, Kongo and Ndongo, were also sites of inveterate resistance and refusal to participate in the colonial and slaving economies. This not only communicates something of the political orientation of Kafuxi Ambari, Kapakasa, Langere, and others who eschewed both state formations and an immersion in the "Atlantic" world, but it suggests something more broadly about the relationship between forms of power and notions of justice in the seventeenth century. A political authority granted by fugitives inherently opposed the kinds of exclusionary ideologies and hierarchies that allowed some rulers to participate in and benefit from commerce in human beings.[60]

As Portuguese demands for enslaved captives increased, in 1611, Portuguese governor Bento Banho Cardoso noted in his longer discussion of the state of the slave trade in Kongo and Angola, "It is not necessary to discuss the part in the south [i.e., south of the Kingdom of Ndongo and the Kwanza River] because slaves do not come from there."[61] It was not only along the Kwanza River that the people of geographical Kisama rejected participation in the slave trade. In 1631, the governor of Benguela complained that the people living along the north bank of the Longa River, that is, southern geographical Kisama, "do not participate in the [slave] trade, nor do they wish to become vassals."[62] Refusing to trade with the Portuguese and *pombeiro* merchants and disobeying the kind of systemic order that the Portuguese believed they had imposed on the region with the establishment of their forts, the actions of the people whose politics are encoded in the archives as that of Kafuxi Ambari, Langere, Kapakasa, and others belied the tenuous Portuguese sense of progress, stability, authority, and permanence that followed in the wake of the construction of

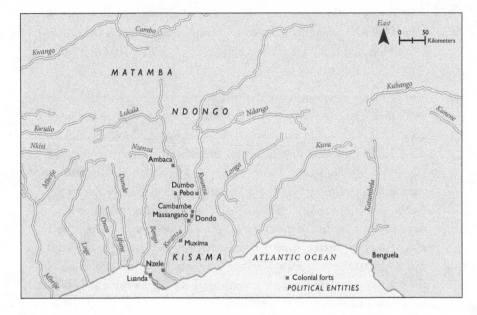

Map 1.1 — Seventeenth-Century Angola. Map by Heather Rosenfeld.

the fort at Cambambe. Despite the many Portuguese attempts to implement the type of warfare/slave raiding system in geographical Kisama that they and their allies used to rend apart communities and capture adults and children throughout the rest of West Central Africa, Kafuxi Ambari and the other sobas' refusal to participate in the slave economy during the early seventeenth century interrupted more than three decades of Portuguese conquests and colonization in Angola and heavily influenced regional notions of the political and social character of Kisama.

As the notion that these lands and their leaders represented a safe haven from the violence of the slave trade expanded beyond merely those lands under Kafuxi Ambari's rule to eventually encompass nearly all of the land between the Kwanza and Longa Rivers, a Kisama politics began to gain salience for local people. The process of transforming from merely an outsiders' ascription or geographic location to an internally relevant and highly politicized identity began with Kafuxi Ambari's use of his power not only to defeat the Portuguese but also to convince other sobas in the region to follow his lead. In Battell's account from 1601, he describes Langere as "one of the greatest Lords . . . [of the] province of

Casama" who was nevertheless loyal to the Imbangala Kalandula, whose forces he guided to Kafuxi Ambari's lands.[63] By "obey[ing]" Kalandula and conveying his enemy force to Kafuxi Ambari's lands, Langere showed that he was certainly no ally of Kafuxi Ambari's. However, by the time of André Velho da Fonseca's account in 1612, he named Langere as a soba who, along with Kafuxi Ambari and Kapakasa refused to participate in the slave trade and reacted with violent hostility to slave merchants, show-ing a certain political alignment of Langere with Kafuxi Ambari that differed from the situation merely a decade before, when Langere led Ka-landula's Imbangala band against Kafuxi Ambari. The same group of three sobas—Kafuxi Ambari, Langere, and Kapakasa—again appear in 1632 in the account of then ex-governor Fernão de Sousa with which I opened the book; he complained that the "souas on whom we border are many and powerful, and warlike; in the province of Kisama, Cafuche, Langere, Ca-paccaça and others, all non-Christians and our enemies."[64] Unlike Kafuxi Ambari's earlier relationship with Soba Ndemba or perhaps those sobas whom Kafuxi Ambari conquered in order to expand his territory and, more importantly, his dependents, these allegiances appear to have been relatively nonhierarchical.

The political dimensions of this common identification are clear from an account of Njinga sending ambassadors to geographical Kisama in an effort to gain allies. The Portuguese captain at Massangano wrote that Soba Malumba, who lived directly south of the fort on the other side of the river, informed him that Njinga's emissaries were on the lands of Kapakasa, where Langere and Kafuxi Ambari, along with other unnamed sobas, had congregated to receive them. Kapakasa's advisors were reti-cent to pass along Njinga's ambassadors' message because they suspected that the Portuguese had sent spies. Indeed, they were correct; the sobas Malumba and Katala, who, in the words of Malumba as reported by the Portuguese captain, "did not want to go to Capacaça to hear the message because they are the sons of the [Portuguese] captain," hurried to report on these events to the captain at Massangano.[65] Through the language of descent and through their actions in providing intelligence to the Portu-guese forces, Malumba and Katala declared themselves on one side of a political chasm that divided this region of Angola in the 1620s through the 1660s into allies of the Portuguese and those who fought against them. While scholars of seventeenth-century Angola have most often re-ified the political contest in the region as one pitting Njinga and affiliates against the Portuguese and their allies or have focused on the turmoil in Kongo, as we will see in the next two chapters, the drama of seventeenth-century Angola was animated far more by the actions and ideologies of fugitives than by states.

The pro-Njinga versus pro-Portuguese division was far from the only axis along which political identities within geographical Kisama region fractured. As early as the 1570s, certain sobas of Kisama who lived along the southern banks of the Kwanza sought the military aid of the Portuguese forces under Paulo Dias de Novais in an effort to maintain their independence from Ndongo.[66] In the early 1580s, long before those living in geographical Kisama acquired the reputation that emerged post-1594, Soba Kamona Kasonga, who lived near the mouth of the Kwanza River, became the first soba south of the Kingdom of Kongo to be baptized. By 1582, his godfather, the governor Paulo Dias de Novais, had him appointed high captain of the native people (*gente da terra*). Novais and the Portuguese colonial and ecclesiastical authorities in the area at the time regarded Kamona Kasonga's conversion and loyalty as particularly valuable, as he was considered a father-in-law to the king of Ndongo, for whom he served as a diviner.[67] Later, Soba Muxima became a vassal on whose lands the Portuguese constructed a fort in 1599; Muxima and Kamona Kasonga had persistent conflicts that each hoped to resolve successfully through an alliance with the Portuguese.[68]

An inveterate commitment to small-scale political autonomy—the factionalism of twentieth-century Angolan nationalist nightmares—characterized Kisama during this and later periods. However, by the beginning of the seventeenth century and certainly by the 1620s, sobas in the region found themselves largely compelled to either actively oppose the Portuguese, their aggressions, their incursions, and their growing trade in people that centered in areas just to the north of the Kwanza River and increasingly in Benguela and the surrounding regions, to align themselves politically with Njinga, or to flee deeper into areas of geographical Kisama that were not accessible by river. By 1612, Kafuxi Ambari emerged as the most formidable of a group of sobas that included Kapakasa, Langere, and others, who positioned themselves against the Portuguese and with Njinga while retaining their independence in relation both to Ndongo and Matamba and to each other. Indeed, independence and autonomy remained primary for these leaders in Kisama, against whom Njinga was prepared to turn after negotiating peace with the Portuguese in the 1650s.[69]

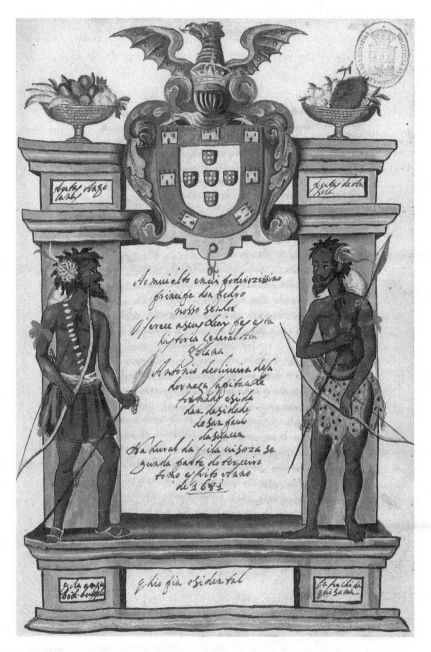

Figure 1.1 — Frontispiece of António de Oliveira de Cadornega, *Historia geral do reino d'Angola,* vol. 3, part 2, 1681. Kafuxi Ambari is on the right, wearing cheetah skin, no shoes, and long hair, and carrying a hunting bow and arrows. Reproduced with permission from the Academia das Ciências de Lisboa, Lisbon, Portugal.

However, Malumba, Katala, and others calculated that being "sons of the Portuguese" better ensured their people's survival in this chaotic, violent period. Sobas, however, did not make such choices absent input from those whom they governed and whose allegiance they commanded. By the late 1620s, an increasing number of fugitives fleeing the Portuguese forts at Muxima, Massangano, and Cambambe as well as Portuguese- and so-called Luso-African-run plantations in the river valleys fled to geographical Kisama. The mere presence of these fugitives and their political will would have a substantial impact on the nature of politics and identity in Kisama for the remainder of the seventeenth century and beyond, and influence the ways in which Kisama political identities traveled in the region and to the Americas.

Conclusions

It was likely around the 1610s or 1620s that the term "Kisama" shifted from an outsider's description of a territory or stereotyped ascription of a "tribal" identity, as evident in texts from BaKongo and Portuguese authors, to a locally meaningful term. While it is impossible to determine from linguistic evidence when the term "Kisama" originated as a label for the region, its prefix is certainly far from common for a place name in the Kimbundu language. Like all languages in the Bantu subfamily, Kimbundu, the language spoken in both geographical Kisama and by neighbors north of the Kwanza River, uses a system of noun classes in which the meaning of a noun word stem can be altered by changing its prefix.[70] For example, the stem -mbundu can be rendered Ki-mbundu, the language, or A-mbundu, the people. The prefix ki- is normally reserved for inanimate objects or languages, as in kima (thing) or Kimbundu the language, though it can also indicate a superlative.[71] When I asked people to explain this origin of the name Kisama, I was told that during the Jita Kwatakwata, the most renowned and mighty of all of the local warriors wore his hair uncombed and uncut. As his tangled and large hair was so distinctive, people began to call him Kisamunu (Comb). Because of this man's skill, the entire region eventually became known by a truncated form of the warrior's nickname, Kisama.[72] While it is possible that Kisama originated as a term in Kikongo, rather than Kimbundu, this local etymology still reflects the historical association of the Kisama identity with a warrior who lived outside of the conventions of a certain kind of social order.[73]

Stories of the founders of societies being men with large, uncombed hair are quite common throughout much of the region of Africa in which Bantu languages are spoken, and Jan Vansina notes that it would be ideal for such a founder to have a name that incorporated the superlative prefix Ki-.[74] While we have evidence of Kisama as a geographical referent by the early sixteenth century, when the king of Kongo (falsely) claimed to rule Kisama the province, this historical memory suggests that Kisama became a legible, intelligible identity for those within the region as it grew to be associated with martial skill, superior ritual power, and a certain alienation: the same circumstances that characterized the rise of Kafuxi Ambari's power in the early seventeenth century.[75] Kisama became a coherent identity which people could adopt as they integrated themselves into Kisama's particular style of politics, modeled after Kafuxi Ambari's turn-of-the-seventeenth-century practices. Kafuxi Ambari—and the meaning of his strength for the vulnerable people whom it attracted to his lands as dependents—forged a Kisama identity that was both profoundly political and also enduring.

It is worth noting that one of the distinct features of the Kimbundu spoken in Kisama is the use of the *ch* sound (as in the English word "change," and written in Angolan national languages as *c*) in places where other dialects of Kimbundu use a hard *k* sound (as in the English word "can"). Though far from universal—many in Kisama today will use the hard sound—it is common to hear someone render "a good thing" as *cima cyambote*, rather than *kima kyambote*, as in the other dialects of Kimbundu. While this is not a sound in any other dialect of Kimbundu, it is common in the neighboring languages spoken to both the east (Cokwe) and the south (Umbunudu). Suggestively, Kisama carries meanings associated with ferocity, strength, and power in lands to the east. In Luvale, a language spoken on both sides of the Angolan/Zambian border and also into the Democratic Republic of Congo, *-sama* means "Cheetah [or] hunting-leopard," or, alternately, "'Grows up to a lion,' i.e., it is like a little lion." These roots are considered by Luvale speakers to be loans from Cokwe, a language spoken to the north and northwest of Luvale.[76] In Cokwe, *-sama* means "leopard."[77] The root of Kafuxi Ambari's name, *-fuxi*, likewise means "quickly [or] swiftly" in Luvale.[78] These glosses point to the profound connections of Kisama with lands to the south and east, and remind us of the importance of resituating this history away from an ever-westward-glancing "Atlantic" view. Further studies of linguistic practices within geographical Kisama will likely yield valuable information about the time depth and nature of these relationships with Cokwe and Umbundu speakers. As I will discuss in the next chapter, however, by the mid-seventeenth century, many speakers of these languages had very likely become Kisama.[79]

While the term "Kisama" appears in written records generated by outsiders from Kongo and Portugal beginning in the 1530s, its relevance for those living in the lands between the Kwanza and Longa Rivers truly emerged in the early seventeenth century. While the soba Kafuxi Ambari of 1588 was compelled by the desperation of drought and crop failure to raid his neighbors, the Kafuxi Ambari of 1594 achieved a profound victory over the Portuguese forces that strove to conquer Angola's interior. Inspired by Kafuxi Ambari's success, many neighboring sobas successfully waged war on the Portuguese. After the turn of the century, Kafuxi Ambari and several of his neighbors, including the previously inimical Langere, found themselves on the same side of a political divide. Beginning in the 1610s, Kafuxi Ambari and other leaders began actively attacking Portuguese and allied slaving interests, gaining a reputation as warlike and resistant. In the following decade, fugitives from the slave trade began recognizing the lands of these leaders as a safe haven. As Njinga fought against the Portuguese north of the Kwanza, sobas south of the river who allied with them—including Kafuxi Ambari, Kapakasa, and Langere— were at odds with those who, like Malumba and Katala, considered themselves "sons" of the Portuguese empire.

For those who suffered the profound tragedy of capture and sale into the trans-Atlantic slave trade but the paradoxical fortune of surviving the Middle Passage to the Americas, the association of Kisama with rebelliousness, a commitment to nonstate politics, and martial skill was a powerful signifier upon which they could draw to reconstitute meaningful political communities in the wake of the social dismemberment of their natal communities; this was the exact purpose for which thousands of fugitives would use Kisama identity during the seventeenth century. Within Angola, the Kisama meme and its signification of effective resistance against the Portuguese and their allies—and a resistance effective in spite of the refusal to institute martial culture and idioms as the dominant social feature, as we will see in the following two chapters—both attracted more fugitives and inspired growing concern from the Portuguese, who, after they negotiated their peace with Njinga, would turn the bulk of their military forces toward Kisama. The public face of Kisama—the warrior—brought many of those who would become Kisama to the lands between the Kwanza and Longa Rivers and, once they were there, helped keep them safe from the predations of the Portuguese and their allies, including the Imbangala. In the next chapter, I will explore the private faces of Kisama and the idioms through which the people of Kisama—fugitive children, soldiers, farmers, fisherpeople, hunters—forged their own fugitive modernities in the context of the arrival of continuous waves of those fleeing violence.

"They Publicize to the Neighboring Nations That the Arms of Your Majesty Do Not Conquer"

Fugitive Politics and Legitimacy, c. 1620–55

In July 1655, Portuguese governor Luis Mendes de Sousa Chicorro accused the "blacks of Quiçama, who more than not desiring the Catholic Faith, [of robbing] the Portuguese of their slaves." Continuing his dire admonishments, he described how,

> in the same Province there are at present more than ten thousand slaves, which is the reason you find the residents of the Forts at Mazangano, Cambambe, and Muchima in poverty. These people seal the routes for the [slave] trade of the Portuguese, attack the *pumbeiros*, take what they carry from them, and they publicize to the neighboring nations that the arms of Your Majesty do not conquer, because theirs [those of the people of Kisama] are the strongest. It is expected that knowledge of these war preparations, without reaching effect, will reduce to obedience the slaves who ran away, that the trade in ivory, and slaves remain open and abundant, [that the troops will] seize the salt mines of Demba, that can give means to pay the infantry and cover

the expenses of the Conquests, that the lines of communication with the Kingdom of Benguella will open, the roads leading to ports on the Coast will be free and people of this Province will be defeated (with their bag[s of salt] the owners will recover a large amount of slaves) . . . while the vassals may stay at home safe from these enemies, who are equally concerned about both the dead and the continuous flights [of slaves].[1]

Sousa Chicorro's accusations here—that the people of Kisama rejected engagement with missionaries, robbed the Portuguese and those trading on their behalf of their captives, that thousands of fugitives found refuge in geographical Kisama, and that Kisama's reputation threatened to undo all Portuguese imperialist endeavors—are equal parts standard colonial litany and fantasy. As early as 1571, the Portuguese dreamed of controlling the salt mines at Ndemba to finance their costly wars in Angola, and by 1594, they identified subduing Kafuxi Ambari and Kisama more broadly as critical to their regional goals. Just as their material aspirations regarding the nonexistent silver mines of Cambambe withered, the Portuguese established a foothold at Benguela in 1617. While in the mid-sixteenth century and certainly before their iconic defeat by Kafuxi Ambari, the Portuguese may have imagined a simplistic political geography of West Central Africa, divided neatly into spheres of control of the Kingdoms of Kongo, Ndongo, and Benguela from north to south, by the time they invaded Benguela, they were certainly well aware of the bewildering multiplicity of peoples and political forms throughout the region, particularly south of the Kwanza.[2] Indeed, the Portuguese preoccupation with subduing the fractured and fugitive people of Kisama had as much to do with their recognition that Kisama both materially and discursively threatened their conquest and slaving enterprises as with the fact that nonstate political forms rendered political control nearly impossible. How could the Portuguese, or any other state power, truly win in Kisama, after all? There was no leader whose death would socially behead Kisama.[3] Kisama's fragmentary nature as much as its obdurate resistance and burgeoning fugitive population continued to frustrate Portuguese desires for direct control of Benguela through Luanda. No colonial geography was possible with Kisama a prominent, illegible disruption at the very center.

That they were heathens who harbored fugitives from the Portuguese slavers in the communities around Massangano, Cambambe, and Muxima, attacked both land- and river-going slave traders, and prevented the Portuguese from conducting their commerce in the region were oft-repeated Portuguese grievances since at least the 1610s. The charge that Kisama was a haven for fugitives, too, was far from exceptional. This had been the justification for intensive Portuguese campaigns against Kasanze and Kongo in the 1610s and 1620s. Sousa Chicorro's emphasis on the impact of Kisama on the regional geography of knowledge and reputation bears some examination, however, for what it can reveal about the translocal influence of Kisama's fugitive politics.

Sousa Chicorro realized that rumors, beliefs, optics, and reputations played just as vital a role in shaping local political perception and practice as did direct experience and observation in the period leading up to the extended Portuguese campaigns in Kisama in 1655–58. Amid the more customary grievances, Sousa Chicorro emphasized the role of Kisama's continued defiance of the Portuguese in shaping regional perceptions of political and military power. According to Sousa Chicorro, the people of Kisama "publicize to the neighboring nations that the arms of Your Majesty do not conquer, because theirs are the strongest." While this may have been a typical fear of states and empires, it also seems to borrow something from the political world of Kongo, or at least a common idiom of state power that Kongo and Portugal jointly constructed through their relationship in the early sixteenth century. Indeed, a full century earlier, in 1549, an embattled King Diogo Nkumbi a Mpundi wrote to the king of Portugal that he should have authority over all residing in his kingdom, including Portuguese subjects and other whites, in order to cultivate the terror that, he argued, was a prerequisite for any king's authority.[4] Ultimate power, for Diogo Nkumbi a Mpundi, and for his Portuguese royal interlocutor, was predicated on inculcating the fear essential to the coercive dimensions of state. Without such authority, Sousa Chicorro recognized, the Portuguese were ill equipped to compel those living throughout the region to continue to participate in the apocalyptic violence of the slave trade. Sousa Chicorro did not elaborate on the places and means by which those of Kisama described their triumphs to their neighbors, nor did he give details that would permit us insight into the political idioms within which these conversations occurred. He did, however, explicitly link the role of Kisama as a haven for fugitives to the reputation for martial acumen of its residents and its disruption of Portuguese political and economic designs for the region.

Beatrix Heintze describes the seventeenth century as "the century of fugitives" in Angola, and the period from the 1610s to 1658 was particularly turbulent.[5] This unprecedented human tsunami was created by the insatiable European hunger for African captives, both to labor on plantations within Angola and also for sale to the Americas—what is too often sanitarily coded as "the Atlantic trade." Their cannibalistic appetite prompted internal conflicts within Kongo and Ndongo, the growth and prevalence of marauding bands of lineageless Imbangala soldiers, and an escalating perversion of judicial and diplomatic institutions throughout the region. Even nobles and those citizens of states who, by treaty, should have been protected from enslavement, often found themselves in chains, sailing across the sea. While nearly 25,000 West Central Africans were torn from their families and communities and put aboard slave ships in 1591–1600, by 1621–30, that number had almost tripled. One-third of these captives were children; one-third of these adults and children died at sea. Two-thirds of those who survived landed in Cartagena, Vera Cruz, or New Spain, with the remaining one-third dispersed to Rio de la Plata, various ports in Brazil, across the Caribbean and Central America, and even New York.[6] This expansion resonates with the "Angolan wave" of captives arriving in the Spanish-colonized Americas.[7]

The Portuguese competed with the Dutch and French along the coast for control of a growing flow of captives leaving for the Americas. As early as the 1620s, Portuguese colonial officials noted widespread mortality from both warfare itself and the famine caused by violence and dislocation.[8] No small part of this pervasive mortality, flight, and depopulation was directly due to the campaigns of the Portuguese and their Imbangala allies. The war against Ndongo, for example, was shocking even to contemporary Portuguese observers, one of whom described the utterly deserted surrounding countryside resulting from the invasion as the unforeseen result of "slaughter" and "butchery."[9] The leaders of Kongo and Ndongo strove to increase their own power through control of an ever-burgeoning number of unfree laborers as crises of political legitimacy wracked both kingdoms. The fractured state of politics in Kongo both generated and attracted fugitives, whose presence was a readily accessible justification for the Portuguese to wage war against the state. Nomadic bands of Imbangala soldiers whose entire social and political being revolved around the ceaseless practice of war and the entrenchment of warrior identities and war-centered rituals began consolidating into a powerful kingdom, Kasanje, that would dominate the organization of violence and commerce in Angola's interior throughout the following century. Subjugated leaders in the interior sought to maintain alliances with the Portuguese by meeting both nominally legal and illegal demands for tribute in bondspeople, and state and nonstate actors alike forged unlikely alliances in an ever more perilous world.[10]

By 1633, Gonçalo de Sousa, superior of the Jesuits in Angola and son of the prolific former governor Fernão de Sousa, complained that there were virtually no captives for sale except at markets distant from Luanda, and these only at high prices. De Sousa reported that the regions immediately surrounding Luanda were almost completely depopulated by slave raiding and warfare—a complaint echoing that of the governor of Benguela two years earlier—and that sobas who were vassals of the Portuguese were fleeing with their people into the bush to escape demands for tribute in captives.[11] Those in flight inevitably found themselves in the midst of others struggling to survive the violence, and these encounters were as often catastrophic as they were cooperative. Conditions of near perpetual warfare and the ever present threat of capture, enslavement, and potential sale made life in seventeenth-century Angola fraught with dangers for the vulnerable, whose ranks only grew. Many thousands were captured; many thousands more fled their homes and lands in an effort to escape, whether to states like Kongo, to the lineageless bands of soldiers known as Imbangala, or to nonstate fugitive societies like Kisama.

As state and nonstate actors alike intensified their coercive pursuits throughout the region, by the late 1620s, it was not merely the structurally vulnerable within each community who fled, but entire communities, including the leadership itself. Former governor Fernão de Sousa described how many sobas abandoned their lands, and those who remained as vassals to the Portuguese were increasingly forced to pay their tribute with elders and children, since their young adults had run away.[12] Many thousands were captured, but an even greater number fled to seek asylum elsewhere. In the fissured political landscape of the early seventeenth century, with the centralized states of Ndongo and Kongo beset by deep divisions and many nominally state affiliated or explicitly nonstate political entities flourishing in the fluid and fractured world, many of these fugitives found their best chance for safety as Kisama. Geographical Kisama functioned as a concrete haven for fugitives; Kisama as a politics worked regionally and globally as a compelling model of the enduring promise of fugitive modernities.

Fugitive Flows, Kasanze, and the Long Seventeenth Century

Just as there is suggestive evidence that Kafuxi Ambari's name and the political idiom within which he operated are linked to deeper histories of thought and imagination in the environs to the east of geographical Kisama, so too is there a broader regional history of fleeing state regimes of power and the devastation of imperial expansion. In the sixteenth and seventeenth centuries, the state power of record was undoubtedly the Kingdom of Kongo. Kongo was an expansionist empire that, over the course of the preceding centuries, had unevenly integrated a number of surrounding territories into its highly centralized provincial structure.[13] Among these, if we can impute from linguistic and political cues and later evidence, was Kasanze, the mainland region adjacent to and north of the island of Luanda.

A campaign against Kasanze was Paulo Dias de Novais's first act of war upon establishing the colony at Luanda in 1575. In this case, he acted on behalf of the king of Kongo, against whose authority the people of Kasanze were rebelling, troubling that monopoly on terror that King Diogo Nkumbi a Mpudi had earlier identified as the defining feature of royal authority. Allying with the Portuguese and other European powers against powerful enemies was a fairly common strategy of leaders throughout Africa through the sixteenth century. Indeed, this was the approach of several sobas living around the mouth of the Kwanza River in geographical Kisama during the same time. In this case, however, the Portuguese served not to aid one soba against another equally or more powerful local leader, but rather to support the most formidable standing army in the region at the time in its efforts to subdue a far smaller, rebelling polity—a confluence of state interests. According to the same Jesuit chronicler who described Kafuxi Ambari's momentous victory of the Portuguese in 1594, the Portuguese were not particularly helpful in this campaign. Kasanze captured the Portuguese captain and all eighty of his soldiers, killing twenty.[14]

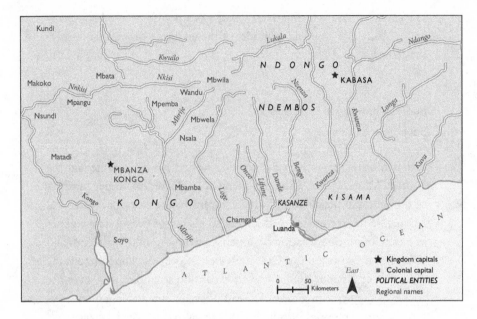

Map 2.1 — Fugitive and State Societies, Seventeenth-Century Angola.
Map by Heather Rosenfeld.

Kasanze was ideally situated to rebel against Kongo authority; not only was it food secure, but it likely also participated in forms of trade outside of Kongo suzerainty. Joseph Miller speculates that Kasanze developed critical relationships with Tomista traders through the early sixteenth century.[15] Tomista traders, themselves often scions of noble families from the Kongo, were keen to avoid the taxation of both the Kingdom of Kongo and Portugal. By eschewing treaties that restricted Portuguese trade to Kongo-controlled sites far to the north and pushing ever further south in their quest for captive adults and children for purchase, Tomista traders were directly responsible for the extension of the slave trade into Angola and its eventual colonization. Indeed, conflict between those in Kongo seeking to deal with metropolitan Portuguese versus Tomista traders was a major source of factional divisions in the mid-sixteenth-century kingdom, eventually leading to Portugal ending its support for a Kongo monopoly in 1560.[16] If it operated as Miller postulates, this economic relationship would have indeed strengthened Kasanze's independence from Kongo, but it was by no means the only potential avenue for autonomy.

Around the turn of the century, Andrew Battell identified Kasanze as the locus of "the greatest store of wild beasts that is in any place of Angola." He claims to have traded fish that he procured from the lake and smoked to the people of Kasanze for maize throughout his six-month sojourn.[17] Two decades later, Portuguese governor João Correia de Sousa depicted Kasanze as "full of many lakes from which they drink and many elephants and beasts that they eat, and they produce a great amount of flour, which is their sustenance, from maize."[18] This suggests that the people of the region were cultivating a food that not only would have greatly augmented local nutrition, but also would have been of significant value in trade with other communities or with the Portuguese, whose settlement in Luanda was endemically undersupplied with food. Battell could not have successfully traded fish to fishing people, so his ability to procure maize in exchange for fish suggests a relatively high degree of subsistence strategy specialization within early seventeenth-century Kasanze. Between hunting, fishing, and cultivating maize for both consumption and possible sale, the people of Kasanze were well capable of surviving and even thriving economically outside of the sphere of Kongo political authority.

However, by the late 1610s and early 1620s, as the Imbangala and Portuguese defeated the forces of the Kingdom of Ndongo and forced the king to seek refuge in an island in the Kwanza River, Kasanze and Kongo had reached a rapprochement. While he was almost certainly overstating the orderliness of the situation, Portuguese governor Correia de Sousa described the *mani* (mani is the Kongo title for the ruler of any people or territory) Kasanze of 1622 as ruling over sixteen sobas and in direct obedience to the king of Kongo under the authority of the dukes of Mbamba.[19] Aside from the mani Kasanze's general aversion to vassalage to the Portuguese or engaging in trade with them, the Portuguese were particularly threatened by Kasanze's close proximity to Luanda and, in particular, to the sources of fresh water upon which residents of the city depended. Indeed, in addition to generally raiding Portuguese plantations and farms and offering refuge to the burgeoning number of fugitives from enslavement not only fleeing Luanda but also the Lukala and Bengo River valleys, the people of Kasanze directly raided the homes of residents of Luanda and helped the enslaved to escape.[20] Enslaved Africans tasked with collecting water and firewood from the countryside surrounding Luanda in particular often found their way to Kasanze.[21] Confident that the Imbangala bands and African auxiliaries would easily lead them to victory over Kasanze, a much smaller polity than Ndongo, and lacking its trained standing army, the Portuguese advanced with artillery and cavalry, in addition to the usual firearms, archers, lancers, and spearmen.

Before attacking Kasanze at their capital, Nsaka, however, the Portuguese identified one strategic necessity: isolating Kasanze—not from their powerful overlords in Mbanza Kongo but rather from Kisama. António de Oliveira de Cadornega describes Kisama as the "Friends and Allies" of Kasanze, ready not only to cross the Kwanza and help them in battle, but also to offer refuge to any fleeing the conflict.[22] To cut off Kasanze from this most threatening ally, the Portuguese stationed forces on elevated points on the right (north) bank of the Kwanza River to act as sentinels.

With significant numbers of their forces dedicated to preventing a Kisama-Kasanze alliance, the Portuguese and their allies turned to Kasanze itself. Nsaka was well protected, situated in "the most closed and defensible woods imaginable."[23] Kasanze used the thick cover of vegetation strategically, forcing the Portuguese to dedicate much of their effort to clearing brush. As the Portuguese struggled to clear the dense brush, the archers of Kasanze quickly and efficiently killed many of their soldiers and prevented the Portuguese from using any closed formation tactics.[24] While inflicting severe losses on the Portuguese and allied forces engaged in intensive defoliation, the people of Kasanze appeared to suffer little mortality. Correia de Sousa surrounded Nsaka, cutting off all aid, trade, and paths for flight to the south and east. Because of Kasanze's well-established food and water security, however, this partial siege, too, had little effect. A full siege, however, did eventually take its toll, and the mani Kasanze planned to flee by swimming across the Bengo River with five of his aides. Many surrendered, and on May 15, 1622, Correia de Sousa took Nsaka. After acknowledging that he "couldn't deny that he was a black of great valor," Correia de Sousa ordered his soldiers to behead and quarter the mani Kasanze and two of his sobas who, by Portuguese reckoning, were most directly responsible for attacking neighboring colonial plantations, stealing livestock, and, critically, liberating enslaved people from Luanda. As was their custom, the Portuguese displayed the dismembered bodies of these leaders on the paths leading out of the city.

However, the battle of Kasanze was far from over. Correia de Sousa ordered his captain to bring him all of the sobas, advisors, nobles, and military officers, along with the four who stood to succeed as mani Kasanze, ostensibly to swear obedience to the Portuguese and be confirmed in their territory. Without informing even his captain of his intention, de Sousa took these leaders and those over whom they ruled, adults and children, and put them onboard slave ships to Brazil, to directly serve the governor, Diogo de Mendonça Furtado, by mining gold in São Vicente.[25] As John Thornton notes, "Of the 1,211 Kongolese [Kasanze] captives who had been sent on five ships to Brazil, almost half (583) died during the Middle Passage and another 68 died shortly after arrival."[26]

A mere nine days after the conquest of Nsaka, the nobles of Kongo chose the Duke of Mbamba to become the new mani Kongo, Pedro II Nkanga Mvika. The mani Kongo and Correia de Sousa were immediately embroiled in conflict, as Pedro rebuked the Portuguese for attacking another of his vassals, a charge which the Portuguese countered by claiming he had supported Kasanze. The absurd demands of the Portuguese escalated, and after a few spectacular battles, Pedro routed them entirely. Pedro's campaign was not exclusively military, however. As sentiments against the Portuguese and their Imbangala allies rose across Kongo, Pedro wrote to the pope and the king of Spain, complaining that the Portuguese and their Imbangala allies were attacking Catholic people. After Correia de Sousa fled for Brazil the following year, the king of Spain wrote to the governor of Brazil, demanding that the captives from Kasanze, subjects of the king of Kongo, be returned. These diplomatic campaigns took years, and, in the interim, most of the original captives from Kasanze died. Some, however, did return.[27]

The spheres of power within which those from Kasanze and those from geographical Kisama moved were far from congruent. While Kasanze, too, served as a vital refuge for fugitives in the early seventeenth century, it was always intimately connected to state power. In the early 1620s, this connection was the source of both decimation and salvation to Kasanze. However, when we view Kasanze at the beginning of this campaign, the archives strongly suggest that while they may have been subjects of the Duke of Mbamba and the King of Kongo, the people of Kasanze looked to Kisama as their natural and inevitable allies in a war that pitted fugitives against state. Here, we have powerful evidence not only of the material importance of Kisama in the political landscape of early 1620s Angola but of the transformative and expansive geography of Kisama's reputation as well. With a documented history of antistate rebellion going back to at least the sixteenth century, Kasanze turned first not to other defiant and marginally allied elements of the Kongo political sphere as allies, but

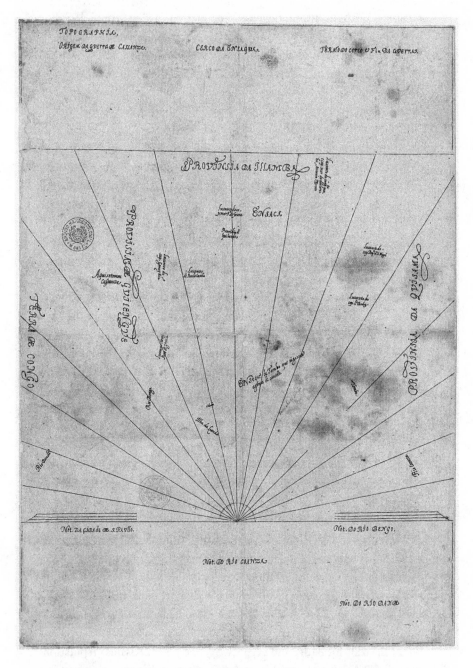

Figure 2.1 and 2.2 — Portuguese military maps in the 1620s campaign against Kasanze. Reproduced with permission from the Arquivo Histórico Ultramarino, Lisbon, Portugal.

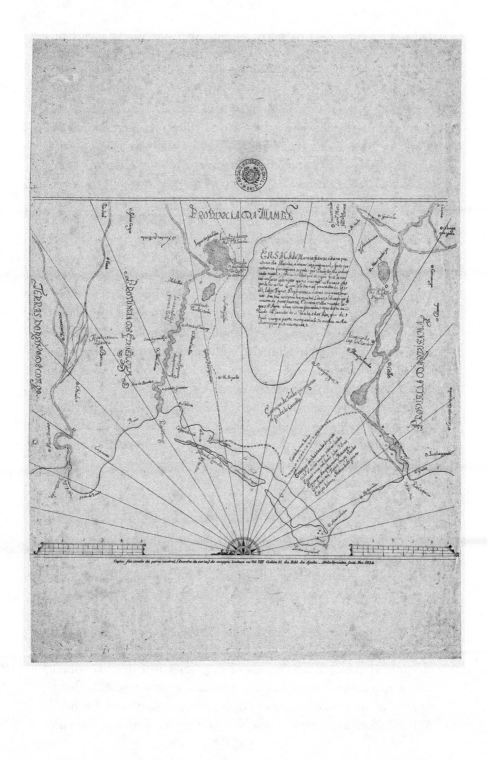

Copia, fac simile da parte central, (desenho da carta) do mappa incluso no Vol. VIII Codice 51 da Bibl. da Ajuda. Abilio Gonçalves, fecit. Nov. 1934.

rather to Kisama. The Portuguese fear that Kisama would welcome fugitives from Kasanze—many of whom were, by the 1620s, *from Kasanze* only and particularly in the sense that they found refuge from enslavement there—is perhaps not surprising. Kisama was already a regionally renowned haven for fugitives from far to the north, south, and east, and likely, at this particular time, many fleeing the atrocities of the Portuguese attack on Ndongo. But the Portuguese preoccupation with the possibility of armed people crossing the Kwanza River to assist Kasanze was remarkable. Scholars and even contemporary observers typically frame the martial activities of nonstate people as either "raiding" behavior, external to their bounded territory, or apolitical "self-defensive" behavior within a circumscribed space. A Kisama campaign in Kasanze fits within neither of those conceptions of politics or geography, instead directing us to consider the ideological underpinnings of war from within Kisama's burgeoning fugitive modernity. Allying with Kasanze was not directed by a desire to control territory or resources or people, nor by the compulsory and reticent martial participation of subjugated people. Rather, it was animated by a political commitment and a fluid geography of reputation and identity centered on the fugitives who were integral to what both Kisama and Kasanze signified.

The first direct mention of geographical Kisama as a refuge for those fleeing enslavement comes from then governor Fernão de Sousa's authorization of the Imbangala leader Nzenza to "wage war on ... the ... rebellious province of Quiçama, [where] the soba Cafuche ... has become very powerful, and is our main enemy ... in order to restore all of the slaves belonging to the Portuguese."[28] While this is the earliest archival reference to Kisama as a refuge for fugitives—in this case those who were among the tens of thousands of bondspeople working the manioc plantations owned by Jesuit or secular Portuguese or those normally identified as Luso-African in the Bengo, Lukala, and Kwanza River valleys—Kafuxi Ambari and other sobas in geographical Kisama had been attracting fugitives as dependents since at least the 1590s, following Kafuxi Ambari's defeat of the Portuguese. Tellingly, in this earliest direct source, however, it is Kafuxi Ambari who is named as the protector of the fugitives and the primary enemy of the Portuguese, suggesting the importance of the connection between his reputation in attracting fugitives and the development of the particular kind of fugitive politics that became Kisama.[29] While Kafuxi Ambari may not have controlled the lands that were the most convenient to those fleeing from the Portuguese forts along the north bank of the Kwanza River and the plantations further north, his unparalleled reputation easily made him the most likely protector for these highly vulnerable people. Kafuxi Ambari's renown as a warrior promised safety for those who could align themselves with him, and the increasing number of fugitive dependents whom he attracted only amplified his reputation and power.

De Sousa's explanation of his authorization of Nzenza's attack on the basis of the need to recapture fugitives speaks directly to the growing political strength of Kafuxi Ambari in the late 1620s aftermath of the defeat of Kasanze, and the role that these maroons played in consolidating his power throughout the region. Just as the fugitives in Kasanze provided the Portuguese with the pretext for invading and ultimately entering into conflict with Kongo itself, so too did the expanding presence and power of fugitives who made Kisama absolutely threaten both Portuguese trade and the monopoly on terror that they sought. By the late 1620s, Kafuxi Ambari's martial aptitude had made him a force with whom to reckon for more than thirty years, allowing him to attract followers from those who freed themselves from captivity on plantations, as well as from among those who fled in advance of the slave raiders. Fugitives came to Kafuxi Ambari for protection, but his ability to provide security from the Portuguese and their allies depended in no small measure on the numerical and military strength of his followers—in essence, a cycle by which large numbers of the weak and vulnerable transformed themselves into autonomous, well-defended, and strong communities of Kisama.

Kafuxi Ambari was not the only soba of Kisama into whose lands fugitives from slavery fled, and their increasing numbers in other sobas' territories dramatically influenced notions of political power, legitimacy, and identity in the region. As Kafuxi Ambari's prestige and reputation spread beyond geographic Kisama, it encouraged more and more fugitives from enslavement to attempt to find security and the opportunity for freedom in Kisama. There is ample evidence that throughout the tumultuous seventeenth century, sobas in Kisama assimilated fugitives through institutions of dependence and social inequality. Certain sobas within geographic Kisama also participated in the slave economy by giving captives to the Portuguese as conditions of their vassalage. However, these conditions of inequality and vulnerability were features of all neighboring state societies as well. What distinguished Kisama was the instrumental role that fugitives and dependents played in shaping notions of political legitimacy and in forging a new form of politics and society in which the individually vulnerable could together reconstitute themselves into well-defended living communities. The central importance and agency of maroons in reconfiguring the political dynamics of Kisama—indeed, of imbuing Kisama identities with political meaning—is not only what separated Kisama from its neighbors, but also what populated the political repertoires of fugitives throughout the region and in the seventeenth-century Americas as well.

The Kisama meme after 1594, and indeed, into the present, may have been largely singular, monolithic, and static; however, the internal social and political dynamics of Kisama were complex, contested, and changing. By the early seventeenth century, the rising tide of fugitives compelled at least some sobas within the region to adapt older social structures in innovative ways to accommodate an ever-increasing influx of people of diverse backgrounds and statuses. From formally trained soldiers to cultivator women, these fugitives affected the evolution of Kisama politics and society, rejecting political authority and alliances that imperiled their freedom.

Violence and Political Legitimacy: Kisama in the Age of the Imbangala

As Africans in the sixteenth and seventeenth centuries developed discourses about cannibalism and zombies who were forced to work beyond death to enrich others as moral and political critiques of the trans-Atlantic slave trade, Europeans involved in this trade recast unrelated nomadic peoples who attacked the established states of Kongo and Ndongo as "Jaga."[30] As John Thornton notes, in contemporary European usage, "it is a name which describes more a way of life than any ethnic group in particular," and, by the mid-seventeenth century, that "way of life" included not only nomadism and lineage-free social reproduction, but also, most infamously, anthropophagy.[31] Being "Jaga," then, meant embodying and enacting a particular extreme form of fugitive modernity, radically rejecting not only the structures of state but also the logic of the lineage and the precepts that typically governed social and cultural life throughout the region. While Imbangala discursively maintained the latter position, from around 1632, the foundation of the Imbangala state of Kasanje and Njinga's formal alliance with Imbangala meant that these radical dimensions of Imbangala politics and culture were incorporated into stable, and statist, social forms.[32]

The lifestyle of the nomadic pillaging Imbangala of late sixteenth- and seventeenth-century Angola, however, was an extreme response to the predatory incursions of slavers, whose raids rent families and communities asunder and made long-term investments in social reproduction—from raising children to tending crops and animals—risky at best, and a costly and futile expenditure of time and resources at worst. After the tidal wave of fugitives from the Imbangala and Portuguese campaigns against Ndongo in the late 1610s and early 1620s, another groundswell of people living around Luanda also ran away. In the early 1630s, entire communities around the city left their homes, their crops, and the graves of their ancestors to flee into the bush.[33] Some of those who fled joined Imbangala communities and moved from place to place, murdering, enslaving, seizing children, livestock, and crops, and cutting down wine palm trees, responding to the violence of the political landscape of seventeenth-century Angola by creating a profoundly antisocial sociability.[34] These reknit and radically reimagined communities in turn prompted a tidal wave of destruction in their wake, severing even more people from their communities and families and compelling them to turn to other fugitive strategies for survival.

While the Portuguese and their allies ripped communities apart through warfare and kidnapping, those who remained alive in Angola no less than those enslaved and transported to the Americas were forced to contend with a world in which older notions of reciprocity and obligation between the powerful and the subordinate were more often violated than they were upheld. In the Congo River basin, for example, those local people who benefitted most from the trans-Atlantic trade established the dynamic drum of affliction called *Lemba* in order to shield local communities from the pernicious spiritual and material illness of capitalism and the commodification of people, redistributing material goods and power.[35] In Imbangala society, however, the rituals through which people forged new communities were distorted mirrors of the very violence through which they had been dispossessed initially; Thornton goes so far as to argue that "Imbangala organization and its initiations, were in fact those of antisocial brigands, and the initiation, like that of child soldiers in modern day Africa required leadership that was ruthless and exploitative."[36] These qualities were useful to both Portuguese and Imbangala who sought to benefit from the commodification and sale of people.

The Portuguese were quite willing to forge alliances with Imbangala groups in order to defeat those whom they deemed difficult or impossible to subjugate. Indeed, Jan Vansina argues that "it is not much of an exaggeration to claim that it was largely due to Jaga support that the Portuguese managed to defeat the Ndongo king by 1620."[37] Already, we have seen Fernão de Sousa's alliance with the Imbangala leader Nzenza in his attempts to defeat Kafuxi Ambari. Sousa Chicorro, too, viewed the Imbangala as crucial allies in his war against the people of Kisama. He enlisted the help of various Imbangala leaders who were camped across the Longa River in Libolo at the time, including Nanboa Ambungo and Lunga dya Kafofo, to whom the Portuguese gave both captives and land as gifts, "which is the same as paying them, as is done with Soldiers of fortune who go where they are paid best . . . this type of people can be compared to the Cantons of Esquizaros who serve one or another Prince for a salary, and go where they are best paid, and perhaps some [will fight] against others."[38] For the Portuguese, this kind of mercenary behavior was intelligible and comparable to their experiences in wars throughout Europe. As inhuman as the Portuguese rendered them, the mercenary Imbangala fit far better within the kind of system that converted people into trade items than sobas and everyday people of Kisama.

In his efforts to understand the incessant resistance of Kisama, Cadornega remarked, "The motive of these powerful Sobas of Quissama to make this revolution, even though they have no need, is that some three hundred slaves of a recently deceased [Portuguese] resident have fled to their lands."[39] While for Cadornega, the continued revolutionary violence of sobas in Kisama in defense of outsiders—those who had only recently fled from Portuguese plantations to their land—was largely incomprehensible, such an act was at the very core of Kisama political philosophy during the seventeenth century. Tautologically, sobas within Kisama, especially Kafuxi Ambari but also others, attracted fugitives such as those who comprised this large group because they were powerful. Their power, in turn, was intimately connected to their ability to defend such people from outside predations, and to assimilate them and their descendants, albeit through relationships of subordination and institutions of social inequality.

Kasanze, Kisama, and the Imbangala represent distinct, overlapping, and interconnected iterations of fugitive modernity in the chaotic and violent world of early seventeenth-century Angola. Kasanze long shifted in and out of the shadow of the Kingdom of Kongo and folded fugitives from Luanda and the Lukala and Bengo River valleys into its adapted hierarchical political infrastructure and terminology. Kasanze's liminality and fugitive orientation made its alliance with Kisama politically workable; its status within the sphere of Kongo allowed it to seek aid within the structures of state during desperate times. Kisama, by contrast, functioned far outside the structures of Kongo or Ndongo, though those within Kisama could nimbly navigate between these poles of power, even, when necessary, allying with the Imbangala. Renouncing the idiom of social reciprocity and reproduction entirely, the Imbangala could serve as mercenaries for states and nonstates alike, pushing no agenda of permanent conquest or domination but rather intense and fleeting violence and totalizing material seizure. These distinctions—far from rigid—inflected the political landscape of the period, and were evident in the language and choreographies of struggles for power within Kisama.

Political Legitimacy, Reputational Geography, and Identity in the Shadow of Chaos: The Langere Succession Struggle

In 1629 or 1630, a man arrived at Massangano, the Portuguese fort on the north banks of the Kwanza River, with his *tendala, mani quizico,* and *makotas,* claiming to be a successor to Soba Langere and petitioning Portuguese captain João Carvalho Mascarenhas to affirm him as the rightful ruler of this soba's lands.[40] After Mascarenhas asked the man whether he would obey the Portuguese, be a vassal of the king of Portugal, and pay his tribute, the pretender Langere and his makotas assented and signed a treaty.[41] He then left for Langere's lands with his advisors and a *kimbare,* or African soldier who had fought as an auxiliary with the Portuguese forces, to ensure the pretender Langere's compliance with the terms of his vassalage. Mascarenhas wrote to de Sousa that he dared not "send a white man, nor a creole, nor a person who wore [European] clothing, for the inconveniences that could result."[42] So eager was Mascarenhas to avoid any conflict with the pretender Langere that he "did not speak of the quimbares who are fugitives in his land, nor of other things in order to not engender distrust."[43]

It is worth noting that in spite of the enduring scholarly insistence that rigid categories of race were nineteenth-century inventions, it is clear that racial ontologies and their phenotypical and sartorial proxies had political currency in the world of seventeenth-century Angola. Not only did Mascarenhas avoid the fraught topic of the runaway *imbare* (plural of *kimbare*)—who represented a uniquely valuable and dangerous type of fugitive in terms of skill and the arms and munitions they would have taken from the perpetually undersupplied Portuguese to Kisama—but he also acknowledged entire racialized categories of people who, by definition, by their very presence, would have endangered or sank the Portuguese diplomatic effort entirely. Here, it is the people of Kisama whose paradigm and racial/political categories determined the contours of interaction. While Joseph Miller, Linda Heywood, John Thornton, and others have cast so-called creoles as liminal figures, in this moment, it seems clear that for those who crafted Kisama, creoles were as inherently untrustworthy as whites or even those who dressed as Europeans.

After passing through the Portuguese fort at Cambambe and Combe Riaquina, the pretender Langere and his delegation attempted to reenter the lands of Langere along with the captain of Cambambe, Miguel Barreiros de Brito.[44] Far from being welcomed home, however, the Portuguese-backed pretender and his delegation found "that in the quisico and those of the banza did not want to obey him [the pretender Langere] because the Jaga Zenza said that he wanted to install the soba who had been cast out of the lands, and [who] had asked him permission to make war against some of his rebellious subjects, and that he [Nzenza] gave him help in this."[45]

This particular Imbangala leader, Nzenza, had already served as an ally of the Portuguese governor Fernão de Sousa, who had authorized his attacks on Kafuxi Ambari. So when the governor informed Nzenza through the captain of Cambambe that the pretender had Portuguese support, the Imbangala leader withdrew.[46] This episode represents a rare occasion on which the colonial archive allows us even the smallest glimpse into the nature of political contestation *within* Kisama. Two distinct groups of people within the lands of Langere—the people of the "quisico" (*ijiko*) and those of the "banza" (*mbanza*)—opposed the Portuguese imposition of a pretender Langere. While the text does not specify under what conditions the other soba had been forced from his lands, he had apparently been pushed out by an unnamed political faction powerful enough that this Langere required Imbangala support to attempt to return.

The people of the ijiko were essentially serfs, or outsiders who were incorporated as dependents and could not be sold.[47] According to Miller, the mbanza describes among the Imbangala as "positions for aliens, which the Imbangala used to assimilate other strangers of various sorts in addition to slaves," while Heintze, drawing on material from Ndongo, defines the mbanza as a "population of certain importance, a principal place, [or] city."[48] Vansina notes that the people of the Kingdom of Ndongo borrowed the term *mbanza* from the Kingdom of Kongo in the fifteenth or sixteenth century.[49] These two glosses for *mbanza* point to the possibility of divergent social and political histories. In the more centralized kingdoms of Kongo and Ndongo, where, though the violence of the trans-Atlantic slave trade irrevocably altered notions of political legitimacy and reciprocity it did not completely sever older forms of social organization, the term *mbanza* maintained the older meaning, referencing a stable, politically powerful people or the geographical location in which such people resided. The Imbangala, however, were essentially *all* outsiders or aliens, until they had undergone martial training and ritual incorporation.[50] Even then, alterity and outsiderness remained an essential part of Imbangala identity. For example, the name of the Imbangala leader Nzenza means "stranger" in both Kimbundu and Kikongo.[51]

Because this snapshot comes from a moment of political flux within the lands of Langere, it may be problematic to interpret the social institutions depicted here as representative of what was actually happening for those who identified as or were identified as Kisama more broadly at the time. Though the Portuguese understood the man who arrived in Massangano as a pretender Langere and his delegation as authorities within Langere's lands, it is impossible to say whether those who identified themselves as subject to Langere's authority at the time would have recognized them as such. However, given the apparent power of the ijiko and mbanza classes in rejecting the Portuguese-backed pretender and supporting the Imbangala-backed soba who had previously been exiled, it seems clear that the social language of ijiko and mbanza worked within the political paradigm of Kisama in the late 1620s, whether or not the particular tendala, mani kijiko, and makotas that the Portuguese-supported pretender brought with him were recognized by the people in Langere's lands.

While it is impossible to know how, precisely, Langere's people would have understood the term *mbanza* in the seventeenth century, its distinction from *ijiko* possibly indicates that those of the mbanza had a higher status than those who were newly fugitive. That the interests of two such seemingly distinct social classes converged in this case, and both of these elements of Langere's populace opposed the Portuguese-endorsed pretender, reveals a certain political cohesion even among socially stratified groups. If fugitives, or those whose interests resonated with fugitives, were part of the mbanza, it suggests that they had been a part of the local political landscape for over a generation—enough time for ijiko to have children who achieved the status of mbanza. This intergenerational mobility, however, was hardly unique to Kisama. Nearly all scholars who have written on institutions of social inequality in Africa have favorably contrasted this feature of slavery and dependency in Africa with the archetypically rigid forms of chattel slavery associated with the Americas. These evaluations, naturally, originate from etic perspectives, asking less about the experiences of the subjugated and more about abstract structures, and we would do well to remain critical, always, of any view that places within a moral or material spectrum the lives of the exploited.

What appears utterly distinctive about Kisama, however, was the *immediate* role that fugitives played in shaping the political orientation of Kisama. The frame of Kisama meaning may well derive from Kafuxi Ambari, but the flesh was entirely fugitive. For those who had been captured by either the Portuguese or the Imbangala and subjected to the violent dimensions of their rule, who had lost everything, risked everything, to become Kisama, someone willing to treat with either of these powers had little claim to political legitimacy, and by the late 1620s, they were powerful enough to challenge Langere's authority. That both the Portuguese-backed pretender and the exiled soba were compelled to seek support from the outside reveals the apparent political power of fugitives in determining the contours of social legitimacy within Kisama.

It is important, too, to note that the only directly, distinctly named fugitive population on Langere's lands at this time that emerges from the archives were the imbare, or trained soldiers who fled from bonded service for either the kings of Ndongo or Kongo or the Portuguese themselves, as seems most likely in this case. The Portuguese were clearly in no position of power in their negotiations with the pretender Langere, and Mascarenhas mentioned to de Sousa that though the Portuguese at Massangano were well aware of the number of fugitive imbare who had fled to Langere's lands, he did not discuss these for fear of causing dissent and discord with his newly sworn vassal. Mascarenhas's hesitation here reveals the significance of this distinct cohort of fugitives in this particular region of Kisama. For the perpetually understaffed, underarmed, and overwhelmed Portuguese forces in the forts of the interior, the loss of even a few soldiers would have taken a tremendous toll. To lose such trained soldiers—and their arms and munitions—not to illness or battle but to the camp of their perpetual enemies in Kisama represented a devastating blow to Portuguese efforts to control the people of the region.

But what did it mean for the people of Langere's lands? We can assume that fugitives arriving with such important skills would have been welcomed in a society whose material survival was predicated largely on martial aptitude. Undoubtedly, their savvy and any supplies that they may have brought with them were important attributes in the evolving martial repertoire of Kisama, and were likely critical in teaching people within Kisama how to use the firearms that they deployed during the war of 1655–58.[52] The knowledge, skills, and supplies that fugitives brought with them to Kisama were as critical to Kisama's political viability as the ever-growing stream of new residents, and the particular military acumen of imbare, their familiarity with firearms, and their intelligence concerning Portuguese tactics would have proven invaluable.

Though the imbare were undoubtedly important to the practice of warfare in Kisama, and the Portuguese recognized them as a distinct class of fugitives, the political imagination of Kisama was less focused on warfare and more focused on relationships of incorporation and social reciprocity. Mascarenhas's use of the terms *tendala*, *mani quizico*, and *makotas* and his familiarity with Ndongo political culture warrant some attention to his claims that the pretender Langere arrived with an entourage that emphasized the centrality of fugitive dependents within his society: a viceroy who was likely drawn from the kijiko class (tendala), an official whose job it was to oversee the ijiko (mani quizico), and elders from various lineage groups (makotas).[53] This seemingly radical change from a more decentralized form of political culture—even if it occurred only within the lands of Langere—may reflect a borrowing from the political culture of Ndongo, or it may simply be a result of the Portuguese tendency to view political institutions in Angola through a monolithic lens shaped by the cultures with which they were most familiar—Ndongo and Kongo. Even if they existed only in the lands of Langere, and other sobas in Kisama found different political strategies for incorporating outsiders that simply did not leave a trace in historical archives, these institutions suggest that political actors in Kisama could adapt and adopt tools of the state for explicitly nonstatist—and indeed, counterstatist—goals. In both Ndongo and the lands of Langere, however, the importance of these three named positions connects directly to slavery and the slave trade.

By inference from Ndongo, the role of the mani kijiko was to oversee those ijiko who were dependents of the soba.[54] To require a titled position in the structure of a relatively small-scale society, the ijiko must have formed a large and powerful class that potentially threatened the legitimacy of the soba, as was clearly the case for this particular pretender whose legitimacy was contested by the ijiko and the mbanza. The Portuguese-backed pretender Langere arrived in Massangano with his tendala, mani quizico, and makotas, pointing to the centrality of social inequality in the world that the fugitives were building. That a leader like Langere who ruled within the notoriously decentralized region of Kisama required a mani kijiko by this period implies the importance of ijiko within his community. If in 1588 the Langere who led the Imbangala leader Kalandula to Kafuxi Ambari's lands was described as powerful, and likely already had a number of dependent ijiko on his land, then the Langere of the late 1620s and early 1630s, who had a titled official simply to oversee the ijiko, must have ruled over even more. The pretender Langere's makotas may have been longer-standing residents of the lands, but after a few generations, even such esteemed titles would inevitably pass to descendants of fugitives. Though fugitives would continue to flee to geographical Kisama well into the nineteenth century, by the late 1620s or early 1630s, the small-scale communities between the Kwanza and Longa Rivers were already at least a couple of generations into the process of becoming mature maroon societies.[55] Whatever the social practices in these regions prior to the sixteenth century, by the mid-seventeenth century, fugitives and their descendants pervaded every aspect of social and political order within Kisama. As much as Kisama was defined by the warlike traits transposed from Kafuxi Ambari onto all of those living in the land, it was also characterized by the political institutions and social mechanisms that allowed for so many thousands of fugitives to form new and enduring communities.

The strife over the pretender Langere's claim—a conflict that should have been unthinkable under the prevailing idioms of personhood—illustrates how the fugitives who fled to Kisama, attracted by the reputation of Kafuxi Ambari and other sobas, were instrumental in shaping the social and political dynamics of the societies to which they fled. While the societies that these maroons built maintained—or perhaps incorporated for the first time—aspects of social inequality, including the division between ijiko and mbanza, the omnipresent turbulence and violence of the slave trade compelled members of different social strata to work together to ensure that they were led by individuals who were capable of defending their autonomy from the Portuguese and Kongo and Ndongo as well as the Imbangala. While the treaty that the pretender Langere signed with the Portuguese was less onerous than comparable treaties signed by other leaders in Angola or maroon leaders in the Americas during the seventeenth century, it still rendered him an illegitimate leader in the eyes of both ijiko and mbanza, who rejected him even as an alternative to the Langere who had been exiled earlier from his own lands. Even in the face of social inequality, fugitive dependents already so pervaded Langere's society as to direct succession and reconceive the contours of political legitimacy. Though the fugitive imbare in Langere's lands and others undoubtedly engaged in violence in defense of their freedom, Kisama's unwillingness to define their social forms through idioms of or reference to the violence so integral to Imbangala society is essential to understanding the distinctive ways in which Kisama politics developed in the early seventeenth century.

While certain families in Kisama are widely reputed to have been active in armed resistance against the Portuguese in more recent times, their honorific names reflect skill in hunting, not warfare.[56] Hunting—always a crucial survival skill in geographical Kisama and particularly in the more agriculturally marginal regions far from the Kwanza and Longa Rivers—is something with which nearly all men and boys who arrived in Kisama would have had experience. Fighting with hunting weapons is far different from using the handheld weapons and combat techniques of the trained armies of state and the Imbangala.[57] Aptitude as a hunter would have allowed for these fugitives to demonstrate their value to the communities they joined as dependents. When game was scarce, and when those practicing agriculture were harried or forced to flee by raids of the Portuguese and their allies, however, turning to "hunting" the Portuguese for supplies could become a crucial strategy for survival.

We have already seen how Kafuxi Ambari used raiding as a strategy for survival in the face of the intensive localized drought conditions of 1588. In fact, he appears to have gone further than merely raiding for supplies and/or captives, moving from the chronically arid Atlantic littoral to seize the more fertile land along the Longa River valley by 1593, and certainly by 1601.[58] In the mid-seventeenth century, however, as Njinga and their Dutch allies and the Portuguese and their allies fought to control Luanda and its hinterlands, the rivers of Angola became increasingly vital sites of conflict, and those living along them bore the brunt of the ill effects of violence and dislocation. By the 1620s, the Portuguese began using the Kwanza River as a major artery through which to export captives from the interior to the Americas in an effort to circumvent the Dutch: "*Pataxos* [two-masted ships], boats, and canoes, the pumbos [*pumbeiros*] would all go up the river, and the same boats would return to the City of Loanda with *pumbieros* and laden on their return with slaves [*peças*] and ivory, and more types of fruit of the land for sustenance."[59] The "fruit of the land" in particular would have made these boats an attractive target for the ever-increasing fugitive population of Kisama.

By midcentury, Captain-General Barreiros, who had served at Massangano for nineteen years, named the sobas Gunga, Songa, Kamoka, and "other rebels who impede the passage of traffic [in] people on the Coanza River because they are confederates of the Dutch."[60] Barreiros's attribution of the motives of these sobas seems dubious, based as it is upon an assumption of supreme European agency. If, however, the food and other supplies on this boat were the primary goal of the canoe-borne raiders from Kisama, freeing the captives on board and augmenting the strength of their societies by adding these additional dependents would have been an extra benefit of such attacks.[61] Indeed, by the eighteenth century, the Portuguese complained explicitly that the people of Kisama attacked the slave ships navigating the Kwanza River in order to free the enslaved captives and bring them back to join Kisama communities.[62]

The succession struggle in the lands of Langere reveals how the fugitives of Kisama reshaped the social and political institutions of the communities within which they sought refuge. Though these men and women may have arrived in the lands of Langere and become ijiko, and the soba had an official specifically responsible for overseeing them, they neverthe-less formed the constituency which determined the shape and meaning of political legitimacy within the territory. Intergenerational assimilation to the mbanza class was entirely beside the point; in this case, the mbanza acted in tandem with the agenda of the ijiko. The ijiko and mbanza, what-ever quotidian, structural, and/or conceptual differences these class labels entailed, here acted in concert to reject both the authority of both the Langere who was exiled and sought Imbangala support and the pretender Langere who attempted to assert his rule through alliance with the Por-tuguese. As the art of ruling the increasing numbers of fugitives in the lands between the Kwanza and Longa Rivers became ever more crucial to maintaining power, these fugitives were able to exercise decisive political agency.

Generations of scholars writing about the distinction between slavery in Africa and chattel slavery in the Americas have focused on the potential for social mobility and intergenerational status alteration for the enslaved and dependent in Africa. This scholarship has been an important correc-tive to the universalizing tendency of those for whom enslavement tends to be synonymous with antebellum North America, though the political implications of the literature can be, at times, ambivalent. A denuncia-tion of centuries of chattel slavery in the Americas shouldn't stem from an incrementalist notion that others *did slavery more kindly*, after all. The generation of African leaders descended from the enslaved and marginal, who came to power in the mid-twentieth century, themselves demon-strate the multigenerational and lingering impact of all forms of social and political stratification. What is distinct about Kisama is not the inter-generational social mobility of the enslaved and/or dependents. Rather, it is that within *a single generation*, Kisama transformed from a vaguely descriptive regional designation to a language of political praxis. Kafuxi Ambari was the spark that ignited what even contemporary Portuguese observers defined as revolutionary. Even for those who were *Kisama* but fought against him at times, the structures of ideology and action pro-voked by his successful campaigns provided the framework within which fugitives made a new world.

The succession struggle in the lands of Soba Langere should have been unthinkable, unimaginable. It would have been if the type of subjectiv-ity that Kafuxi Ambari occupied were more widespread, a general quality of leadership, rather than unique and particular to him. An enduring subjectivity, after all, is not subject to the pressures of local constituencies, however powerful. Instead, in this provocative sliver from the colonial archives, we see how multiple strands of political language and worldview intersected, intertwined, and pulled in tension with each other during this chaotic period. For Kisama-identifying and/or identified people in the lands of Langere, the adjacent Kafuxi Ambari was at the center of the reputation that drew fugitives to become Kisama. However, in the lands of another soba, who made choices that directly threatened not only the lives and well-being of those over whom he exercised authority but that also directly contradicted the political ideology at the core of the world the fugitives were creating, it was entirely possible and even necessary to reject the right to authority. Here, fugitive dependents did not just work quietly to integrate into preexisting social structures. Rather, they radically and decisively remade them in their own image.

Conclusions

By the 1620s, thousands of fugitives, attracted by the compelling reputation of Kafuxi Ambari and, by extension, Kisama, as the bastion of resistance against the Portuguese, fled slavery and sought refuge in the lands between the Kwanza and Longa Rivers, geographical Kisama. There, they found no centralized states, but rather autonomous communities within which they could play important roles as hunters, fishers, farmers, and those who practiced combat. These fugitives found the fragmented political terrain foreign, perhaps, but not alien; they did not lose their social identities here, and could, and in fact did, reforge political identities, at times even using the language and structures of state. While those fugitives who had formal military backgrounds (imbare) were essential in the training of those who would defend the vulnerable within Kisama—as shown by the transference of the name "imbare" from the soldiers themselves to the fortified supplied pits so vital to Kisama's defense—the people of Kisama continued to identify and understand themselves through reciprocal social relationships. Despite the fact that much of Kisama was on nearly constant war footing throughout the seventeenth century, unlike in Imbangala society, where diverse and unrelated outsiders were assimilated into a society that cohered exclusively around a warrior ethos, life in Kisama centered more on forging reciprocal social bonds and the politics and economics of cultivation. Those who fled to Kisama might be fisherpeople who attacked Portuguese slave boats on the Kwanza River to procure supplies, or they might be former imbare who taught their peers how to use firearms and construct defensive pits, or they might be women who farmed manioc and maize on fertile lowland soils. Those who fled to Kisama may have initially been ijiko, but even ijiko asserted sufficient political agency to reject a soba who attempted to impose an unacceptable form of political dependency on his people.

In the unprecedented terrorscape of early seventeenth-century Angola, thousands of adults and children fled from their communities, seeking refuge in new lands, among new people, and in new social and political forms. For some, powerful centralized states like Kongo and Ndongo proved compelling, offering the protection, however tenuous and often violently ruptured, of treaties and standing armies. Some rejected the older institutions of social life and reproduction entirely to form roving martial bands, the Imbangala. Others found haven in close proximity to both the city of Luanda and the plantations of the Bengo River valley, transforming the Kongo province of Kasanze to a maroon society in the direct crosshairs of Portuguese colonial retribution. Even for Kasanze, however, the most important, most reliably revolutionary fugitive-driven society in the region was Kisama, their ally.

Kisama's strong reputation by the early seventeenth century not only attracted legions of fugitives, from cultivators to hunters to imbare, or trained auxiliary soldiers, but it also shaped the actions of other political powers in the region. As the king of Ndongo faced a devastating crisis of authority within his own territory and a threat from the Imbangala and the Portuguese, he instead fixated on the potential for Kafuxi Ambari to usurp his rule. And the Portuguese themselves, after decades of conflict with the formidable armies of regional empires, instead were concerned that the enduring, nonstate politics of Kisama inspired resistance throughout the region, publicizing to neighboring people that power lay not in firearms but in the collective action of the vulnerable. Kisama presented the gravest material, rhetorical, and ideological challenge, not just to the totalizing destructive capitalist logic and violence of the transAtlantic traffic in human beings, but also to the attendant transformation of governing social idioms to center on warriors and warfare.

CHAPTER 3

"The Husbands Having First Laid Down Their Lives in Their Defense"

Gender, Food, and Politics in the

War of 1655–58

In December of 1655, as Njinga negotiated an end to decades of conflict with the Portuguese, they wrote to the governor of Angola, Luís Martins de Sousa Chicorro, "I trust with God that Your Lordship [Sousa Chicorro] will be in His Majesty's good graces only if you leave me in peace and tranquility and conquer Quissama, a thing that no governor has earned the glory of accomplishing. I offer Your Lordship my assistance in the conquest of Quissama. If it refuses to pay obeisance to you, and if it pleases Your Lordship, I will dispatch one of my grandees with as large a force as can be mustered."[1] For Njinga, Sousa Chicorro, and various African and European actors in the region at the time, the association between a rapprochement and jointly turning their armed forces against Kisama would have required little explanation. Throughout the 1640s and early 1650s, as the Portuguese and their allies focused on wars against Ndongo and Matamba, Kongo, and their Dutch allies, refugees continued to flee to geographical Kisama, creating political Kisama in the process. Indeed, this flight was likely facilitated by an ephemeral collaboration between sobas along the southern bank of the Kwanza River and those in Illamba, a region between the Bengo and Dande Rivers that, by the 1640s, was already home to many Portuguese-run plantations, mirroring the alliance of Kisama and Kasanze two decades earlier.[2] During the 1640s, the rivers in Angola's interior—particularly the highly navigable Kwanza River along which the Portuguese located most of their important forts and local powers situated their slave markets—became both increasingly important to Portuguese strategic interests and impossible for them to control. As those living along the southern bank of the Kwanza River attacked Portuguese river traffic between Luanda and the forts at Muxima, Massangano, and Cambambe, those living along the northern bank of the Longa River impeded all Portuguese attempts to open a land route for communication between Luanda and Benguela.[3] If the notoriety of Kafuxi Ambari had helped shape the regional reputation of Kisama as an identity of the invariably recalcitrant, brave, and martially adept, the actions of those who identified as or were identified as Kisama in the 1640s and 1650s only reinforced this notion. While some of the sobas of geographic Kisama nominally allied with Njinga, some allied with the Portuguese, and some with the Dutch in the 1640s, nearly all continued to defend their autonomy from outsiders, European and African alike.[4] This was by no means a unique facet of Kisama politics; what was distinctive was the inherent and ongoing rejection of larger-scale, more hierarchical social forms and the role of fugitives in shaping Kisama political culture.

Even before he left Portugal for Luanda, Sousa Chicorro remarked on the paucity of captives available in Angola and the centrality of the slave trade in the economic life of the residents, proposing the necessity of "wars against the King of Congo, Queen Ginga and the Province of Quiçama, all persecutors of my vassal sovas for participating in commerce with the Portuguese."[5] Unlike the centralized states of Kongo and Ndongo, with whom the Portuguese had regular if problematic diplomatic relations since the late fifteenth and early sixteenth centuries, respectively, even a nominally vassal soba like Muxima in Kisama did not participate in the kinds of letter writing and diplomatic activities that made the politics of Kongo and Ndongo legible in Lisbon, Seville, the Hague, or the Vatican.[6] That an official in Portugal was aware of the reputation of the people of Kisama and the ways in which their actions impeded the Portuguese commerce in people—and influenced the exercise of political power in the region to the same degree as the standing, trained armies of the states of

Kongo and Ndongo and Matamba—is testimony to the centrality of this putatively marginal space in early modern global consciousness, African and European alike. Even by this period, those in Lisbon and elsewhere around the globe were intimately acquainted with Kisama's geography of reputation.

The Kisama meme and the praxis of fugitive modernities emerging in Kisama had already begun to resonate globally, well beyond the lands between the Kwanza and Longa Rivers. Kongo, Ndongo and Matamba, the Dutch, and the Portuguese all perceived the threat of Kisama in essentially the same terms: it was fragmented, ungoverned and ungovernable, and not swayed by the kinds of hierarchical negotiations that allowed for states to shape the political behaviors of those who worked within their idioms. After decades of conflict and negotiation with various factions in the Kingdom of Kongo and Njinga, the Portuguese knew well the complexities of West Central African statecraft, and were well versed, if clumsy, at negotiating with heads of state.[7] Kisama, however, was a different matter. Its very existence was nebulous and porous, and it was not, in any meaningful way, conquerable, though this did not dissuade state actors from Ndongo, Matamba, or Portugal from trying.[8] The same promise that Kisama represented to the vulnerable, alienated fugitives throughout the region reverberated as threat through the state political cultures to which it represented such a challenge.

After arriving in Angola, Sousa Chicorro fulfilled both his wish and that of Njinga. After lengthy negotiations, he finally signed a peace treaty with Njinga on October 12, 1656; the Portuguese recognized Njinga's sovereignty but gained access to the lucrative markets in which bondspeople were sold in Matamba. With Njinga no longer a barrier to the Portuguese and their voracious appetite for captives, Sousa Chicorro followed Njinga's counsel and initiated a prolonged and devastating war in Kisama lasting from 1655 until 1658, in many ways echoing the three-year campaign against Kasanze three decades earlier. Outside the orbit of Kongo politics or state protection, however, Kisama's response to invasion would unfold and resonate differently than had Kasanze's.

Linda Heywood and John Thornton describe Sousa Chicorro's campaign as "more like a great slave raid than an attempt to bring the area into submission," despite acknowledging António de Oliveira de Cadornega's comparison of this campaign to great battles of Mediterranean antiquity.[9] Though violence and rupture had marked the lived realities of all in the region for the better part of a century, the war of 1655–58 represented a critical point during which the political, social, and environmental topography of Kisama changed in ways that would reverberate for centuries to follow. While for those in Matamba and Ndongo and for their Portuguese allies the war may have appeared as naught but an extended and intensive slave raid—and are slave raids less of a totalizing terror, or less globally/politically imbricated than other types of conflict, anyway?—for Kisama, this war would reify divisions in political ideology, sharpen notions about the relationship between violence and political legitimacy, and demonstrate the various approaches through which different people across the region assimilated fugitives into their communities. It also highlights the ways in which state- and nonstate fugitives were instrumental in refashioning gender roles in the tumultuous seventeenth century, and the role of environment and subsistence practices in creating, sustaining, and defending fugitive landscapes. In this moment of tremendous flux and turmoil, we can access further snapshots of Kisama politics and society after a few generations as a fugitive-centered society.

A detailed exploration of the war of 1655–58 in all of its complexities, too, allows us to view fugitive modernities through another critical lens: that of social health and healing. For more than three decades, the literature on social health and healing has proliferated within Africanist scholarship, vastly enriching our understanding of the multiple idioms of power and social cohesion. While many of these foundational texts are in fact based in West Central Africa in the era of the trans-Atlantic slave trade, including John Janzen's seminal *Lemba*, few other than James Sweet and Pablo Gómez have applied the theoretical and methodological tools of this extensive literature to the contiguous world of rupture, violence, and dislocation within which many Africans and their descendants from West, West Central, and Southeastern Africa and the Americas found themselves from the fifteenth through the nineteenth centuries.[10] In this chapter and the one that follows, I interpret illness and health as an essential part of the repertoires of political thought and praxis in seventeenth-century Angola and the Americas, attempting to center the experiential dimensions of the epistemological work of Kisama. What more clearly articulates the topographies of power and thought in a society than the ways in which it defines the nature of illness and the means through which people and communities can be brought back to health?

As we have seen, in the decades leading up to the war of 1655–58, Kisama's reputation as a unique fugitive space and praxis spread far beyond the boundaries of geographic Kisama and shaped politics in states throughout the region, and even in Europe and the Americas. The crux of this reputation, of course, was Kafuxi Ambari's power and his iconic defeat of the Portuguese in 1594. However, power has many idioms of articulation. For the vulnerable people who were inclined to become Kisama, the spiritual and healing aptitudes that were an integral part of martial skill may have been crucial to the language through which the people of Kisama publicized their supremacy over the Portuguese. Suggestively, Giovanni Antonio Cavazzi, who wrote extensively about the world of mid-seventeenth-century Ndongo and its neighbors, mentions that the region of Kisama (and neighboring Libolo) were home to

> renowned [priests of] *navieza* and *cassumba*, his woman, called thus after the name of their idols. For the first, the Jagas built a house and for the second a veranda, amply supplied with everything they need: food, drink, weapons, skins, cloths, and containers. In the house of *navieza* I often saw large numbers of musical instruments, barbarous of sound and rough of manufacture. I also saw many heads and, among others, one particularly dedicated to the idol, full of feathers and hair. However, I could never penetrate their significance. In these dwellings they sacrifice goats, chickens and other animals. All come here to seek cures for their illnesses. In case of death, the bodies of the men are taken to the *navieza*'s home and the women to the *cassumba*'s veranda. They are all given the highest tribute, consisting of feasts, debauchery, dances and songs for eight continuous days, so that the two possession priests [*xinguila*] pass all of their lives at parties, with no troubles.[11]

Structurally and formally, there is nothing that particularly distinguishes Cavazzi's description of the navieza and cassumba in Kisama from the practices of possession priests and healers throughout the region. However, Kisama's reputation as the locus of the most powerful healing priests—following only a few decades after Kafuxi Ambari vanquishing the Portuguese governor Coutinho by attacking him with an "illness of the country"—points to the profound and vital connection between these languages of power.[12]

It is worth noting that Cavazzi, the seventeenth-century Italian Capuchin whose description and acknowledgment of his own inability to decipher the meaning of the navieza and cassumba practices constitutes the only known primary source that refers to these priests, believed that their origins lay to the east of geographic Kisama, in Grande or Alta Ganguela. This again troubles the forever state-centered focus of historians, and, like Kafuxi Ambari's name, hints at the possibilities of deeper historical connections between the fugitive peoples of geographic Kisama and those to the east. These tantalizing clues compel us to continue questioning the "Atlantic" origin of historical scholarship and the primordialist nature of both academic and popular thought concerning ethnolinguistic and political identities in Angola and beyond. If we center "the Atlantic" in West Central African histories, we again elevate the colonial, obfuscating the violence and rupture of the Jita Kwatakwata behind language that conflates the ease of archival access to historical actors entangled in capitalist enterprises with their centrality in the world of the past. If we continue to use the ethnolinguistic identities that featured so prominently in twentieth-century conflicts in Angola as hollow proxies for political identities in the seventeenth century—or to even assume that there is ever a natural, unproblematic correspondence between language and politics—then we impose the vexed logic of states onto the very people who so assiduously shunned them. Languages and choreographies of power and identification throughout the region had complex, nonlinear, and winding paths, often moving back and forth among nonstate people.[13]

The categories through which we understand illness are certainly as defined by politics as they are by any kind of objective, universal science or omniscient etiology, and it is conceptually misguided to conceive of the biomedical nature of an illness and people's experiences of it as fundamentally different. Indeed, in Cavazzi's account, what those in a twenty-first-century biomedical hegemony might categorize as "germ theory" and "therapeutic quarantine" sit comfortably and equitably alongside notions of personhood and time that are far less familiar. Cavazzi describes how "those afflicted and deformed by the bubonic plague, leave their country and, crossing to the region of Quissama, are put in an isolated hut. When they die, the people venerate them as protective deities against this illness. This cult, introduced by the ancestors, and still retained by their descendants, attributes the punishment of this illness to irreverence for these idols [navieza and cassumba]. Truly, the cases of the plague are numerous, whether due to the quality of the food, or whether due to the nature of the climate."[14] It is of course by no means clear that what Cavazzi describes as the bubonic plague was actually *Yersinia pestis*. However, given Cavazzi's upbringing in Italy and undoubted familiarity with the waves of bubonic plague that devastated much of the country from 1629 to 1633, and again from 1656 to 1657, it is likely that he knew the plague's symptoms and presentation well.[15] The DNA of *Yersinia pestis* from Angola is unique, virulent, and ancient, and endemic in rodents, but other genetic studies suggest that the roots of all global *human* outbreaks of the plague since the 1300s lie in the infamous first European epidemic.[16] Regardless of the biomedical etiology of what drew the afflicted to geographical Kisama and enshrined those who perished as protective spirits, it is clear from Cavazzi's description that navieza and cassumba drew significant numbers of suffering people from across the region to relocate to geographical Kisama in search of both a cure and a community.[17] While Cavazzi details how those who died remained in the community as protective deities, he does not describe what happened to those who survived. Perhaps they became priests, or other specialists, serving the growing community of the afflicted. This common practice in therapeutic communities throughout Africa forged a particular economy of knowledge and power, often outside of and in tension with more hierarchical and statist forms.[18]

Both along the Kwanza River and further south in the region of Benguela, people suffered rampant illness, drought, and famine in the period leading up to and during the war of 1655–58.[19] In August 1656, Sousa Chicorro reported that many of his infantry soldiers were dying of the "many and grave illnesses . . . that continue in this army. [It is] more than that the climate is unhealthy, it appears that is already a pestilent year."[20] If the Portuguese forces were suffering, then undoubtedly the much more numerous troops from Ndongo and elsewhere fighting alongside them were, too, and these fighters in turn likely spread disease through the countryside.[21] In such conditions, the famed navieza and cassumba, who attracted followers from far and wide, may have been instrumental in amplifying Kisama's renown and prestige throughout the region. The presence of large numbers of troops and the violence and social dislocation they wrought moving through geographic Kisama only exacerbated these typical ills of war, and they may themselves have been the most potent illness from which the vulnerable in the region sought a cure, often through the political medicine of becoming Kisama.[22] The peril of being alienated from one's natal community and the dense and protective fabric of ancestors and local spirits was an affliction nearly all in West Central Africa suffered in the seventeenth century. Navieza and cassumba worked effectively in tandem with the medicine of Kafuxi Ambari and others who rewove the regionally unraveled fabric of political and social life.

Whether the reputation of Kisama spread primarily through idioms of warfare or ritual power and healing—or, more likely and interrelatedly, both—given the wide geographical area from which fugitives fled to become Kisama, awareness of its peoples' resistance stretched from north of Luanda, into Kasanze, south to at least to Benguela, and far to the east. To counter this, Sousa Chicorro devised a counterpropaganda campaign, suggesting that the mere knowledge that the Portuguese were preparing for conflict would be enough to compel the people of Kisama to return fugitives and allow for the Portuguese to trade in adults and children, as well as in ivory. For those in geographical Kisama who publicized the frailty of the Portuguese military in comparison to their might, however, rumor and anticipation alone were not enough to coerce obedience. In present-day terms, Kisama had by far the most effective viral public relations machine, with a truly unmatched global reputation.

Diplomacy, Strategy, and the Fugitive Life of Plants

While in the period leading up to the war in 1655, some sobas did send ambassadors to the Portuguese promising allegiance and to return those fugitives who were in their lands, none of those who attempted to escape Portuguese depredations through diplomacy actually followed through on their promises. Instead, they used these diplomatic missions as a strategic stalling technique.[23] To return fugitives would have meant losing political power and claim to legitimacy to rule for these sobas, as seeking affirmation from and alliance with outside powers who would have imperiled fugitives had some twenty years earlier for two pretender Langere. It would have also necessitated tearing apart multiple generations of families. Those sobas who did seek to negotiate vassalage with the Portuguese did so only after observing the devastating impact of the war on their people and neighbors and concluding that jeopardizing legitimacy and power was necessary to ensure the survival of even a few.

In the first offensive campaign of the war, the Portuguese left the fort at Cambambe with hundreds of soldiers, including the king of Ndongo and his son, the prince, to attack the nearby lands of Soba Langere. Langere's forces used the woods as "their fortress and principal defense," engaging the Portuguese artillery and musketeers from within the security of their densely wooded fortifications.[24] The Portuguese intended to pass through Langere's lands to those of Kafuxi Ambari, which were not only populous and fertile, but were also the least densely wooded in the region—a distinct advantage to a Portuguese force that was determined to use a cavalry and to fight in formation.[25] However, as they attempted to pass through Langere's lands, the Portuguese discovered that though the leaders of Kisama ardently defended their autonomy, they were still quite capable of working together against an immediate danger like that presented by Sousa Chicorro's soldiers.

By the 1650s, Kafuxi Ambari was still "the most powerful Lord in Quisama,"[26] and he had also apparently transformed his relationship with Soba Langere from the enmity of the 1580s and the shared political positions of the earlier seventeenth century into a more durable alliance. Indeed, as the Portuguese attempted to march into Kafuxi Ambari's lands, those living on the lands of Soba Karindo attacked the Portuguese from within the cover of thick vegetation "to impede the passage of the Portuguese Army[,] and there was a great skirmish with many deaths and injuries on both sides."[27] Karindo's people recognized the threat that both cavalry and formation fighting posed, and so manipulated the landscape to force the Portuguese soldiers and their allies—including the king of Ndongo and his son—to march single file.[28] Other people within Kisama employed similar tactics during this war, planting thorny grasses across the paths that forced the Portuguese to stop and clear the passages with machetes.[29]

In many ways, the strategic use of vegetation mirrors not only the tactics of Kafuxi Ambari in 1594, but also, intriguingly, those employed so effectively by Kisama ally Kasanze during their war against the Portuguese in the early 1620s. The final stage of the Portuguese campaign against Kasanze involved them closing their siege and attacking the capital, Nsaka, located in "the most closed and defensible woods imaginable."[30] Much as in Kafuxi Ambari's victory in 1594, Kasanze was able to deploy the dense vegetation as part of an ingenious combat strategy, preventing the Portuguese from using any type of closed formation tactic.[31] Recognizing that vegetation was a critical part of the battle, Correia de Sousa ordered "a great quantity of axes, scythes, and cleavers" for each of his officers, mandating that each one clear fifty-five meters (sixty yards) of the brush. The Portuguese soldiers and their allies cleared the brush under cover of guards with firearms, who were nevertheless ineffective against the arrows that the people of Kasanze shot. According to de Sousa, "There were many days on which 25 or 30 Portuguese were shot, and these were by armor better defended than the black auxiliaries, of whom they killed many."[32]

In the case of the Portuguese attack on Kisama in the opening days of the war of 1655–58, assaults from the woods and the disruption of the Portuguese formation were so formidable that the Portuguese had to change their route and turn from their intended assault of Kafuxi Ambari to instead attack the people of Soba Kimbambala. Cadornega describes Kimbambala as being one of the sobas who sheltered the greatest number of fugitives from Portuguese captivity in the period leading up to the war of 1655–58. Indeed, some twenty years earlier, the Portuguese attempted to attack Kimbambala in order to recapture these fugitives, but Kimbambala's forces were alerted to the Portuguese advance by the noise and disruption resulting from an auxiliary's beating of his bondsmen.[33] By the mid-seventeenth century, then, fugitives were numerous far beyond the lands of Kafuxi Ambari and were central to the political and quotidian life of all within geographical Kisama. It is tempting to assume that this common orientation toward harboring fugitives engendered a sense of a shared political agenda among the diffuse and distinct people in geographical Kisama. However, as ever, alliances were temporary and shifting, and conflicts could and did endure.

From existing sources, we can discern that Kafuxi Ambari, Langere, Karindo, and indeed even Kimbambala worked together as allies during this period of intensive conflict, though Cadornega does claim that Karindo was in a more permanent position of vassalage to Langere. What, beyond the obvious exigencies of war, promoted this kind of cooperation among leaders who were committed to their own autonomy? Given the role that fugitives apparently played in reshaping the contours of political legitimacy in the lands of Langere, and the centrality of fugitives to the political positions of both Kafuxi Ambari and Kimbambala, it is likely that these maroons themselves wove the social fabric that permitted this kind of durable alliance during the mid-seventeenth century.

Fugitives were the common element within Kisama's fragmented political landscape, and the ramifications of harboring fugitives helped align the interests of various sobas, at least during times of more exacerbated and direct violence in a climate in which apocalyptic violence was the baseline, such as in the war of 1655–58. This balance of power moved beyond mere accountability to the ruled; indeed, it rendered sobas less important to the exercise of power of the contours of political ideology than those over whom they nominally exerted authority. We should not assume that the contemporary archival sources' glossing of politics through the names of sobas is an accurate rendering of the dynamics of power within each society. It is not enough to merely note the absence of these thousands of fugitives in the archive, or to theorize their silencing. Instead, it is imperative to engage their politics by taking seriously the ideology underlying their actions.

After passing through Kimbambala's lands, the Portuguese moved toward the lacustrine areas in the eastern part of the region, near the Kwanza River. Already, the people of the region had essentially besieged the Portuguese at Massangano, and they continued to plague the Portuguese military with continuous waves of archery, projectile spear, shotgun, and musket fire from their fishing and trading canoes.[34] While it is impossible to definitively date the adoption of firearms within Kisama, their use at this juncture likely resulted from instruction by the fugitive imbare who were present in Kisama by the early 1630s, and the firearms, munitions, and supplies they brought and/or seized from Portuguese forts and ships.[35] While the armed forces of centralized states like Kongo and Ndongo, who had professional, trained soldiers, relied more on hand-to-hand combat techniques, the irregular and essentially guerilla forces of various sobas of Kisama depended upon these long-distance projectile weapons.[36] For nonprofessional fighters with backgrounds as hunters, using these more common weapons combined with evasive techniques based on mastery of the land would have been tremendously effective. There were undoubtedly tactical and material reasons for martial strategy that depended on the use of projectile weapons. However, given the prevailing association of hand-to-hand combat with professional soldiers and a particular form of statist martial masculinity in seventeenth-century Angola, it is important to read these tactical choices as political ones, as well. Turning the weapons of the hunt to war is rooted in a different ideology than turning hunters into warriors.

Kafuxi Ambari and the Politics of Thirst

In the early seventeenth century, Soba Kafuxi Ambari was instrumental in forging the kind of revolutionary identity with which Kisama was associated. By the time of the war of 1655–58, Kafuxi Ambari was forced to adapt to the dire situation within which he found himself and his people, making alliances with the socially unpalatable and politically problematic Imbangala from the other side of the Longa River—the same Imbangala whose support of one of the pretender Langere had illegitimated his claim to authority twenty years earlier.[37] Like Njinga's alliance with the Imbangala when their rule was under such threat from both internal opponents within Ndongo and Matamba and external attacks from the Portuguese and their (Imbangala) allies, during this war, Kafuxi Ambari was forced to come to terms with this strikingly different practice of fugitive modernity in order to defend his largely fugitive society.

The Portuguese acknowledged that the defeat of Kafuxi Ambari was essential to their campaign against Kisama, as he was "the greatest power, and . . . King of this Province."[38] Kafuxi Ambari was so powerful at this time that he exercised authority from his more recently conquered territory along the inland Longa River valley all the way to his old territory on the Atlantic coast, where the Portuguese and their allies were camped. That he conquered the fertile land of the Longa River valley illustrates the fragmentary nature of politics in early seventeenth-century Kisama. While Kafuxi Ambari's leadership played an essential role in the discourses about Kisama identity from the late sixteenth century onward, those who shared in this common identity as Kisama did not necessarily also share a common political allegiance to each other. Kisama meant independence, as much from neighbors as from centralized states.

From within his newly conquered lands, Kafuxi Ambari's forces ardently guarded the *imbondeiro* tree cisterns that were the only sources of potable water inland from the Longa River, forcing the Portuguese to depend entirely on ported water. Kafuxi Ambari's strategy of monopolizing the only source of drinking water drove the Portuguese into a desperate situation once they were in the region. Defeating Kafuxi Ambari was no longer a question of pride or political maneuver, but rather of life or death. According to Cadornega, the Portuguese and their allies from Ndongo "proceeded so desperately because they realized that they had to win, or perish from thirst."[39] In confronting the Portuguese and their allies, including the king of Ndongo, his son, and a significant contingent of imbare from Ndongo, Kafuxi Ambari employed both psychological and martial tactics. Kafuxi Ambari's forces "scream[ed] and taunt[ed] that we [the Portuguese] could not drink their water." Kafuxi Ambari's forces and their Imbangala allies then "let loose torrents of arrows, barrages of spears, and shots from Muskets; the arrows were . . . let loose from very long Bows drawn with force, with the ends on the ground . . . to prevent slipping." Arrows shot from these bows "ripped holes in bodies that were awesome [to behold]." According to Cadornega, these arrows were the most notably effective weapons used in this battle, and "those who most used this kind of cruel and ferocious arrows were those Jaga from the other bank of the Longa River." The Portuguese were confident that their military response, however, had killed a great number of the Imbangala and driven the remainder across the Longa River. Kafuxi Ambari's people continued to fight until the Portuguese shot them at point blank range, thus gaining access to the imbondeiro tree cisterns.[40]

The tactics that Kafuxi Ambari and his Imbangala allies used throughout this conflict demonstrate military training and organization. For Kafuxi Ambari's forces to mount an effective archery and projectile assault, complete with the use of firearms, a certain degree of drilling would have been necessary. These are, after all, different methods than hunters use, and coordinating with Imbangala would have required even more training. In his examination of warfare in seventeenth-century Angola, John Thornton notes how both Kongo and Ndongo forces typically relied on a single volley of arrows before engaging in hand-to-hand combat. Because of this, commanders normally adopted a more dispersed pattern that would allow individual, professionally trained soldiers the opportunity to parry, dodge, jump, and otherwise acrobatically and skillfully maneuver against an enemy's strikes. If the commander of one army perceived that they were losing, he would typically order his soldiers to disperse, only to re-form in a few days.[41] Kafuxi Ambari's approach here, however, reflects a variation on the strategy. Though his forces used firearms, Cadornega believed that it was the extraordinarily long-range longbows that were the most effective weapon. While Kafuxi Ambari's Imbangala allies may have possessed more of these weapons or used them more skillfully, their employment in this conflict belies a certain material departure from the weapons of hunting in favor of the weapons of war. Such long bows would have been unwieldy hunting weapons, but they were well suited to a more stationary defensive battle, such as this last-ditch defense of an essential resource like the imbondeiro tree cisterns. For Kafuxi Ambari's forces to stand in defense of the cisterns until the Portuguese shot them at point-blank range, rather than dispersing and reforming as was typical throughout the region or as they had done in 1594, reveals both the organized military training necessary to wage such a campaign and the high stakes of the conflict.

Even as narratives of Kafuxi Ambari's individual battles may be lost to oral history, the centrality of these imbondeiro conflicts to the sovereignty—and survival—of the region's residents almost certainly informed the way in which they figured in the political and social life of communities in Kisama. It is possible that people have maintained memories of these trees and the connection of their defense in this and perhaps other conflicts to the histories of enslavement and the judicial practices they understand as "traditional." António Sondoka described the *imbondo ya mbumbu*, an imbondeiro tree under which those accused of crimes such as murder, adultery, witchcraft, and theft were tried. If the tree began to ooze blood, the accused was deemed guilty and killed immediately.[42] During the period of the trans-Atlantic slave trade, rulers often replaced the death penalty for offenders with the punishment of sale to the Europeans and their agents.[43] While I have found no written accounts of the use of the imbondo ya mbumbu in Kisama or elsewhere in the seventeenth century, it is possible to imagine how the capture of significant numbers of Kafuxi Ambari's forces—those who were not shot lethally at point-blank range—in defense of the imbondeiro-tree cisterns could have led to the ritual association of imbondeiro trees with bloodshed and slavery/death.

It is clear that Europeans maintained a memory of this desperate combat even into the nineteenth century, and it informed their perceptions of the nature of the people of Kisama. In 1858, the Scottish missionary and traveler David Livingstone wrote, "The Kisama are brave; and when the Portuguese army followed them into their forests, they reduced the invaders to extremity by tapping all the reservoirs of water, which were no other than the enormous baobabs of the country hollowed into cisterns. As the Kisama country is ill supplied with water otherwise, the Portuguese were soon obliged to retreat."[44]

While Livingstone appears here to have conflated the water-centered battle of the mid-seventeenth century with the Portuguese retreat during the conflict with Kafuxi Ambari at the end of the sixteenth century discussed in chapter 1, that this particular strategy endured for centuries as a symbol of the bravery of the people of Kisama in the minds of Europeans and their local interlocutors is a testament to its material and discursive efficacy. Unfortunately, there is no clear record of how Kafuxi Ambari himself or those of his people who lived outside the immediate area of the battle and survived it viewed the alliance with the Imbangala or the aftermath of the battle. The fact that after the conflict, the Imbangala retreated back across the Longa River suggests that this alliance was temporary and that Kafuxi Ambari was able to maintain his position of authority, rather than being ousted by the Imbangala or by people who objected to his alliance, as had been the case with Langere two decades earlier.[45]

Though we do not know the direct ramifications of Kafuxi Ambari's losses or of his alliance with the Imbangala, we do know that he continued as a prominent leader throughout the region even after his alliance with the Imbangala during the war. Cavazzi observed that, following the war, the Portuguese sought to open the slave trade and expand their missionary activities into "various provinces, especially that of Cafuxi, situated on the side [of the Kwanza River] of Quissama. . . . He [the missionary] related that this prince [Kafuxi Ambari] presented him with thirty seven sons, all of them beautiful, and well maintained. After this, when Mr. Bravo [the translator and guide] presented some bottles of European wine and a very expensive umbrella, the prince [Kafuxi Ambari] offered the wine to a large idol and put the umbrella on the head of the same idol before using it."[46] Though the war of 1655–58 was indeed devastating for many of the people between the Kwanza and Longa Rivers, Kafuxi Ambari appears to have weathered both his conflict with the Portuguese and his situational alliance with several Imbangala bands with minimal impact to his status. His many "sons" may well have been personal dependents—likely fugitives—rather than biological offspring, demonstrating how Kafuxi Ambari's authority derived from the dependence of those whom he was able to attract to his lands. Indeed, Kafuxi Ambari's power, and that of Kisama writ large, was connected to the ability to facilitate the transformation of dispossessed, alienated individuals into materially and discursively powerful new communities. While the Portuguese yearned to establish a trading relationship with Kafuxi Ambari, even after the war he was unwilling to enter into any sort of alliance with those against whom he had struggled, and from whom many of those who were the base of his power had fled. As Cavazzi notes, "But all of their [the Portuguese governor's emissaries'] efforts were useless, especially because of that chief [Kafuxi Ambari]."[47] His use of the foreign wine to libate a local spiritual figure demonstrates that he recognized how rooted his political legitimacy was in his spiritual power and its military manifestations. While his personal charisma and status allowed him to endure both his conflicts with the Portuguese and his engagement with those who, in other contexts, called the political legitimacy of other sobas into question, Kafuxi Ambari remained keenly aware of the ultimate sources of his power and of the importance of retaining political legitimacy among the expanding constituency of fugitive dependents in his land.

Though in the immediate aftermath of the war, Kafuxi Ambari appears to have retained his autonomy and to have continued to derive his political power from his ability to assimilate large numbers of dependents who were attracted by his martial skill—even as he apparently surrendered some of these dependents to the Portuguese—later in the seventeenth century, and perhaps as a consequence, Kafuxi Ambari's power waned. While Cadornega describes him as "ruler of a large number of people, from which he derives his greatest power, as king of this province [Kisama] . . . all of these sovas [in Kisama] recognize and pay tribute to him as their king and lord," he also includes him among the sobas who "call themselves sons of *Maniputo* [the king of Portugal], but are hardly obedient."[48] Thus, by the beginning of the eighteenth century, while the discourse of fugitive modernities forged in the early seventeenth century in Kisama remained critical, actual practices within much of Kisama were different. The early seventeenth century, however, remained the point of reference for political discourses both within Kisama and about Kisama for centuries to come.

Wars of Plenty and Wars of Starvation: The Role of Food Surpluses and Shortages in the War of 1655–58

Violence was omnipresent within Kisama as it was for all throughout the region in the seventeenth century, but unlike in Imbangala society, the incorporation of outsiders into local communities within Kisama was predicated on social, rather than military, reproduction. While hunting, fishing, and the gathering of wild produce and honey were important survival strategies throughout the lands between the Kwanza and Longa Rivers, the people of Kisama who lived in lands where intensive agriculture was possible, particularly near rivers, took full advantage of these opportunities. In the war of 1655–58, Sousa Chicorro and his troops passed through a "very fertile lowland in which there were many houses in which lived the greater part of the Cultivators, and where there were many fugitives from the Portuguese that because of its fertility lived there mixed with the Quisamas."[49] Here, Sousa Chicorro distinguishes between these fugitive cultivators and "the Quisamas." While it is unclear as to whether or not the local people made such distinctions, it is certainly likely that full-fledged membership in local society came only with time, or that different avenues to incorporation were available to hunting/fishing/fighting men and to women. These groups of cultivators, then, may have been comprised of large numbers of women, including those discussed in previous chapters who fled Portuguese plantations.[50]

Women and the food they produced appear to have played a much greater role in the war of 1655–58 than scholars have previously recognized. While Beatrix Heintze does not discuss the conflict in any detail, Aurora da Fonseca Ferreira argues that Sousa Chicorro was motivated primarily by the desire for captives for sale in the slave trade.[51] Heywood and Thornton contend that Sousa Chicorro was compelled to fight this expensive, high-casualty conflict by the role of Kisama as a refuge for fugitives from Portuguese enslavement and as a constant impediment to Kwanza River traffic.[52] There is no doubt that seizing captives, recapturing fugitives, and putting an end to the incessant attacks on Portuguese river boats were priorities for Sousa Chicorro. However, the importance of the independent salt and food merchants of Kisama in the local economy—and the role of fugitive women in particular in producing manioc, millet, and maize for market—remains an unexplored and essential aspect of the conflict of 1655–58.

Already by the early 1630s, Portuguese colonial governor Fernão de Sousa had concerns about the presence of merchants from Kisama in Lembo, a market town on the Lukala River, where rock salt from Ndemba served as currency in a trade centered on the acquisition of captives.[53] De Sousa ordered the captain of Massangano to clear Lembo of free people from Kisama, free people attached to residents, and all others, "without exception of Christians, pretenders to titles, *cassueas*, and others who have been attached to us for many years, and are already naturalized."[54] When the local officials protested the governor's orders, de Sousa modified them to require that they expel only "those black brigands of Quiçama who were not Christians, pretenders to titles, *cassueas*, or naturalized."[55] De Sousa's insistence on the expulsion of "those black brigands of Quiçama" points to the unique position that these merchants held in the local economy. Since the sixteenth century, the Portuguese had sought control of the rock salt from Ndemba that functioned as currency throughout the region. They used this Kisama-produced and -controlled commodity to both purchase bondspeople and to pay their own soldiers. Expelling independent salt merchants from Kisama from the markets at Lembo was a logical strategy for Portuguese authorities who were constantly preoccupied with usurping the independent production and circulation of this saline currency.

No less than salt, however, maize, manioc, and millet were essential elements of the economy of war- and slavery-ravaged seventeenth-century Angola. These American crops—save millet, which was an earlier local cultigen—compelled a true agricultural revolution throughout Africa, changing everything from gender and seasonal labor patterns to population densities to relationships between rulers and dependents to epidemiology to regional power dynamics.[56] Joseph Miller emphasizes the role of manioc cultivation in particular in promoting population growth in previously marginal and relatively arid regions with sandy soils, and the role of such increased production in "nourish[ing] children, captives, and slaves to ages at which they could be sold profitably to Europeans," as well as the vital role of manioc flour—either locally produced or imported from Brazil—in (barely) sustaining the captives aboard the slave ships that left from Angola to the Americas.[57] While many communities throughout the region added to or replaced earlier agricultural repertoires based on sorghum, millet, beans, and plantains with the introduced manioc and maize (and, by the nineteenth century, sweet potatoes) for domestic consumption, in the seventeenth century, the commercial production of manioc and manioc flour was limited to plantations, with one exception. Drawing from Cadornega, Jan Vansina notes that just as enslaved people grew manioc and processed it into flour for consumption by the Portuguese plantation communities along the Kwanza, Lukala, and Bengo Rivers and for sale in Luanda, so too did cultivators grow and process manioc in Kisama.[58]

According to Olfert Dapper, who likely drew from sources dating to the Dutch occupation, Kisama was "a land fertile in millet & in manioc."[59] This fertility supported not only the local population but also a class of highly active merchants, because of whom, Dapper argued, "the Quisames must be of better extraction than the other Blacks, they do not work themselves into the ground. They just carry salt & millet to the market, where the people of the Northern bank of the Quasa [Kwanza] come to exchange [the salt and millet of Kisama] for slaves."[60] These Kisama merchants not only participated in regular markets but also took advantage of sporadic droughts and famines in other parts of the region. Dapper contrasts the diligent cultivators and merchants of Kisama with the putatively lazy people of the regions directly surrounding Luanda, who were reduced to hunger by poor harvests and were forced to sell vulnerable members of their communities to the people of Kisama in exchange for food.[61] This type of market exchange stands in great contrast to the situation described by André Velho da Fonseca in 1612, when Kafuxi Ambari, Langere, Kapakasa, and others refused to trade with the Portuguese and their African merchants at all.[62] Mobilizing salt and agricultural products into a capacity to procure more dependents represents a different approach to building political power than the attraction of fugitives through military might, but these strategies could well have been complimentary within the repertoire of Kisama's fugitive modernities.

The presence of bondspeople in Kisama who were acquired through commodity and currency exchange throws into sharp relief the contingent nature of fugitive modernities. It would be wrong to assume that Kisama's opposition to participation in the trans-Atlantic slave trade meant an ideological opposition to social inequality in general; objection to strategies of state does not equate to a romantic, idealized notion of primitive equality. As we have already seen, fugitives often found themselves in the position of dependency to powerful leaders like Kafuxi Ambari, who represented their best—and often only—hope for defense from Portuguese predations and the threat of capture and sale, whether locally or across the Atlantic. From the perspective of those facing starvation and repeated Portuguese and Imbangala predations around Luanda, Kisama may simply have been the least oppressive alternative among several crushing possibilities that were never really choices. However, it is also possible to view inequality within Kisama as the social and intellectual opposite of the practice of slavery on Portuguese-run plantations in Angola and in all of its varied forms throughout the Atlantic islands and in the Americas. While enslaved Africans and their descendants forged new political cultures through their enduring struggles against the threat of social death in these contexts, social inequality within Kisama itself was part of the process of social life. Purchased captives were not the social equals of those who had purchased them in Kisama, but neither were they alien others. Instead, they were integral to the social life of Kisama and the political practices that emerged to defend it.

Adding purchased adults and children to the growing flood of fugitives who fled to the lands between the Kwanza and Longa Rivers allowed for these capitalizing merchants to initiate something of a positive feedback loop. The purchased bondspeople could produce more maize, millet, and manioc, as well as serving as important assets in the defense of these communities. These communities could support not only the growing population but also produce more salt and crops for sale in markets such as Lembo, where they were traded for more people. While the exchange of salt and crops for people in seventeenth-century markets contributed to the development of unique social and political forms in Kisama, where these dependents helped build a new society renowned throughout the region for the ferocity and bellicosity of its members, these economic transactions also helped Kisama society on a much more rudimentary level. While manioc supported the growth of populations in areas that had previously been entirely marginal due to aridity and poor soil quality, the tubers alone are nutritionally poor, providing an abundance of carbohydrates with limited protein, fat, or other nutrients. Though consuming the leaves of the plant together with the tubers adds vitamins, including iron, and protein, a near-exclusive reliance on manioc can lead to serious health concerns due to malnutrition. Those Kisama merchants who traded salt and wild-gathered honey and wax—and possibly those who traded manioc, millet, and maize as well—exchanged their goods for "oil, vegetables, flour, and other things necessary for their survival."[63] These market-procured items would have proven an essential supplement to carbohydrate-heavy and nutrient-poor diets comprised largely of manioc, millet, and maize. Thus, though the people of Kisama faced significant environmental challenges, their reliance on hunting and fishing, the collection of wild honey, the cultivation of manioc, millet, and maize, and the exchange of both salt and agricultural products in the market allowed for those living between the Kwanza and Longa Rivers to experience a certain degree of food security and nutritional adequacy before the war.[64] Aridity and sporadic rainfall were certainly enduring features of Kisama's natural environment. Even Dapper mentions the characteristic imbondeiro-tree cisterns used by those living far from rivers to trap rainfall for the dry season and the crucial invocation of spirits designed to protect these reservoirs from discovery by outsiders.[65] While it is clear that adapting to the aridity of the region has a deep history, it is critical to locate the detrimental demographic impact of seemingly natural causes in the violence of the slave trade rather than in the agentless machinations of the environment, as Miller tends to do. *Famine* in Kisama was neither natural nor inevitable, but rather was politically and socially produced through the violence of the trans-Atlantic slave trade. As Mariana Candido argues in the case of Benguela, "For the local population, the threat was the colonial presence, not because of disease or drought. . . . Famine that affected the Ndombe and others cannot be disassociated from the actions of the Portuguese agents and the pressures of the trans-Atlantic slave trade."[66]

Food and food procurement played a central role in the conflict of 1655–58, and the Portuguese were driven as much by the quest to secure enough nourishment for their troops as by any strategic vision. Sousa Chicorro complained repeatedly of the difficulties his troops experienced due to lack of food. For example, marching through the lands of Soba Kimbambala, he noted that the people of the principal village had fled, taking all of their crops with them deep into the forests save a few houses where his troops found small amounts of millet; he distinguished between the scarcity of the millet left behind and the larger quantity of maize that the residents of Soba Kimbambala had taken to the forests. Instead of being able to subsist through plunder of the crops of Kimbambala's people, the Portuguese were left with only this meager millet and the palm tree groves on the lands of Soba Langere from which the imbare of the Portuguese plundered hearts of palm and palm oil.[67] When the Portuguese marched on the fertile lowland mentioned above, it was in pursuit of its "abundant maize and some manioc, of which there was news of its ripeness" as much as it was to take captives for sale or to punish those who attacked the Portuguese.[68] When they reached this oasis, the people there "resisted some but because they were assaulted by our war, they avoided any involvement, the foot [soldiers] like wind passing through their woods." Both the Portuguese soldiers and their local allies capitalized on the flight of the local residents by "roast[ing] corn cobs, making them taste like they were Chestnuts."[69]

Just as the residents of this once-fertile lowland learned that the presence of the Portuguese army meant utter devastation and fled to protect themselves, so too did other people within geographical Kisama seek to avoid the violence of the Portuguese campaign. By June of 1656, Sousa Chicorro remarked that the sobas who pledged obedience to him did so because of the "hunger that they suffer[, and that] because [of the war] they are not cultivating [crops]."[70] One month later, Sousa Chicorro noted more explicitly that "hunger was the worst ill" suffered by the people of Kisama, and attributed their desperation to the fact that the war was depriving the people of Kisama of the "slaves that they force to cultivate" crops.[71] Those whom the Portuguese understood as slaves were either those whom merchants had purchased in exchange for either salt or crops, or those who had been enslaved by the Portuguese and had fled to Kisama, and whose status within Kisama, while not equal, was certainly not the same as that of a racialized and permanently bonded class.

The capture or murder of these fugitives and/or dependents by the Portuguese undermined a critical element of the food production system within Kisama. The human toll of the war, combined with the drastic impact of Portuguese depredations on the land, compelled Soba Langere to attempt to negotiate with the Portuguese after a particularly fierce battle with many casualties. Langere claimed that "he wanted to be [a] Vassal of the King of Portugal, who would not destroy their lands and Palm Groves, from which they sustain themselves; that the Sheep could not leave before the Wolf, [so] that he would go back to his Quilombo, that within three days he would come in obedience to recognize the vassalage."[72] With this deft diplomacy, Langere was able to save his lands and people from total devastation. Other sobas in Kisama, "fearing the war that was at their door, said through their Ambassadors or Envoys that they were the sons of Mueno Puto [the king of Portugal] and they wanted peace and friendship with his vassal Portuguese and to turn over the Slaves that were in the lands that belonged to them."[73] The sobas who made such deals with the Portuguese bought their tenuous peace with the lives and freedom of those who had fled to their lands for safety. The threat of devastation forced them to define clearly who was and who was not a full member of their society. By offering to return these fugitives, these sobas revealed the boundaries of membership in their societies and the contingency of social integration during times of intense conflict.[74]

Not all communities within Kisama, however, were willing to sacrifice some or all of their most vulnerable members in exchange for the fleeting promise of safety and security of the others, as the Portuguese learned when their cavalry and imbare, along with their leaders, entered a part of Kisama that Sousa Chicorro and Cadornega do not specifically name. There, the people of Kisama fought fiercely, resisting the Portuguese cavalry and auxiliary infantry with all of their might. According to Cadornega, the Portuguese forces returned during the night with "some prizes of people, mostly women, that we captured from the woods where they had run as fugitives; because these Heathens resisted so much that they were all weakened [to the point of death], the Husbands having first laid down their lives in their defense, they are very zealous about their Consorts, more than any other People in these Kingdoms."

After another battle the following morning, the Portuguese captured more than one hundred women—Cadornega notes this as a record for any forces fighting in Kisama—and set the village and its fields and crops on fire, decapitated all of the fugitives they could identify, and feasted on the chicken and cattle they took from the devastated village.[75]

One of the most poignant scenes in Cadornega's description of the war of 1655–58, this episode encapsulates the relationship between food production and security, women's labor, and warfare. The crops that sustained this nameless village were undoubtedly produced by the same one hundred women who were captured by the Portuguese and almost certainly sold into trans-Atlantic slavery from Luanda, if they survived the harrowing journey to the coast. Through warfare and fire, the Portuguese devastated this community in which women worked rich lands and had woven relationships with men whom even the Portuguese identified as their husbands (*maridos*). For the one hundred women who were taken as captives, the memory of the land of Kisama as a refuge wherein the reconstruction of family and reciprocal relationships with other members of the community was possible, and the violation of this asylum by the Portuguese troops, must have profoundly shaped their understanding of their own subjectivities.

Intriguingly, of the seven slave ships listed in the Trans-Atlantic Slave Trade Database that left Luanda between 1656 and 1659, the years for which we can presume captives from the campaign in Kisama would have been sold from Luanda, four sailed to the Rio de la Plata, one to Puerto Rico, one to the Dutch Guianas, and one to Hispaniola. The four voyages to the Rio de la Plata in 1656 all encountered storms at sea, but three of these had very few Africans on board.[76] Twenty-three Africans boarded the *Nossa Senhora da Candelaria* in Luanda, and eighteen survived the storms to be sold in Buenos Aires; seventeen boarded the *São João de Deus e Nossa Senhora da Concieção*, and fourteen disembarked; and in the case of the *Nossa Senhora do Popolo e São Antônio*, twenty embarked, and sixteen arrived. The only significant number of Africans who were put in slave ships in chains in Luanda who next touched land in Buenos Aires during this period from Luanda came aboard the *Nossa Senhora dos Remédos e São Antônio*, on which 563 people watched 142 of their brethren die at sea. The ship that arrived in Hispanola in 1657, the *Nossa Senhora de Guadalupe*, also encountered storms at sea, and 455 men, women, and children died, leaving only 225 of the original 680 to disembark. Of these, 62.5 percent were children, and 27.5 percent were girls. The voyage of the British slave ship the *Brazil Frigate* in 1658 was interrupted by Dutch pirates, who took the 1,200 surviving Africans of the 1,304 who embarked in Luanda to Essequibo. In 1659, Dutch pirates likewise captured a Portuguese slave ship leaving from Luanda and sold the 207 men, women, and children who withstood the Middle Passage of the original 259 in Puerto Rico.[77]

There were certainly no optimal variations on the terror of the Middle Passage. However, the experiences of those departing Luanda during this three-year period were exceptionally traumatic and unpredictable. While we cannot know for certain upon which ships the one hundred captured women, or any of the hundreds and perhaps thousands of other adults and children of Kisama left African shores, we can imagine how terrifying these voyages must have been. Beyond the incomprehensible specter of human violence, there are simply no equivalents within the interior of Angola to the storms these ships encountered on the open sea. Even within the realm of pure speculation, it is easy to see how for the few that survived, incorporating their experiences at sea into life and political narrative arcs that were shaped by rupture, alienation, and the reconfiguration of living communities would have been the project of much intellectual and social labor. These were the stories bondswomen, men, and, largely, children imagined on the auction block and told in the slave quarters and maroon communities of the Americas.

Conclusions

While the martial aptitude of many sobas within Kisama and the reputation their skill engendered did in fact protect its people for much of the early seventeenth century, during the war of 1655–58, Sousa Chicorro set out to prove himself capable of what no other Portuguese or African commander had yet accomplished: conquering the lands of geographical Kisama. Like those before him, Sousa Chicorro, too, failed. He did not conquer the territory of Kisama, but his war devastated many of the communities in which fugitive and fugitive-descended adults and children sought security, peace, and networks of kinship and reciprocal relations from which they had previously been severed. For those who found even a few years of security in the lands between the Kwanza and Longa Rivers—or who knew of those who did—the reputation of Kisama as a land where martial skill and spiritual acumen provided the conditions necessary to form relationships based not on idioms of warfare but rather on those of community and kinship would have informed their notions of what was possible in the Americas. As much as the events of 1594 set Kisama's reputational geography in motion, the war of 1655–58 propelled new waves of people familiar with Kisama's ideological repertoires throughout the region and into the Americas.

CHAPTER 4

(Mis)Taken Identities

Kisama and the Politics of Naming in the Palenque Limón, New Kingdom of Grenada, c. 1570–1634

> However, the violent domination of slavery generated political action; it
> was not antithetical to it. If one sees power as productive and the fear of
> social death not as incapacity but as a generative force—a peril that moti-
> vated enslaved activity—a different image of slavery slides into view, one in
> which the object of slave politics is not simply the power of slaveholders,
> but the very terms and conditions of social existence.
>
> — VINCENT BROWN, "Social Death and Political Life in the Study of
>   Slavery," 2009

In 1633, Perico Quisama and his companion Malemba fled from the farm
of Francisco Martín Garruchena outside of Cartagena de Indias, New
Grenada (present-day Colombia), to Limón, a palenque (maroon community) located in the mountainous forested region approximately fifty
miles outside of the city.[1] There, they told the leader of the community,
Queen Leonor, and other authorities that their master had accepted silver from the government in Cartagena in order to pay the people of the
indigenous community of Chambacú to attack the palenque. Queen Leonor decided that "it would be better if the ... Indians didn't come to

their land [Limón,] but that the palenqueros [maroons] should go to their *pueblo* and burn it and kill [them]." The queen mobilized several Limoneses to attack Chambacú, including palenque-born and fugitive men identified as Malemba, as well as Upper Guinea– and West Central Africa–identified palenquerxs. Perico guided them to Chambacú, stopping first at the farm of his erstwhile master in order to kill several pigs. Not only did those who had lived in Limón for some time participate in this attack, but so did those whom the Limoneses had recently freed from bondage during a raid on another Spanish farm. Most of the men and women brought along their bows, arrows, and machetes, though Francisco de la Fuente and Captain Francisco availed themselves of their shotguns and munitions.[2]

All of the captured palenquerxs who testified about these attacks describe Perico Quisama and his companion Malemba as the impetus for the action. Indeed, the testimonies on this topic are remarkably congruent on the details of what Perico and Malemba said and how leaders in Limón reacted to their news. Even the Spanish who testified about their role in the attack on Limón recounted a nearly identical narrative. However, despite the obvious importance of Perico and Malemba's flight and the intelligence that they brought to Limón, those who related these events in their testimonies did not concur on one critical detail: Perico Quisama's name.

While all who testified agreed that Perico's less *ladino* (Iberian-acculturated) companion was named Malemba, not all concurred on Perico's name. Sergeant Miguel Antunes, who led the Spanish attack on Limón, and neighboring Spanish farmers Francisco Julián de Piña and Juan Ortíz, both of whom likewise participated in the assault on the palenque, all name the man who fled Garruchena's farm and brought news of the impending government-sponsored campaign against Limón as Perico Quisama.[3] Juan Criollo de la Margarita, a leader within Limón, and two palenquera women, Catalina Angola and Francisca Criolla, call the same man Perico Angola.[4] Palenque leaders Francisco de la Fuente and Juan de la Mar refer to him simply as Perico.[5] Four Angola-identified men—Gaspar, Lázaro, Jacinto, and Juan—use the more formal name Pedro Angola to describe the same figure who fled from Garruchena's farm with Malemba, brought news of the impending assaults to the palenque leaders, and then lead the attack on Chambacú.[6] Perico himself testifies as Pedro Angola, and it is under this appellation that the Spanish judge sentenced him to hang in the gallows until he died, at which point they quartered him, decapitated him, and displayed his dismembered body publically in Cartagena.[7]

It is not only Perico Quisama, however, who appears through the records by more than one name. The two other Kisama-identified men about whom we have the most information, Lázaro and Manuel, are also inconsistently identified throughout the testimonies. To regard these variations as inconsequential errors, however, would be to lose sight of the vital texture that transforms these names into a map of the social and political topographies of the community that generated them. These apparent contradictions serve as an important window into the dynamic ideological processes that flourished in resistance to the threat of physical and social death in Africa and in the Americas during the mid-seventeenth century. The testimony that these captured palenquerxs offered, often as a brief interlude between their torture by Spanish captors and their eventual murder and dismemberment, and the terms by which they described themselves and other members of their community, both within and without the palenque, help illuminate the political tensions and competing ideologies that operated within this maroon community and the broader social world within which it was imbricated.

Here, I take seriously the words of contemporary observer of mid-seventeenth-century Angola, António de Oliveira de Cadornega, who described the resistance of Kisama to the Portuguese and to its existence as a seventeenth-century maroon society in Angola as revolutionary.[8] While in the first part of the book, I have focused on the impact of Kisama's evolving fugitive politics both on social and political practices in geographical Kisama and on regional politics in West Central Africa more broadly, in this part of the book, I follow these ideologies across the Atlantic. Kisama engendered a cartography linking the interior of Angola to the New Kingdom of Grenada, Brazil, and beyond—not through the normal routes of capital and violence, but rather through the dynamic, fluid movement of ideologies we can recover from shadows and echoes.

In Angola, as Kisama, fugitives eschewed both the bondage that many of them had endured either on Portuguese plantations or as imbare and also the morally repugnant response of the Imbangala to the Portuguese violence. Refusing both the institutionalized warrior-centered social ethos of the Imbangala and the tenuous promise of safety in centralized states such as Kongo or Ndongo, those who forged new political forms as Kisama instead consciously disavowed any but the most fleeting alliances to nonlocal political authority. In the Americas, those familiar with the political ideologies and praxis of Kisama, whether through direct experience, or, more commonly, through traversing Kisama's broad reputational geographies, encountered a variety of other fugitive and nonfugitive politics, including those of the obdurately nonstate peoples of Upper Guinea, as well as Native Americans. The seventeenth-century Americas were a veritable crossroads of fugitive modernities emanating from all corners of the globe.

As David Wheat reminds us, in the lands colonized by the Spanish prior to the nineteenth century, the overwhelming majority of those performing the day-to-day labor of colonial society were African. While scholars have often focused on the importance of enslaved Africans in extractive- and export-oriented economies, Wheat demonstrates that not only small-scale ranching and provision agriculture but also the totality of labor in colonial urban society was performed by Africans. Seventeenth-century Cartagena, much like other port cities on either side of the Atlantic littoral, was a city nominally ruled by Spanish colonists but run by Africans. This did not abrogate the violence that deformed, dismembered, and disordered the lives and all too quickly engineered the deaths of enslaved people in any of these contexts. It did, however, mean that the primary political and cultural lingua franca in these societies was African. And, as Wheat shows, the early seventeenth century, too, was a time of shift, as the former Upper Guineas majority gave way to a rising tide of West Central Africans.[9] The history of the seventeenth-century Americas is inherently an African and indigenous history.

By investigating the trial records from the captured palenquerxs of the maroon society of Limón, we understand aspects of Kisama's past that no Angolan sources can reveal. In the century and a half from Kisama's first appearance in archival records (1535) to the end of Luis Mendes de Sousa Chicorro's war in 1658, the meaning of the term "Kisama" changed both within and without geographical Kisama's porous, nebulous boundaries. After Kafuxi Ambari's dramatic defeat of the Portuguese in 1594, the primary significance of "Kisama" shifted from geographical to political. While from the late sixteenth century on the residents of Kisama remained infamous within the region and beyond for their intractability, this reputation paradoxically emphasized the politically, socially, and culturally fragmented nature of life between the Kwanza and Longa Rivers. During the mid-seventeenth century, Giovanni Antonio Cavazzi described the residents of Kisama as "glorify[ing] in a certain independence," and by 1825, Portuguese governor Nicolau de Abreu Castelo Branco complained that Kisama's "many inhabitants, and proliferating rulers, who have the title of soba, profess a reciprocal rage against each other."[10] The renown for resistance of the notoriously autonomous people of Kisama helped attract thousands of diverse fugitives, who, by the early 1630s, themselves participated in reconfiguring the notion of Kisama identities in Angola. The enduring challenge of telling such stories, of course, is to find a critical mass of sources that allow for a glimpse—however mediated, distorted, and patchy—of changes in and contestations about the practice and conception of political authority, violence, and community over time.

In the case of sixteenth- and seventeenth-century Kisama, it is possible to weave together fragmented sources generated by imperial and slaving interests and neighboring kingdoms, oral histories and local etymologies, and linguistics to reconstruct a political, intellectual, cultural, and social historical narrative. However, in Angola, these sources do not reveal much about the histories of named individuals, aside from sobas. Kafuxi Ambari emerges clearly from both oral and written accounts, but the equally vital histories of all of those who fought by his side, who tended the crops he consumed, and who accepted or contested his authority are all but invisible. Royalty of Kongo, Ndongo, and Matamba, Portuguese military officers, colonial officials, and European missionaries named only those with whom they interacted on a macropolitical scale, and all other adults and children appear in aggregate, if at all. It is difficult enough to access the histories of subaltern people within states during this period; finding insight into the lives of everyday fugitives and common people outside of the boundaries of states is far more challenging. Historians working in all corners of the world who seek to craft less elite-centered histories of the pre-nineteenth-century world face similar challenges.[11]

However, what if it were possible to find answers to some of the more complex questions about sixteenth- and seventeenth-century Kisama history outside of Angola? Do sources from the Americas allow us to glimpse otherwise inaccessible fragments of early modern African histories? Can an interrogation of the ways in which other local African histories intersect with Kisama histories in the Americas help illuminate dynamics of Kisama history that would otherwise remain obscure? Throughout the seventeenth century, Kisama identities in Angola were forged largely within and among communities formed by thousands of individually weak, vulnerable fugitives from a broad region of West Central Africa. Thus, those living far beyond the Kwanza and Longa Rivers knew of Kisama's reputation and of the prospect for shelter from the raids of the Portuguese and their allies and the prospect of capture, sale, forced labor, and possible transport across the Atlantic. However, not all who yearned for the relative safety that a life in/as Kisama represented were able to flee there successfully; even for those living in geographical Kisama, the prospect of capture in the endless wars against the Portuguese and their allies, such as the extended conflict of 1655–58, transport to the coast, and sale to the Americas—or bonded labor in Luanda or on Portuguese-owned plantations in Angola or São Tomé—was an enduring threat. Even today, those living in geographical Kisama can identify caves along the coast where the Portuguese kept their captives while they waited for the slave ships to take them on their harrowing journey.[12] For the most part, those most susceptible to such capture and sale were the very same unnamed, nonelite actors who fled to the lands between the Kwanza and Longa Rivers and helped create new political and social forms, and about whose lives the sources from Angola are the most silent. While records from the Americas contain less information about the lives, experiences, and beliefs of individual enslaved and free Africans and their descendants than we would like, American sources nevertheless allow us to understand far more about Kisama society than we can learn from African sources alone.

Scholars have recently begun to recognize the situational nature of expressions of African identities in the pre-twentieth-century world. Building on the scholarship of Mariza de Carvalho Soares and Luis Nicolau Parés, James Sweet argues that depending on context, Africans in the Atlantic world could identify in the broadest terms, reflecting region of provenance (like Angola or Mina), in "metaethnic" terms (such as Bioho or Kisama), or in very specific terms (like Massangano or Savalu). Sweet acknowledges that these choices carried political meanings, particularly in the case of an identity like Mahi, "an 'ethnic' identity born in the fires of war, in resistance to the privations wrought by the army of Dahomey."[13] Extending Sweet's formulation, I argue that examining the relationships between members of the palenque Limón and its broader community and the idioms within which they evoked political difference allows us a rare opportunity to more fully grasp the intellectual work of fugitive modernities in seventeenth-century Africa and the African Diaspora.[14] As Kathryn McKnight suggests in her writing about Limón, "Thinking about identity can transform long lists of names with brief identifiers into challenging but vital sources of palenque thought."[15]

Advancing my previous discussion of the nature of political development in mid-seventeenth-century Kisama, I argue that the fugitive modernities constructed by and contested as Kisama constituted a revolutionary current with global implications. Here, I do not mean that Kisama ideologies were revolutionary in the sense that they were concerted efforts to overturn an existing order and to replace or even repopulate the machinery of state. Rather, I mean that Kisama's deliberately fractured, nonstate political forms and overall rejection of an economic and political order centered on the capture, commodification, and sale of human beings represented not only an important counterideology, but also a highly mobile, adaptable set of practices and logics that could be employed or evoked in lands far beyond the Kwanza and Longa Rivers. Since at least the late sixteenth century, resistance against the Portuguese by Kafuxi Ambari, other sobas, and, most importantly, the unnamed thousands who successfully evaded capture by slave raiders and archival technologies in geographical Kisama not only inspired revolt among neighboring people but also encouraged the vulnerable and enslaved from other parts of the region to flee to and become Kisama.[16] By the 1620s and 1630s, these fugitives had constructed a new social order and demarcated their own boundaries of political legitimacy within Kisama. Not only did these actions influence regional political histories within Angola, but they also shaped the practice of politics in maroon societies throughout the Americas. While this particular revolutionary current did not lead to the establishment of liberal democracy or republican governance—it has no obvious teleological link to the present—it was no less transformative for the relationships between state and nonstate actors in Angola and between the enslaved and the enslavers in the Americas.

In this chapter, I follow the discourses about political legitimacy, community, and violence in Kisama through its articulations in the palenque Limón outside of Cartagena. Our information about the events within and around Limón comes from the nearly thousand pages of documentation generated by the trial in 1634 of nineteen maroons captured by the Spanish.[17] Limón was far from the only palenque community troubling the Spanish settlements in and around Cartagena at the time. Juan de Sotomayor, a Spaniard who owned a farm worked by enslaved Africans outside of Cartagena, testified to the existence of at least one larger palenque (led by Maria Angola), three of equal size, three smaller, and four smaller yet, of which three were indigenous communities and one African.[18] Because of Limón's recently adopted policy of overt aggression toward the Spanish, however—in effect, popularizing to the still-enslaved Africans and their descendants in and around Cartagena that Spanish power was fragile—the colonial government prioritized attacking Limón and killing or capturing its residents. Like many colonial raids of communities of fugitive Africans and indigenous people, this one was not particularly successful; most of the palenquerxs escaped, including the (in)famous Queen Leonor and many of the other leaders of the community. In fact, the queen was one of the principal targets of the Spanish raid. The Spanish were interested in capturing the queen not only because of her leadership role within the palenque, but also because of her putative participation in the ritual killings of several Spaniards and indigenous people.[19]

Queen Leonor was undoubtedly instrumental in a political shift within the Limón community, which had existed since at least the 1570s and had apparently remained relatively under the radar while the Spanish were preoccupied with the raiding activities of other maroon communities, including the notable palenque of King Domingo Bioho. Those who founded Limón were both African- and American-born fugitives from slavery; after some years, their numbers were augmented not only by a perpetual trickle of runaways and those who were ostensibly "captured" from Spanish farms, but also by a substantial cohort of free-born children and grandchildren who knew no life outside of the fugitive community. In the years leading up to the Spanish assault on the palenque Limón in 1634, members of the community attacked the Spanish slave-holding farms of Diego Márquez, Francisco Martin Garruchena, Gomes Hernandez, Francisco Julian de Piña, and Alonso Martin Hidalgo, as well as the indigenous community of Chambacú.

While the maroons of Limón had lived in the area outside of Cartagena for several decades and had coexisted with the neighboring Spanish landowners and indigenous communities, in the 1620s and 1630s, just as fugitives in Kisama began to profoundly reshape the political contours of their communities, newer arrivals in Limón likewise began to reorient the politics of the palenque.[20] Leaders of the larger Limón attacked the smaller neighboring community of Polín and compelled all of those whom they captured to join them, albeit in subservient or servile roles.[21] The palenquerxs whom the Spaniards caught claimed that their attacks on the white farms and the indigenous community were motivated by self-defense; they had learned that the Spaniards planned to pay the indigenous residents of Chambacú to attack them while they were negotiating a peace treaty with the government.[22] Tautologically, the Spanish claimed justification for attacking the palenque because of the attacks on the farms of Garruchena and Márquez as well as Chambacú.

The palenquerxs who testified themselves identified a relatively recent change within Limón, and they connected these developments to Queen Leonor and a newly arrived cohort of Malemba-identified men. Sebastián Angola argued that "the palenque residents were peaceful until Cristóbal Malemba, Francisco Malemba, Moriungo Malemba, Gaspar Malemba and Pedro Buila stirred up the queen with herbs."[23] Who was Leonor, and how was she "stirred up"? What kind of political change did this spiritual coronation initiate, and what were the intellectual, social, and cultural topographies of the communities within which this new politics operated? How can understanding the dynamic political situation of a seventeenth-century maroon community outside of Cartagena help illuminate the history of Kisama, and what can Kisama tell us about this palenque?

While the rich documentary record of Limón is certainly compelling in its own right, intriguingly, prior to the nineteenth century, the richest written historical source of information about the lives of individual Kisama-identified people comes not from Angola, but rather from the nearly one thousand pages of records generated through the trial of the captured Limoneses.[24] Of these seven Kisama-identified members of the community, only one—Perico—testified; all others besides he and Luis Quisama evaded capture by the Spanish.[25] No one who testified self-identified as Kisama, and Perico Quisama, who testified as Pedro Angola, was called Quisama only by the Spanish. However, in the case of the others, their fellow palenquerxs—African- and American-born alike—did name seven individuals in total whom they identified as Kisama; besides Perico, Lázaro, Manuel, and Luis, they also named another Manuel (from Matute), Juan, and Maria.[26] While those who testified mentioned some, such as Luis, Manuel from Matute, Maria, and Juan, only in passing, they discussed others who appear to have played a prominent role in the political, cultural, and social life of the community, like Perico, Lázaro, and Manuel, who had fled from the farm of Garruchena, in some detail. From these testimonies, we can ascertain important dimensions of the ways in which Kisama political identities functioned in a fugitive community in

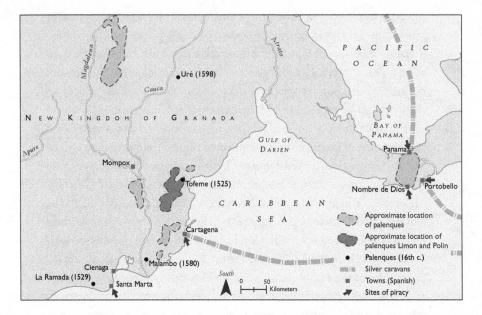

Map 4.1 — Fugitive and Colonial Sites in Sixteenth- and Seventeenth-Century
New Kingdom of Grenada. Map by Heather Rosenfeld.

the early seventeenth-century New Kingdom of Grenada. And while these
Kisama-identified individuals do not themselves speak, through the narrative about life within the palenque that it is possible to piece together
through these documents, we can discern parallel discourses and debates
to those in Kisama, linking changes in Limón to a more widespread Age of
Revolution originating in the fugitive modernities of Kisama.

I explore how political ideologies and practices forged in Kisama and
similar communities in West and West Central Africa informed the nature of maroon communities in the Americas through an examination
of the trial record from Limón. I argue that approaching the history of
Limón from the perspective of Kisama history—and using Limón to help
understand Kisama—reveals the interconnected, contiguous nature of
these seventeenth-century spaces and demonstrates the flows of fugitive
ideologies through them. Indeed, just as the world of Kisama extended far
beyond the Kwanza and Longa Rivers, as reputation and rumor drew fugitives from throughout the region and the news of each successful repu-
diation of Portuguese military incursions increased Kisama's renown, so
too did the world of Limón reach far beyond the palenque's boundaries.

As a close reading of these documents reveals, Limoneses imagined them-selves as part of a community that included not only the diverse adults and children who lived inside the palenque, but also an extensive network of bondspeople in the surrounding region, neighboring indigenous peoples, and also spirits from Africa. They also linked themselves, both through direct interaction and through discursive mobilization, to other maroon communities in the region, both contemporary and historical. To truly understand the political shift in Limón in the years leading up to 1634—and the vital role of Kisama-identified people and Kisama-oriented poli-tics within that shift—requires an African-rooted, processual approach equally sensitive to local histories in the Americas.

The New Kingdom of Grenada and Fugitive Modernities: Maroons and Pirates in the Sixteenth Century

In shaping the political and social contours of their palenque, Limoneses drew from experiences and discourses not only from Africa but also from the political traditions of maroonage in the region. Indeed, such geo-graphical terms obscure the fact that violence and social rupture were the common language of many parts of Africa and the Americas in the seven-teenth century, and many of those who fled enslavement in New Grenada to try to reform autonomous communities were likely not doing so for the first time in their lives.[27] As the African population of the New Kingdom of Grenada shifted from being dominated by those from Upper Guinea to those from West Central Africa in the second decade of the seventeenth century, enslaved and self-liberated people incorporated new political ideologies and historical precedents into their concepts of freedom.[28] Lo-cally, however, there was also a deep tradition of maroonage, stretching back for over a century. Long before fugitives founded the community that would become Limón, enslaved Africans throughout the region fled urban-, plantation-, and mine-based bondage and founded free societies. Maroon communities predate Spanish settlements in present-day Co-lombia; even before Pedro de Heredia officially founded the colonial city of Cartagena da Indias on June 1, 1532, Africans fleeing enslavement in Panamá and surrounding regions had formed maroon settlements near the indigenous town of Tofeme. This settlement expanded after 1532 and the subsequent influx of Africans into the city.[29] By 1540, less than a decade after the Spanish founded the colonial city and port of Cartagena, a decree of the Council of the Indies forecasted that "many blacks flee into the mountains, where they do much damage to the Indians who live there: this has not been and cannot be remedied unless blacks are pardoned."[30] These words would prove prophetic in the years to follow.

In neighboring Panamá, thousands of enslaved Africans fled to the mountains and jungles in the isthmus's interior in the mid-sixteenth century, and the fugitives who comprised the palenques of sixteenth-century Panamá developed a variety of political forms, drawing from diverse African intellectual traditions.[31] Rather than staying in remote, interior locales—a stereotype of maroon societies that has always contradicted the evidence—these fugitives moved between the mountains and the coast, targeting the mule trains that carried Peruvian silver from Panamá City on the Pacific coast to the port of Nombre de Dios on the Atlantic coast and sent Spanish imports back in return. In 1573, the Spanish factor at Nombre de Dios wrote to the king, "This place is so alarmed and in such need . . . of people to garrison it against the numerous cimarrones [maroons], and other negroes who run away to join them daily, that, unless the situation be remedied, they can readily enter it. . . . [O]n the twenty-ninth of the month of January they went so far as the Venta de Chagre, and burned it, and in it killed four soldiers of the guard of the mule-train. They took a pack-train coming from Panamá, and stole the silver it was carrying, killed some mules, and badly wounded a friar."[32] In May of the same year, a group of fifty maroons and thirty French and English pirates attacked yet another pack train, seizing "30,000 [*pesos*] and . . . all the gold and some bars."[33] These raids not only enriched the English and French pirates, but also greatly benefitted the maroons, who negotiated their relationships with the corsairs from a relative position of power, setting the terms under which they would be willing to help those attempting to cross from Atlantic to Pacific. Despite the differences in linguistic and political backgrounds, these maroons and pirates shared a fundamentally nonstate ethos.

By the 1570s, Panamanian maroons already had a trans-Atlantic, transnational reputation. When the Spanish captured the English pirate John Oxenham in 1577, he testified at length about the relationship between his men and the maroons in Panamá, claiming that Captain Francis [Sir Francis Drake], Englishman, who sailed along these coasts of the Indies with another captain, a Frenchman, and returned to England, to the port of Plymouth ... told deponent [Oxenham] that in this Vallano there were *cimarrones* rich in gold and silver, and he described the country, and said that he could barter to them whatever he might bring; and it was about two years ago that he told him this; And deponent came with the intention of bartering to the said negroes much merchandize which he brought from England—cloths, hatchets, *machetes* and other things of different sorts—which he intended to barter for gold and silver, and so return rich to his own country.[34]

From Oxenham's deposition, it is clear that the leader of Vallano, King Domingo Congo, ruled over a large number of people who inhabited not only the primary village at Rincóncholon but also many affiliated villages. While this kind of settled life permitted the palenquerxs to practice agriculture, planting banana groves and maize fields, they were mobile enough to have a well-developed plan for flight.[35] Such social organization required not only an intimate familiarity with the land and both martial and subsistence strategies suited to the location, but also the ability to use and distribute the machetes, hatchets, iron, cloth, and other goods that those in 1570s Plymouth knew the maroons desired. These events also indicate a well-developed political system that, while hierarchical, enabled individual communities to respond to potential threats.

Domingo Congo, king of this palenque society, governed a community with an established system of relative local autonomy within a broader political structure. When, after years of flight and battle, he sought to negotiate peace terms with the Spanish, he sent fourteen captains to Panamá City to negotiate with them in his name. Among these delegates was Antón Mandinga, a man both trusted by Domingo Congo and conversant in Spanish language and culture, whom the other captains relied on to convey much of their message to the Spanish, as well as "Juan Jolofo, captain of the Piñas River and Vicente Sape, captain of the Manta River and Gaspar Bran, captain of the Gallinasas River."[36] King Domingo Congo appears to have been familiar with Kongo court culture, negotiating absolution for his sins and for those of his followers. Indeed, the ways in which his captains were tied to particular regions is reminiscent of the political structure of the fifteenth- and sixteenth-century Kingdom of

Kongo, where the king delegated control of formerly independent provinces to family members and supporters, thus ensuring their loyalty.[37] However, his captains were not fellow BaKongo, nor were they even West Central Africans. Instead, they were Mandinga, Jolof, Zape, and Bran—identities that point to geographical origins in present-day Senegambia, Sierra Leone, and Guinea-Bissau. These maroons appear to have adapted a very particular political culture from Kongo to their new social environment, using the tools and language of state to forge their own particular society.

Maroons in Panamá attacked Spanish caravans crossing from the Pacific to the Atlantic side of the isthmus and allied with English and French pirates intent on capturing wealth from Peruvian silver mines as well as the cargoes of Portuguese slave ships. In the New Kingdom of Grenada, however, much as was the case in turn-of-the-century Kisama, maroons began to incorporate assaults on Spanish riverine trade into their strategies. Coinciding with what historian Enriqueta Vila Vilar calls "the first great wave of Africans to come to the Spanish Indies," in the 1570s, maroons living along the Magdalena River began to attack the Spanish settlement at Barranca de Malambo, four days distant from Cartagena by mule, which served as the primary customs, mercantile storehouse, and lodging point for those bringing goods from the interior.[38] Between occupying the mountainous territory in between Barranca de Malambo and Cartagena and mounting these effective attacks, in combination with the omnipresent threat from pirates along the coast, maroons ensured that Cartagenerxs lived under a virtual blockade, cut off from supplies from both the interior and the sea.[39] By 1575, a Spanish doctor passing through Cartagena on his way to Santa Fe de Bogotá wrote to the king that the situation was so desperate that he did not recommend "that any more blacks come to Cartagena until there is a remedy for the maroons in the mountains."[40] In the midst of the turbulent situation in Panamá, it must have seemed to the Spanish that the New Kingdom of Grenada could also soon be embroiled in a costly, drawn-out conflict with self-liberated Africans.[41]

The king of Spain did not officially respond to the doctor's recommendations. However, the Trans-Atlantic Slave Trade Database has no record of any slave ships landing in Cartagena between 1576 and 1584.[42] Of course, there are many gaps in the data, and a lack of records does not indicate that all human traffic to Cartagena ceased during these nine years.[43] However, once records resume in 1585, the number of Africans who arrived—762—more than doubled the number that arrived in 1575

(289). For the remainder of the sixteenth century, the trend continued toward a dramatic increase in Africans arriving in Cartagena, so that by 1600, three to four thousand enslaved Africans regularly disembarked each year.[44] Until 1590, the overwhelming majority of those who arrived in Cartagena were from Upper Guinea; while captives from other regions continued to arrive in Cartagena, it was only after 1617 that Angolans comprised the majority of all newly arrived captives, and by 1626, two out of every three Africans disembarking in Cartagena had left Africa from Angola.[45] For the political life of Limón, the fact that the "Angolan wave" of bondsmen and women began arriving in Cartagena just as fugitive politics began to emerge as a revolutionary current in Kisama is significant.

Even after the dire cautions of Spanish observers in the 1570s, Africans continued to flee captivity in Cartagena and neighboring areas, and the Spanish had little success in enforcing draconian legislation intended to prevent maroonage.[46] By the turn of the seventeenth century, Spanish officials throughout the circum-Caribbean were terrified that the multitude of fugitive Africans throughout Tierra Firma (present-day Venezuela), Panamá, and the New Kingdom of Grenada would unite in an armed struggle against the Spanish. Just as the Portuguese feared Kafuxi Ambari's martial skill and charisma, so, too, did the Spanish in the Americas focus their anxieties on a series of charismatic maroon leaders who appear to have organized hundreds or even thousands of fugitives in palenque communities that, in many cases, predated their leadership. By the early 1600s, while those in Limón lived without direct conflict with their Spanish and indigenous neighbors, the Spanish governor in Cartagena described a dire plot in which Domingo Bioho, a fugitive from the Spanish king's galleys and the leader of yet another large palenque community outside of Cartagena, would unite "a large quantity of blacks and go to Monopox [a town] and from there they could unite with [the revolted African miners in] Zaragosa and take it and with the remainder and with the blacks from the mines that they could raise to take this city [Cartagena] and do harm and Pass to Panama with more maroons."[47]

This type of collective action and political unity among disparate groups of fugitives seemed possible to the Spanish because this was how palenque communities operated throughout the sixteenth century. Time and time again, small groups of people would flee from a single farm, or master in the city, or particular mine, run to the mountains, and join with other such groups of people to form a viable community. I do not mean to imply here that all fugitives inherently identified with a common cause, or that the fugitive politics of different groups of maroons, or maroons and pirates, were intrinsically congruent. In Limón, as in Kisama, political conflicts between various fugitive constituencies could at times drive armed confrontations; while all who lived in Limón certainly escaped the lethal life of slavery and the threat of imminent social death, not all palenquerxs enjoyed the benefits of that liberty in the same way. Just as in Kisama, Limón was a society marked by social inequality. However, in spite of these inequalities, as we will see in the case of Limón, oftentimes those who claimed a common political identity or who had common experiences of enslavement by the same master would return to free their companions.

Shaping Community in Limón

Perhaps no individual within Limón's life story better illustrates the social ties that bound palenquerxs and those still enslaved together than that of Francisco de la Fuente, called "el Morisco" ("the Moor") by both his fellow Limoneses and the Spanish. De la Fuente, like Domingo Bioho before him, came to Cartagena on a galley ship, marked with the distinctive facial brands of those enslaved by the king.[48] After he discovered another bondsman speaking with his beloved, he killed his rival. Fearful of the consequences of his rash actions, he fled first to the indigenous community at Chambacú and then by boat to Bahayre, and, after another boat ride and foot journey, he made contact with those enslaved on the farm of Piña, where he remained for more than fourteen months. After Francisco "the Hunchback" Criollo, who was enslaved on the neighboring farm of Juan de Sotomayor, notified de la Fuente that other Spanish in the area were going to capture him, he helped him escape to an indigenous community where he waited for men from the palenque Limón. Francisco Criollo contacted the palenquerxs, who claimed that they were desperate for more soldiers and would treat de la Fuente well; they escorted him to the palenque, where he appears to have rapidly ascended to a position of power. When the Spanish later captured him in the wake of the Limoneses' attacks on neighboring farms, they seized him from Bañon's hut on Ortencio's farm.[49] Not only did de la Fuente's personal relationships with these two men transcend the divide between enslaved and maroon, but

Bañon and Criollo had enduring connections with others in the palenque as well.

Indeed, Francisco Criollo seems to have facilitated contact between many who wished to escape slavery, like de la Fuente, and the palenquerxs of Limón. Juan de la Mar, born into captivity in Cartagena, testified that he worked for his master transporting maize by boat. One day, he found that he was lacking some of the maize that he was supposed to bring to the city, and he had no way of compensating his master for the loss. He told Francisco Criollo what had happened, and then, "out of fear of his [de la Mar's] master," Juan de la Mar fled with Francisco Criollo to the farm of Juan de Sotomayor, where Criollo was enslaved, and where Juan de la Mar stayed for "seven months without the said [D]on Juan seeing him." Then, five Limoneses—one of the Chale brothers (Domingo or Gonzalo), Simon, Juan Angola, Nicolas, who was born in the palenque, and Tunba Criollo—came to Francisco Criollo on Sotomayor's farm to bring de la Mar to Limón, where he had lived for the two and half years preceding the Spanish attack and his capture. De la Mar claimed that "only the aforementioned Francisco Criollo the Hunchback and his friends and the Indians of [A]lferez Piña were there the two days when the maroons were on the farm of the aforementioned [D]on Juan and no one else," suggesting that, as in the case of Francisco de la Fuente, Criollo and Bañon were adept at hiding fugitives from their masters.[50] De la Mar confirms that Francisco Criollo and Francisco Bañon brought de la Fuente to the palenque, along with others, including "Juan Criollo[, who was enslaved by] Francisco Lopez Nieto[,] and also another black[,] Garcia Angola [who was enslaved by] Pedro Destrada."[51]

Juan Criollo de la Margarita, whom de la Mar named, also escaped from the brutal treatment he received as a bondsman on the farm of Francisco Lopez Nieto with the help of Francisco Criollo. He may have attempted to run before, as he testified that Lopez kept him in shackles. While still shackled, however, he managed to flee to Juan de Sotomayor's farm, where he stayed in a hut belonging to the elderly Manuel Angola with Francisco Criollo, and "other Anchicos and a Malemba who was in the palenque of [P]olín [who] helped him remove the iron ring that he had on his foot[,] and as the blacks of the palenque of Limón . . . communicated with the people on the farm of the said [D]on Juan [de Sotomayor] and they saw the declarant [Juan Criollo de la Margarita] . . . Francisco Criollo took him to a Criollo from there [the palenque] named Gonçalo Chale took him to the palenque of Limon."[52]

Francisco Criollo and Francisco Bañon's regular roles in facilitating the flight of enslaved Cartagenerxs to palenque Limón demonstrate how they occupied vital positions in the political and social life of the community, even while living outside of it. Their knowledge about the activities of the palenquerxs and their intimate relationship with its leadership over the course of many years meant that they were trusted members of the community. In fact, their remaining on the farms of Juan de Sotomayor and Andres Ortencio conferred distinct advantages to the palenquerxs in terms of access to supplies—including gunpowder and bullets—a never-ending stream of those wishing to join their community, and also vital intelligence.[53] The Limones leadership acknowledged the importance of Criollo and Bañon's relationship with the palenque in the wake of their attack on Diego Marquez's farm, when Queen Leonor mandated that the palenquerxs share the pigs they captured with these two allies.[54] Criollo, Bañon, and others like them cemented the solid links between the political life inside the palenque and the lived experiences of individual bondsmen and women in Cartagena and surrounding areas. The relationship of Criollo and Bañon to the palenque parallels the situation in eighteenth-century Angola, where bondsmen and women who had served Portuguese masters in Luanda "found a particular welcome among the lords of Kisama, who used them as spies who could return undetected to the city, dressed like its other African residents, and report back on Portuguese military capacities and intentions."[55]

Even as they remained enslaved, Francisco Criollo and Francisco Bañon appear to have represented and participated in one type of political response to their enslavement by regularly helping those who wished to flee bondage make contact with the palenquerxs and by shaping both the discourse and population of the community itself. They seem to have advocated a more direct confrontation with the Spanish than the leadership in Limón prior to the 1620s supported. In a conversation with de la Fuente, they inquired why the people of Limón had been "very quiet[,] and why didn't they go out and rob and kill people like Domingo Bioho and his soldiers did[?]" This inquiry came in the context of a warning about an impending attack by the Spanish on the palenque in the coming summer. Since an attack by the Spanish was inevitable, Criollo and Bañon argued, it made sense to gather as many people together as possible to inflict the greatest possible damage against them.[56]

Referencing Domingo Bioho as an idiom for a particular kind of political action drew upon the reputation of a leader whose fame was widespread in the early seventeenth-century New Kingdom of Grenada. While the palenque Limón certainly existed while Bioho was at the height of his power, it is unclear the degree of contact that community members had with this other leader; none of the palenquerxs themselves directly mention Bioho in their testimony, aside from de la Fuente recalling Francisco Criollo and Francisco Bañon's question. Nearly all of the Spanish who testified, however, compare the threat of Limón to that of Bioho, indicating that for many, Bioho served as a revolutionary archetype. Bioho, like Kafuxi Ambari, became a charismatic symbol of aggressive and effective martial resistance against slavery. Bioho's reputational geography intersected with Kisama's and that of others in Limón.

Whatever political divisions existed within Limón in the sixteenth century and the first few decades of the seventeenth century, it appears that those advocating a more conciliatory approach to the Spanish prevailed. However, in the 1620s and 1630s, the arrival of a new group of West Central Africans in the palenque and the rising prominence of a cohort of Malemba-identified men within Limón, along with an influential group of Kisama-identified men both within and without the palenque, would push the community in an entirely new direction. It is certainly no coincidence that just as political shifts within West Central Africa dramatically reconfigured the social landscape of the region, as waves of fugitives to Kisama asserted their own notions of political legitimacy and the previously nomadic bands of Imbangala consolidated their power into the Kingdom of Kasanje, West Central Africans in the Americas, too, promoted political changes. Those driving these changes not only bridged the still-enslaved/self-liberated divide, but their political repertoires also stretched across the Atlantic and the boundaries between the world of the living and the world of the dead to place royal authority inside the body of a young woman born in Limón, Leonor Criolla.[57] By examining the spiritual and military articulations of this new political orientation within the palenque and the critical role that Kisama-identified people played within this change, it is possible to trace how the language of identity served as an idiom of political orientation in the early modern Africa and in African communities in the Americas.

By the time of the 1634 trial of the captured Limoneses, there were clear distinctions within the palenque between those who advocated a more aggressive policy toward the Spanish—and who controlled the ritual practices necessary to successfully sustain these attacks—and those who advocated a more conciliatory approach. As we have already seen, such political divides transcended the physical boundaries of the palenque, and many who remained enslaved on farms surrounding Cartagena were central to the transformation of Limón's politics. Francisco Criollo and Francisco Bañon certainly advocated Bioho-like militarism. However, the attacks on the neighboring palenque Polín, the farms of Diego Márquez and Francisco Martin Garruchena, as well as on Chambacú, were prompted by the growing support both within the palenque and its extended community for increased aggression. These palenquerxs and their allies used politico-ritual identities to articulate their common membership in a broad community that connected bondspeople to maroons, Americans to Africans, and the living to the dead. Queen Leonor's rule was the nexus of this shift, and through her and those connected to her, it is possible to discern the contours of these changing identities.

Remarkably, Leonor herself was almost certainly born in the palenque. Sebastian Angola identifies Leonor's father, Domingo, as a "criollo del palenque." Leonor's sons Marcos and Cristóbal then represented at least the third generation of this family living within Limón.[58] None of those who testify name Leonor's mother, while they identify Leonor's father, Domingo, as both Domingo Angola and Domingo Bondondo, a name that may link him to certain ritual powers.[59] Domingo's appellations, just like those of Perico and the other Kisama-identified palenquerxs, further demonstrates the absurdity of the origins-obsessed scholarship that treats colonial ascriptions as static signifiers. How could Domingo be both a *criollo* (American born) and an Angola and also Bondondo, unless these terms were political signifiers rather than geographical tags? While some of Domingo's names suggest that he was born in Africa, and that his daughter was born in the Americas and probably within Limón, both participated actively in the ritual practices that emerge from the problematic transcripts of the trial as the decisive marker of their new, more radical political orientation.

While the Spanish were prone to conflating all African and indigenous practices as "witchcraft," it is clear from the records that those within the extended community of Limón categorized ritual practice according to moral and political valence. Indeed, Limoneses articulated the emergent political tensions within their community through the idiom of witch-craft. Gaspar Angola identifies Leonor as a *mohana*. This word appears only one other time in all of the documents, when Juan de la Mar notes that Captain Francisco's elderly, Angola-identified mother "was said [to be a] Mohongo."[60] The Limoneses understood the practice of mohans and witches as occupying two separate moral and political universes. Queen Leonor and Francisco's elderly mother were both mohans whose practices supported and were supported by the increasingly powerful constituency within Limón that advocated direct action against the Spanish. Because their ritual practices—however abhorrent they may have appeared to the Spanish—were perceived by the dominant segments of Limón as promoting the community's welfare, community members described them with terminology that appears, at the very least, neutral.

Given the growing tensions between different elements within Limón's extended community, however, those in power within the community did not condone all ritual practices. Though each claimed to know about the event only secondhand, through rumors that they heard within the palenque, Juan Criollo de la Margarita and Lorenzo Criollo both re-counted a case in which Limoneses had killed an Arará-identified man.[61] According to Juan Criollo de la Margarita, they burned him because "they said he was a witch [*bruxo*]," while Lorenzo Criollo recounted that "they burned after killing an [A]rara man because he was an herbalist [*yerbat-ero*] and he wanted to kill the children." Juan says that the Arará man was with Tunba, another name for Francisco Criollo (not "the Hunchback," who was still enslaved, but another man by the same name), a powerful leader within Limón, and that he was killed outside of Limón as those who attacked Chambacú returned.[62] However, from the sparse descrip-tion of the events, it is impossible to determine if this Arará is the same Arará, Francisco, who went back to the farm of Piña where he had been enslaved and helped carry off Sebastian Angola, or if he was indeed an outsider to the extended community of Limón.[63] Knowing whether or not this particular Arará-identified man had previously lived in Limón or not, however, would not ultimately clarify his insider/outsider status.

As Leonor became queen and the palenquerxs adopted a more aggressive stance toward their Spanish and indigenous neighbors, they increasingly articulated political tensions in language that could be construed as "ethnic."[64] However, those who used ostensibly "ethnic" language did so, as ever, as shorthand for political ideology and moral practice, commenting on the growing tensions within the community. These were not primarily conversations about origins or essential and essentialized loyalties, but rather about political legitimacy and the relationship of various forms of violence to social formation and cohesion.

Juan de la Mar, the Cartagena-born man whom Francisco Criollo had helped escape slavery and join Limón, testified that in

> truth ... the criollos of the palenque were peaceful when the declarant [Juan de la Mar] arrived and for a long time afterwards[,] without doing harm or ill to anyone[,] and the declarant swears that it went well until the Malembas of Juan Ramos and Sebastian Congo [their] companion who stirred them up and later others came from the palenque of Polín[,] and Marques's negro named Lasaro who came from the same [palenque] and those of Alonso Martin Hidalgo ... who declared that [the palenqueros should no longer] work for [the Spanish] nor [trade for] blankets[,] they wanted to teach the criollos del palenque to weave.[65]

The antagonism here was not between so-called criollos and West Central African *bozales* (African born). Indeed, the fact that Queen Leonor was herself a criolla who was probably born in the palenque and whom the Malembas ceremonially invested with the spiritual essence of a queen means that such terms have limited value in describing the social and political dynamics of Limón and African societies in the Americas during the seventeenth century. The discord in Limón stemmed not from different origins or essential cultural incompatibilities but rather from antithetical political ideologies that were often articulated through terms of origin. A fugitive imbare from Kisama and a citizen of Mbanza Kongo (the Kingdom of Kongo) might both be captured in war and shipped to the Americas from Luanda. In most records, that would render them both "Angola." These two captives, perhaps shackled together below the decks of a slave ship, may have come to understand each other. They would likely not, however, share the same political ideologies. While political tensions emerged from local circumstances, people understood them through the kaleidoscopic lenses of their prior political ideologies and knowledge.

In the situation Juan de la Mar describes, the Malemba-identified men, Sebastian Congo, and others from Polín advocated economic activities that would afford Limón greater autonomy from the Spanish. Weaving textiles would help free the Limoneses from the need to work for and trade with their neighbors—a political and economic policy reminiscent of the approach adopted some twenty years earlier by the sobas Kapakasa, Langere, and Kafuxi Ambari in Kisama, who refused to trade with the Portuguese.[66] Given that the palenquerxs had long worked for and traded with Garruchena and Marquez, two of the Spanish whose farms they ultimately attacked, this effort to increase local production was prudent. However, not all in Limón were receptive to the ideas of those from Polín, which was a far smaller palenque; by de la Fuente's account, only eight or ten men and perhaps four or five women lived there.[67] That such a small group of people would have a distinct, separate identity from the larger palenque of Limón—at least until the Limoneses attacked Polín and compelled its residents to join them in subservient roles, performing agricultural labor and carting wood and water—suggests that there were important political differences between the two palenques.[68]

Continuing his description of the riven political climate within Limón, Juan de la Mar explains,

> The men [who had been enslaved by] Alonso Martin [Hidalgo] and Lasaro [who had been enslaved by] Marques insisted that they [Limoneses] go to burn the farms of their masters and to rob them and to carry off some of the people [still enslaved there who were from] Angola[.] They asked why they didn't want to carry off the people from the rivers [of Guinea; Upper Guinea, and they responded] that they had bad intentions[.] And thus they went and did all of the evil and damages that they had said they were going to do, but the declarant [Juan de la Mar] doesn't know what they had attempted, because he lived apart from the Malembas and Angolas with the Criollo people who were in the Chale band.[69]

In the period leading up to the attacks on the neighboring Spanish farms and the pueblo Chambacú, there were apparently at least two distinct residential divisions within Limón, reflecting differing political ideologies, as demonstrated in Juan de la Mar's description. He lived with the "Chale band," ostensibly so named because it was headed by the leader Captain Diego Chale and/or his brother Gonzalo, who were palenque-born children of Pedro Biafara, a name that suggests connections to the non-state politics of Upper Guinea.[70] While Diego Chale still exercised some degree of authority within Limón as a recognized captain, it is clear that this group was losing power relative to Queen Leonor and the Malemba-, Angola-, and ultimately, Kisama-identified constituency that had begun to change the orientation of the community, even opposing the likewise Malemba-, Angola-, and Congo-identified members of the neighboring community of Polín. They targeted the farms of their former masters not simply out of revenge but also in order to free particular people to whom they felt connected and whose political inclinations supported the new authority within Limón.

These complex politics were far from natural outgrowths of straight-forward antagonism between people from different regions; indeed, those who were gaining power in Limón were, like those in the palenque Polín whom they attacked, apparently mostly of West Central African origins. It is important to remember that not only are names such as Angola broad, but that they encompassed individuals whose presence in the Americas could be traced to conflicts with each other. There was no natural affinity among "Angolas" or "Criollos" any more than those from Upper Guinea enjoyed solidarity with each other and a political in-clination toward accommodation with the Spanish ostensibly shared by the American- and palenque-born. Indeed, it is significant that the name Domingo Bioho itself—which connoted the same type of aggressive po-litical orientation that both the still-enslaved, American-born Francisco Criollo and the West Central African-born maroon Malembas and An-golas advocated in Limón—suggests origins in Upper Guinea. Upper Guineans and the American-born were not essential pacifists, nor were they inherent enemies of West Central Africans; the sixteenth-century Panamanian maroon leader Domingo Congo's trusted captains, after all, were all Upper Guinea–identified. Instead, these claims reflected grow-ing political divisions within Limón and the degree to which the exercise of particular forms of violence defined membership in the community. The political ideologies articulated as Malemba and Kisama identities best illustrate the contours of these political divisions and their connec-tions to seventeenth-century African fugitive modernities.

The Politics of Naming: Lemba, Kisama, and
Community in Limón

Just as so-called ethnicity cannot be deracinated from politics, neither can
we understand the "politics of practical behavior" without considering
"people's strategies for using cultural practices to fulfill a variety of press-
ing needs in difficult and dangerous circumstances."[71] Limoneses used
terms like "Angola" and "rivers of Guinea" to articulate very concrete political differences, and they distinguished between various forms of ritual
behavior not by their points of origin in Africa but rather by their role in
supporting the increasingly martial agenda of the palenque. Differences
in the choreographies and provenance of ritual seem to have mattered
far less than the relationship between its practitioner and the political
will of the community at large. Mohans became queens and respected
elders; brujos and yerbateros were killed and burned. Throughout the extensive trial documents, the term of identity that palenquerxs most often
evoked in connection with ritual practice was "Malemba." But what did
"Malemba" mean, how did it relate to Kisama, and what can these terms
and the multiple and often contradictory ways in which they are deployed
tell us about life in Limón and in the seventeenth-century worlds of
Africa and the Americas?

Malemba-identified individuals appear fairly frequently in these documents, most often in conjunction with the radical political changes inside the palenque. Sebastián Angola argued that "the palenque residents
were peaceful until Cristóbal Malemba, Francisco Malemba, Moriungo
Malemba, Gaspar Malemba and Pedro Buila stirred up the queen with
herbs."[72] According to palenque leader Juan de la Mar, "When they arrived, Juan Ramos's black men put some devil in Leonor's head, because
from then on she began to command. And all obeyed her, even the captain and commander, because something happened to her in the head
that made her walk as if crazy, falling down and hitting herself before she
spoke. And when she came back to her senses, she made a thousand wild
statements and in effect everyone feared her and obeyed her as queen."[73]

McKnight argues that the change in Limón's political orientation followed the arrival of the Malemba men and their installation of potent
spiritual forces inside of the American-born Leonor's head—a contention
well supported by the evidence. Our divergent interpretations of the same
materials stem from an epistemological disagreement. McKnight, like

the majority of scholars of Africans in the Americas until very recently, interprets claims of identity as straightforward attributions of original African provenance. For McKnight, "Malemba," like "Angola," is a place. Citing Alonso de Sandoval's connection of "Malembas" from east of the Kwanza River to those who were often taken from Luanda, McKnight claims that it is more likely that those whom other palenquerxs identify as "Malemba" (no self-identified Malemba testified) hailed from east of the Kwanza River valley rather than the port north of the Congo River bearing that name.[74]

However, it is unclear why we should assume the basis for African identity in the Americas is primarily or exclusively geographical. If McKnight favors Sandoval's explanation, then why would the other palenquerxs identify these men specifically as "Malemba" rather than "Angola," as those who left from Luanda supposedly normally did? While it is certainly possible that these men came from either of the Malembas McKnight cites, the role of these particular Malemba-identified men in altering the ritual and political practices of Limón and in initiating a new form of leadership indicate that in Limón, Malemba, like Kisama, is yet another African identity better understood through the lens of (ritual-)politics rather than of origins; place and region provide the matrix within which these ritual and political practices were performed, contested, and re-shaped. Cristóbal, Francisco, Moriungo, Gaspar, and the other Malembas of Limón may have been from nearly anywhere in West Central Africa or beyond. Their actions in the New Kingdom of Grenada, however, suggest that they were familiar with Lemba.

Lemba—"'a medicine of the village'; 'a medicine of family and its perpetuation'; fertility medicine'; 'the sacred medicine of governing' . . . ; 'the government of multiplication and reproduction' . . . and 'sacred medicine integrating people, villages, and markets'"—proliferated throughout the northern Congo region from the seventeenth to the nineteenth centuries as elites across nonstate societies sought to mediate and manage the unprecedented moral crisis of increasing danger and social stratification ushered in by the trans-Atlantic slave trade.[75] In John Janzen's seminal study of this widespread "drum of affliction," he found that Lemba not only transcended ethnic, linguistic, and political boundaries throughout Central Africa, but that it also crossed the Atlantic, where he sees extensive evidence of the practice of Lemba ritual and the prominence of Lemba identities in both Haiti and Brazil. In Haitian Vodoun, practitioners associate Lemba with particularly volatile spirits and, according to Jean Price-Mars, it is the only rite "celebrated secretly, deep in the forest, rather than in the village or town."[76] Janzen further identifies continuities between Price-Mars's account of the role of pig blood and sacrifice in the Haitian Lemba rite with communal Lemba practices in the northernmost regions of its practice in the Congo.[77] It is perhaps not coincidental, then, that of the many important articulations of Leonor's new, Malemba-vested authority, one of the most prominent was an attack on Diego Márquez's pig farm. As we have already seen, the palenquerxs did not simply slaughter, smoke, and consume the pig meat within their own community, as we would expect from those whose material survival was always perilous, but they also shared some pig meat—and no other provisions that they captured—with Francisco Criollo and Francisco Bañon. As was the case in Congo, Haiti, and Brazil, the slaughtered pigs helped delineate the boundaries and nature of the ritual-political community of Limón.

As a rituo-political identity, however, Malemba was neither singular nor monolithic; Limoneses situated Malemba within a West Central African political context by connecting and conflating it time and time again with "Angola." While those who testified named Perico Quisama in four separate but interrelated ways, his companion was always described simply as Malemba—none offers any details about his background, his ties to any save Perico, or his fate. Malemba remains virtually unfathomable save through his connection to the ritual politics of Lemba and his role in promoting targeted militarized activism within Limón. His constant association with Perico Quisama suggests that within the general regional category of Angola, those who identified as Malemba and Kisama occupied adjacent and overlapping spaces—both concretely, as evident in the testimony of Juan de la Mar, but also ideologically. Indeed, as in the case of the Limones leader Manuel, sometimes Kisamas *were* Malembas.

Nearly all of the palenquerxs who testified named Manuel Quisama as one of the most important figures in Limón. He was instrumental in leading the attacks on the smaller palenque Polín and in bringing enslaved Africans from neighboring farms into Limón. Juan Criollo de la Margarita characterizes him as the overall "leader of the people of Guinea [those born in Africa]," sharing authority with Queen Leonor, Francisco de la Fuente, Juan de la Mar, Captain Francisco Criollo, Tunba, and Lorenço.[78] Gaspar Angola describes him as one of two "executioners" in Limón.[79]

It was likely in this capacity that he participated in the ritual killing of the Spanish overseer and the indigenous worker whom the palenquerxs captured at Márquez's farm.

The description of his participation in this ritual killing, however, reveals an important ambiguity in the trial records. In his account of these events, Juan Criollo de la Margarita describes Manuel Quisama as "a black Malemba that was called Quisama."[80] If Malemba indeed meant a place, rather than a political or ritual identity, however, how could a "Malemba" be "called Quisama"? Why was he called Kisama only when he was acting in a capacity that foregrounded the social domestication of ritual violence?[81] In the context of Limón and its extended community in the late 1620s and early 1630s, palenquerxs appear to have understood and articulated the political valences of Malemba through ritual idioms and military action. Not only did the Malembas in Limón dramatically alter the leadership structure of the community by ceremonially elevating Leonor to the level of a queen, but they also promoted both an increasingly assertive military approach to relations with neighboring communities— Spanish, indigenous, and African alike—and also an increasingly radical ritual articulation of these politics. By all accounts, Manuel participated actively in these practices, leading raids and serving in a ritually sanctioned role as the community's executioner. He was thus a Malemba in practice. While it is certainly possible that Manuel was "called Quisama" because he claimed origins between the Kwanza and Longa Rivers, it is impossible to deracinate these putative geographic origins from the dynamic political climate of early seventeenth-century Kisama. Whether Manuel was "from" Kisama, or claimed Kisama, or had a Kisama identity imposed upon him by other members of the community, in the charged and increasingly West Central African-dominated world of Limón, being a "Malemba called Quisama" combined multiple strains of ritual power and the politics of resistance. The existence of such concatenated identities in a maroon community in the Americas reveals the durability of fugitive politics in parallel but distinct political spheres. In a post-Bioho period in Limón, "Malemba" and "Kisama" represented two distinct but synergistic political ideologies that those who advocated a more direct confrontation with the colonial state could mobilize.

In seventeenth-century Angola, Kisama and Imbangala exemplified two radically different forms of fugitive modernities, drawing on diametrically opposed ideologies of political legitimacy and social organization in response to the pervasive chaos and proliferation of violence that characterized the period. For those fortunate enough to survive the murder of their family members, the capture and sale of their children, and the destruction of their homes, fields, and sacred spaces by the Portuguese and their allies, fleeing to an ostensibly more secure space was often their only option.[82] Those who crossed the Kwanza River from the north or the Longa River from the south, or the mountains from the east, joined a society whose political culture emphasized idioms of kinship and eschewed the institutionalization of violence, if not its necessary and highly effective practice in defense of the community. The thousands of vulnerable fugitives who comprised the backbone of seventeenth-century Kisama society valued martial skill to the extent that it kept them safe from outside predation, but they did not make it the defining idiom of social organization. Kafuxi Ambari—the only named warrior who persists in oral tradition and historical memory in the region—and the pseudonymous, eponymous Kisamunu figure, who is likely the same person—are remembered as dangerous, powerful outsiders whose martial skills helped forge Kisama society even as they defined these figures outside of its social boundaries.[83] By contrast, Imbangala society placed violence and warrior identities at the very core of their political and cultural life. By disavowing kinship and settled agrarian life as organizing idioms for society and instead promoting rootless, pillaging war camps, the Imbangala kilombos were lenses that refracted and concentrated the extremity of African life in the era of the trans-Atlantic slave trade.[84] Even after 1630, when the Imbangala formed the state of Kasanje, violence remained at the core of their social practices, and slave raiding and trading the root of their economy.

In most respects, Limones society was far closer to the Kisama end of the spectrum of responses to violence and dislocation than the Imbangala pole. Nearly all who testified mentioned familial connections within the palenque, from Queen Leonor's relationship with her father Domingo, her husband Manuel, and her sons Marcos and Cristóbal to Pedro Biafara's sons Diego and Gonçalo Chale to the extensive list of grandparents, parents, and children that Juan de la Mar offers.[85] Even the contours of who was "carried off" in the attacks against the Spanish farms seem to reveal the power of the very social relations and sense of kinship that the Imbangala rejected. Those who fled often returned to help free those still in bondage on the farms where they had served. For example, Lázaro Quisama, who had fled Márquez's pig farm for the palenque two years prior to the Spanish attacks, "asked . . . [the Queen] Leonor to go and burn the farm of his master because he treated his blacks badly and he had threatened the people of Limon."[86] After attacking and burning Márquez's farm, Lázaro Quisama and the other palenquerxs brought several of those enslaved by Márquez back to Limón, among them Juan Quisama.[87]

Like Perico and Manuel, Lázaro was yet another Kisama-identified man who appears under multiple names in the testimonies. Indeed, of all who mention Lázaro, it is only Jacinto Angola who calls him Lázaro Quisama, though he also calls him Lázaro Angola. Otherwise, Lázaro Angola (not the same person), Juan Carabali, Juan Angola, Catalina Angola, Juan de la Mar, and Sebastian Angola call him Lázaro Angola exclusively.[88] Like Lázaro, Jacinto Angola had been enslaved on the farm of Diego Marquez, and Jacinto clearly remembered Lázaro from their time together on Marquez's farm. He testifies that "it had been more than two years already since he [Lázaro] had left and went to the said palenque," and describes how Lázaro participated in carrying off him, Miguel Bran, Juan Carabali, Juan Quisama, and Gaspar Congo. It is within the context of this recollection that Jacinto calls him Lázaro Quisama. However, when reporting generally on Lázaro's participation in the raid on Marquez's farm, he refers to him as Lázaro Angola.[89] For Jacinto, then, "Quisama" appears to have carried a more familiar connotation than did "Angola." He had lived and worked with Lázaro Quisama before he fled two years earlier, and this familiar man returned to bring not only Jacinto but another Kisama-identified man (Juan) to freedom as well.

The kind of familiarity Jacinto's use of the appellation Kisama seems to indicate in the case of Lázaro helps underscore Limón's political proximity to the range of fugitive modernities developing in Kisama at that time and distance from Imbangala politics. This similarity reveals less about some ostensible retention of essential ethnic characteristics between Africa and the Americas and more about the kinds of practices conducive to the establishment of socially and politically sustainable communities. In critiquing the continuing insistence of scholars writing about Palmares and other maroon societies in Brazil and the Americas in general regarding Imbangala kilombos as their antecedents, John Thornton writes that the states of Kongo, Ndongo, and Matamba, "or smaller political entities in the [West Central African] region," were far more likely models.[90] Indeed, the fugitive nature of Kisama politics makes it a prime candidate for a model of political practice, ideology, and culture in maroon communities throughout the Americas. Accounts from the sixteenth through the nineteenth centuries, from North America through the Caribbean and Latin America, concur: when and wherever possible, fugitives endeavored to establish settled, agrarian communities and family systems—practices that were anathema to the Imbangala social model. However, just as I argue that in spite of Kisama's static reputation and representation across five centuries, the nature and meaning of Kisama identity was always changing—as one might expect from an endemically nonstate society whose survival was predicated on attracting and incorporating ever-expanding numbers of diverse fugitives—so, too, was Limones politics always in flux.

The convergence of radical shifts in the political orientation of communities both between the Kwanza and Longa Rivers and outside of Cartagena in the late 1620s and early 1630s, however, suggests that this was a resonant moment of political transformation in West Central Africa and in Limón. While the experiences of violence, rupture, and dislocation were common in seventeenth-century Africa and the Americas, the local histories of maroonage and the different African intellectual, political, social, and cultural strands woven through life in Limón ensured that those living within and connected to its community—however much they drew on the reputation of Kisama or actual experience within it—created a distinct, though related, fugitive modernity. Influenced by earlier maroon societies in the region, such as those led by Domingo Congo and Domingo Bioho, as well as by the political cultures of Upper Guinea, Kongo, and Ndongo, when Limoneses shifted their political orientation, they did so through the idiom of sacred royalty. By placing a particular African spirit into Leonor's head, the Malemba-identified men ensured that political authority in Limón would remain intimately connected to particular African ritual and spiritual discourses designed to abrogate the social and moral ills of slavery.

Still, it is only from the trial of the Limoneses that we can hear any form, however distorted, of direct testimony from a nonelite, Kisama-identified actor in the seventeenth century. So, we return finally to Perico Quisama, whom the Spanish identify as Pedro Angola in his own testimony. Just as was the case with Francisco Bañon and Francisco Criollo, Perico's testimony reveals that when he and Malemba brought news of the impending attack to Limón, they were not entering a community of strangers. Perico and other bondsmen and women knew many of the Limoneses because they worked on their master Garruchena's farm. In exchange for general agricultural labor and help with the maize harvest in particular, Garruchena gave the maroons "salt and tobacco and catiba de mangle to cure those who had sores."[91] In direct contradiction to every other deponent's account of the raid on Garruchena's farm and Chambacú—in which Perico and Malemba hasten to Limón to bring news of an impending attack—Perico claims in his own testimony that he ran to Limón in an attempt to recover the "two [pairs of] pants and three head cloths and one cloth that is worn on the belly and three bars of soap" that the previously amicable palenquerxs supposedly stole from his hut. According to Perico, once he arrived in Limón, he complained to Captain Francisco about the theft and was kept waiting for several days. Juan de la Mar asked him if he wished to return to his master, and he said yes. De la Mar responded that they would not allow him to return, since he "already knew the way to the palenque and would teach it to the whites." After three days, Queen Leonor and other soldiers told Perico that they were "angry with his master Francisco Martin [Garruchena] because they had come to work on his farm and brought sticks to make his huts[, and] he had sent them a box of salt filled with straw."[92] This is not the only time that the box of salt filled with straw that Perico represents as the source of the palenquerxs' anger toward Garruchena appears in the testimonies, however. According to Lázaro Angola, when Captain Francisco and others returned to Limón bearing a box of salt from Garruchena, Perico, who had just arrived with his news of the impending assault on Limón, told the palenquerxs that "in the said salt there were lethal herbs and no one [should] eat it."[93]

The key to understanding Perico's multiple identifications and the elaborate and apparent lie that he told during his trial may come from a careful consideration of the role of this box of salt. Of course, by describing himself as the dual victim of theft and kidnapping, Perico sought to portray himself as less culpable in the eyes of the Spanish trying him, and in response to the consistent testimony by all others that he and Malemba had instigated the attack on Garruchena's farm; he did not succeed, and the Spanish indeed executed him. When Perico characterizes the outrage in Limón over the box of salt as resulting from Garruchena's deception of those who had performed hard labor on his farm and expected compensation—valuable salt, rather than worthless straw—he depicts a world populated by those driven by economic self-interest. Especially given the role of rock salt, and rock salt from Ndemba in Kisama in particular, as currency in the regional economies of West Central Africa, Perico's claim has prima facie credibility. Salt was valuable for Africans, indigenous people, and Europeans alike in the seventeenth-century New Kingdom of Grenada and the Caribbean world, where colonial powers fought to control salt production on various islands and contraband in salt trading led to repeated, unsuccessful attempts by the Spanish crown to establish monopolistic control over its production and trade.[94] However, Lázaro Angola's account moves the box of salt from the realm of the purely economic to that of the rituo-political. Lázaro portrays Perico as saving the leadership of Limón from assassination through the consumption of poisoned salt.

Throughout Africa and the Americas, Africans articulated many of their critiques of the direct and indirect violence of the trans-Atlantic slave trade through discourses about the powers of salt. In West Central Africa, salt not only carried economic value, but it also has the capacity to protect from malevolent witchcraft. For the Haitian *zonbi*—a chilling figure, a dead captive laborer whose soul is controlled by a powerful priest— salt has the power to reanimate. "If they happen to taste salt, they drop their crushed attitude, raise their heads and look their tormentor in the eyes. They even recover the strength to escape."[95] Whereas salt is a liberatory force in Haiti, in Jamaica, those who consume salt in life are unable to return to Africa after death; for this reason, Rastafarians traditionally abstain from cooking with it.[96] When Perico Quisama warned the Limoneses about the peril of consuming the adulterated salt, he evoked powerful discourses about malevolent power and liberty. While such beliefs about salt were indeed widespread throughout Africa and the Americas, Perico's role in revealing that what could be powerful medicine or wealth in one context had been transformed into an instrument of destruction by Garruchena lends further credence to his association with Kisama. The lands between the Kwanza and Longa Rivers were such an appealing refuge for vulnerable people from throughout West Central Africa because of the reputation of its leaders for martial and spiritual efficacy and staunch defense of fugitives; Kisama's appeal to powerful outsiders, by contrast, was linked primarily to the allure of the rock salt mines of Ndemba. By warning the Limoneses that the salt was adulterated, Perico not only saved the palenquerxs from poisoning but also evoked a prescient warning about the perils of resource wealth and entanglement in global capital. In his actions in the New Kingdom of Grenada, Perico traveled a parallel path to many in Kisama, like the imbare who fled from violence, brought important knowledge to the communities between the Kwanza and Longa Rivers, and were then instrumental in helping fight their former masters.

The social and political underpinnings of Perico's ascribed identity seem the diametric opposite of Lázaro's. In Lázaro's case, he is called Kisama by the deponent who knew him best, who remembered him from their shared experience of enslavement on Diego Marquez's farm, and who owed his fleeting freedom to him. In Perico's case, however, it is only Sergeant Miguel Auntunes, Captain Francisco Julian de Piña, and Juan Ortiz—the Spanish officials responsible for his capture—who call him Perico Quisama. According to Piña, when he captured Perico in the palenque, Perico told him that he had fled to Limón and reported that his master had received money to pay the people of Chambacú to kill them. When Piña asked him "why he said this lie[, he] responded that the devil had deceived him and that what he said happened and that the majority of the blacks that he [Piña] caught said that they were determined to burn all of the farms in [the mountains of] Maria."[97]

Perico directly rebuked Piña's accusation that he lied; more importantly, however, he linked the "devil [who] had deceived him" to the political practices and resistance of those whom the Spanish captured and, by implication, the many more whom they did not. Was Perico's "devil" the same as that which the Malemba-identified men has put in Leonor's head to make her queen? We can only speculate that this might be the case. However, regardless of whether Perico meant to describe the same spirit or a distinct one, the meaning was the same. In the words of Gaspar Angola, who had fled from captivity on the farm of Alonso Martin Hidalgo because the overseer Gregorio Lonva repeatedly beat and whipped him, and threatened him with castration, the attacks on the Spanish farms and the pueblo and the ritual sacrifice of captives was intended as "a warning from Guinea."[98]

This warning from Guinea was articulated less through speech than through the actions of those in the extended community of Limón, who responded to their individual and collective experiences of violence and alienation by forming their own viable society. Their close relationships with those still enslaved not only ensured the palenquerxs access to valuable resources and intelligence, but it also helped combat the threat of imminent social death that slavery represented. Clearly, the Limoneses who lived, worked, and raised multiple generations of children in the mountains outside of Cartagena were far from socially dead; Francisco Bañon and Francisco Criollo, though still enslaved, were equally socially alive. Limón was riven by political and social cleavages, often articulated through terms that scholars understand as ethnic. To the Limoneses, however, it seems more likely that this was a language of politics, not of apolitical provenance. Domingo Bioho represented a particular kind of militarism diametrically opposed to the ostensible passivity of those in the Chale band with whom he shared a region of provenance in Upper Guinea. Those who identified as Malemba did so through their use of ritual to advance a particular vision for Limón. Fragments of ideologies that can be connected to early seventeenth-century Kisama politics appear in the testimonies of the Limoneses, who strove to use martial and spiritual practices to maintain the integrity of a community in which idioms of kinship prevailed. This combination of practices and radical strategies for incorporating outsiders into the fabric of a settled community nevertheless forced to survive through aggressive military actions bears more than a coincidental similarity to parallel processes in Kisama during the same period. Thus, the late 1620s and early 1630s indeed constituted an important historical node in the practice of fugitive modernities on either side of the Atlantic. If the purpose of fugitive politics as practiced in the lands between the Kwanza and Longa Rivers was to help alienated, dispossessed individuals reestablish a meaningful form of personhood through forging stable communities and redrawing the structures of kinship, then the multigenerational family structures within Limón attest to the resonant power of such practices.

CHAPTER 5

Fugitive Angola

Toward a New History of Palmares

Palmares plays an outsized role in the racial geography and cultural bi-ography of the Brazilian state; it stands as the iconic example of a kind of heroic, resistant Blackness and untainted Africanity to which scholars and activists alike recur time and time again.[1] However, while much space has been devoted to tracing the African cultural antecedents to Palmares, there has been little critical examination of the intellectual and ideological repertoires of the community itself.[2] As I argued in the previous chapter, the Atlantic Ocean and the profound dislocation of the Middle Passage and of enslavement in the Americas were no barriers to the continuation of a fugitive politics already deeply rooted in multiple experiences of rup-ture in Africa. For seventeenth-century West Central Africans, Kisama was not only or even primarily a place. More significantly, it was a set of practices and ideologies rooted in the fugitive politics that emerged after 1594 and through the late 1620s and 1630s, and continued to change, frag-ment, and reform during the war of 1655–58 and after. Kisama's reputation, forged initially through Kafuxi Ambari's victory in 1594 and subsequent welcoming of fugitives, dispersed during the war on Kasanze, and spread even further through the region and the world during the disastrous war of 1655–58, transcended the Atlantic Ocean and was in no way centered on it. Thus, rather than viewing Kisama as a putative point of origin for the people of Palmares or centering the history of Palmares on a search for African antecedents, I instead regard it as a source of political logics.

What are the stakes of moving a discussion of African identities in the Americas out of the realm of origins and firmly into the discursive territory of politics? Perhaps this question is nowhere more relevant than in Brazil and around the case of Palmares. Palmares and Zumbi have lent their names to Black student–focused schools, an airport, sports teams, capoeira and dance groups, and community initiatives too numerous to name. If the northeast serves as imagined homeland of Brazilian Blackness, then Palmares is equally the most renowned quilombo. Indeed, the public institution within the Ministry of Culture established in the wake of the constitution of 1988 that is responsible for "promoting the preservation of the cultural values and social and economic impacts of the Black influence in the formation of Brazilian society" is named the Fundação Cultural Palmares; this is the governmental body charged with implementing affirmative action and overseeing the integration of African history and culture into school curricula. In 2006, activists in São Paulo established a private university dedicated to serving low-income Black students, which they named the Universidade Zumbi do Palämares (Unipalmares).[3] An international airport in Alagoas is likewise named after Zumbi. In 1978, the Brazilian government established Black Consciousness Day (Dia da Consciência Negra) as a national holiday on the anniversary of Zumbi's murder on November 20, and in 1997, finally canonized him as a national hero.[4] There are now several commemorative statues, from the Freyrian one in Brasilia to the embodiment of heroic resistant masculinity in the Pelourinho of Bahia. Assertions of a politics of Blackness in Brazil are inextricably bound to the history of Palmares, and yet the histories of Palmares through which scholars and activists alike mobilize action concerning the dire conditions of Black people in Brazil today are limited in the scope of their political imagination.

What made Kisama meaningful in the seventeenth-century world and beyond was not the degree to which the practices of those who claimed it qualified them for entry in museums or textbooks on civilization. There are no elaborate masquerades or images of royal authority to venerate, no lists of heroic deeds. The decidedly unromantic practical politics of Kisama revolved around the constant negotiation between the importance of the practice of violence and the equal necessity of not weaving violence into the fabric of the society, around the balance between rejecting forms of outside political authority and statism, of entanglement with capital economies, while navigating the need to negotiate with such powers for survival.

Approaching the history of Palmares as part of a study of fugitive modernities frees us from the imperative to prove that the children of enslaved Africans merit inclusion in the modern world or the institutions of rights of nation-states by virtue of origins in African empires.[5] From the vantage point of Kisama, we can claim a modernity that was always that of farmers and fisherpeople, hunters and herders, those with no aspirations for gain and no desire to do anything but avoid the Jita Kwatakwata. We walk away from the golden stool of Asante, we abandon the resplendent courts of Kongo, we turn our back on the wives of the leopard of Dahomey. We begin to ask questions about which structures of political imagination allowed people to reconstitute community and family time and time again, in the face of unfathomable violence and multiple experiences of catastrophic rupture. We place our faith in the creative intellectual labor of everyday people whose names we will never know to have dreamed up a world where survival was possible. Some of these dreamers called that work Kisama, and many more called it by other names, but it is this labor, these contestations and conversations, that promises to offer more both to our understanding of the past and our capacity to view any kind of way forward than the endless recursion to origins can ever do. There is no evidentiary smoking gun linking Kisama origins to Brazilian practices, but the lack of such evidence compels us to view trans-Atlantic fugitive history as process, rather than through the mechanistic lens of origins and retentions. By reinterrogating the political structure of Palmares from the standpoint of Kisama, I am able to offer a new perspective of the political ideologies that operated within this famous maroon community in particular, and maroon societies and African communities in both Africa and the Americas more broadly.

The Remarkable Odyssey of the Kisama Meme in Palmares

Perhaps the most oft-quoted document generated through the multiple colonial assaults on Palmares throughout the seventeenth century is the anonymous 1678 manuscript, "Relação das guerras feitas aos Palmares de Pernambuco no tempo do Governador D. Pedro de Almeida." Written to glorify the *bandeirante* leader Fernão Carillho's unprecedented military success against the quilombo and to celebrate the negotiation of the peace accords between Ngana Zumba and the colonial government, this document is rich in details and includes the most extensive discussion of the political geography of Palmares found in any of the known contemporary sources.[6] The author describes the settlements that comprised the overall quilombo as follows:

> In the Northwest, the Mocambo of *Zambi*, sixteen leagues from Porto Calvo; to the North of this at five leagues' distance that of *Arotireue*; and next to the East of these two named Mucambos is *Tabocas*; fourteen leagues to the Northwest of these *Dombrabanga*; and eight leagues North of this the village called *Subupira*; and six leagues North of this the Royal Enclave called *Macaco*; five leagues West of it the Mucambo of *Osenga*, and nine leagues Northwest of our [Portuguese] town of Serinhaem the village of *Amaro*; and **twenty leagues Northwest of Alagôas the Palmar of *Andalaquituxe*; Brother of Zambi**; and between these which are the largest and most defensible, are others of less consequence, and with fewer people.[7]

Of all of the place names on the list, Andalaquituxe stands out as somewhat unique. It is the only one of the communities described as a "palmar"; it is the only *mocambo* (maroon community) other than that of the well-known Zumbi whose leader is named explicitly, and, like Zumbi's mocambo, the leader's name and that of the community are the same; the community's leader is identified through his putative family relation to Zumbi. Thus, it is not surprising that during the proliferation of geographic and historical studies in nineteenth- and early twentieth-century Brazil, regionalist scholars like the Alagoans João Severiano da Fonseca and Alfredo Brandão sought to explain the origins of this incongruous name and toponym.

Even from the first efforts to explain the Andalaquituxe of the document, however, scholars began to subtly distort the material. The doctor and brigadier general João Severiano da Fonseca, who spent three years studying the Brazilian border with Bolivia in the 1870s and wrote extensively about indigenous communities in Mato Grosso, predictably claimed that "the word Cafuchy comes from tupi [an indigenous language]—*caa*, forest and *fuchy*, ugly."[8] Writing some forty years later, Brandão contested Severiano's claim, arguing,

> The word *Andalaquituche* appears altered in the manuscript: it must be *Zalaquituche*, which is comprised of two parts: *Zala*—[a] word

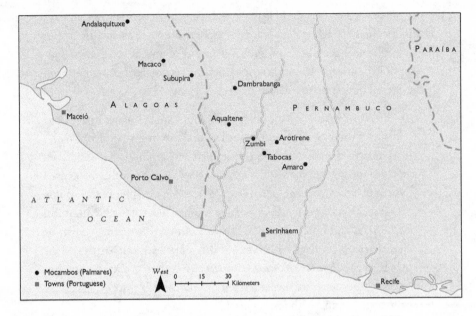

Map 5.1 — Seventeenth-Century Palmares. Map by Heather Rosenfeld.

from the *kimbund[u]* language of Angola, that signifies residence, house or group of houses[,] and *Quituche* or *Cafuche*—a proper name that must be that of the chief of the mocambo. Furthermore the mountain of Cafuchy can be found northeast of the city of Alagoas, at a distance of more or less 25 leagues, a distance that also concords with the manuscript. [In the accompanying footnote:] The existence of the word *cafuche* in the *kimbund[u]* language, the name of the mocambo signaled by the manuscript and the additional fact of being verified in an ancient document (see document n. 1) that Cafuchy mountain appears with the name *Caxefe*, a name that appears like an alteration of *Cafuche*, induces me to give this word an African origin.[9]

The document that Brandão cited is a petition Domingos João Carvalho, the captain of infantry during the final raid on Palmares, had written seven to eight years after the destruction of the community. In soliciting more compensation, Carvalho described which leaders directed which elements of the attack and mentions the "mountain of Caxefe."[10] Both Severiano and Brandão correctly parsed "Andalaquituxe" into its appropriate morphemes, "Ndala" and "Kituxi," though Severiano further divided his interpretation of the latter. While they disagreed on whether the word is Tupi or African, both concurred that *quituxe* is simply a mistranscribed *kafuxe*. Brandão's justification rested on the existence of *kafuxi* as a word in Kimbundu and for the correlation he made between this name and the mountain of Caxefe in another contemporary document. In other words, *quituxe* became equivalent to *caxefe* because both seemed similar to *kafuxi*, a word that exists in Kimbundu, an African language with which Brandão was acquainted. Thus, with his publication in 1915, Brandão linked the term "Andalaquituxe" to "Kimbundu," and to the proper name "Kafuxi," which he also associated with a mountain named in the original source as "Caxefe."

Some thirty years later, Edison Carneiro, who called Brandão's scholarship on Palmares "the best, without a doubt . . . he most approximates the truth, working with the few documents he had," adopted his gloss of the term "Andalaquituxe." Carneiro cautioned that many of the Bantu linguistic subfamily origin names in the 1678 "Relação" were likely rendered incorrectly by the anonymous author, and cited Brandão's analysis of "Andalquituxe" as an example of this. Carneiro relates: "Alfredo Brandão calculates, for example, that the name Andalquituche must be an alteration of Zala-Quituche or Zala-Cafuche, or, the residence of Cafuche, the name of the chief of the mocambo,—a hypothesis supported by the location of this mocambo in the Mountains of Cafuchi, again in accord with the manuscript."[11] Thus, Carneiro uncritically and fully replicated and endorsed Brandão's interpretation of the original material. While both insisted that Andalaquituxe was really Ndala Kafuxi, and that "Kafuxi" was a proper name in Kimbundu, neither attempted to further historicize or contextualize the name.

Indeed, it wasn't until 1965, when an American, R. K. Kent, published an article in the *Journal of African History* in which he famously described Palmares as "an African state in Brazil," that any scholar would establish such a link. Like Severiano, Brandão, and Carneiro before him, Kent believed that "Andalaquituche" was a mistranscription of "Ndala Kafuche." In a long list of putative connections between individual mocambos and particular places and people in Africa in support of his argument that the majority of Palmares leadership was not Brazilian-born, Kent linked Ndala Kafuche to Kisama on the basis of a personal communication with Jan Vansina. Because Kent's intention was to prove that "Palmares did not spring from a single social structure . . . [but] was, rather, an African political system which came to govern a plural society and thus give continuity to what could have been at best a group of scattered hideouts," he did not elaborate on what the connection of Andalquituche to Kisama—or any of the other named mocambos to Loango, Benguela, or any of the other places or people in Africa whom he mentioned—might signify.[12] Kent argued rather that the diversity of possible origins of the names of different mocambos within Palmares meant that only a nonspecific "African" governing system could function, anticipating by more than a decade the argument that Sidney Mintz and Richard Price famously articulated in *An Anthropological Approach to the Afro-American Past* regarding "heterogeneous African crowds."[13] The fact that Kent did not pursue the political histories of the regions of Angola that he cited as the sources for the majority of Palmarinos undermined his larger argument. By drawing on etymology alone to direct his focus in Africa, Kent missed the implications of particular dynamics of political practices within Palmares. In uncritically accepting the transformation of *kituxi* to Kafuxi from earlier sources, Kent merely reproduced the errors of scholars before him. However, despite the fact that Vansina linked Kafuxi to Kisama for Kent, Kent did not interrogate the potential ways in which Kisama political ideology—or the particular political ideologies of any of the other places in West Central Africa—informed the practice of fugitive politics in Palmares, nor did he even reference the widely circulating Kisama meme to speculate on the role of Kisama politics in Palmares. Neglecting these kinds of comparisons allowed Kent to see Palmares as "an African political system . . . transferred to a different continent," rather than as a case of political logics that were dynamic within both seventeenth-century Africa and the Americas.[14]

While he does not, for the most part, cite his sources, Nei Lopes appears to have adopted and amplified Kent's claim. In his *Enciclopédia brasileira da diáspora africana* (2004), Lopes included three Kisama-related entries. First, he described Andalaquituxe as the seventeenth-century "leader of Palmares killed by Fernão Carrilho in the onslaught on the quilombo of Garahuns." Next, he located the mountains of Cafuxi "180 kilometers northeast of the capital of Alagoas, where there was the citadel of Andalaquituxe, leader of Palmares. In precolonial Angola, Kafuxi was the name of a region south of the Kwanza River, governed by a soba of the same name." Finally, Lopes wrote that in the sixteenth century [*sic*, this mocambo was a seventeenth-century polity], Kisama "in Palmares, [was] the name of a ruler of a quilombo of the same name, located in the mountains of Cafuxi. In ancient Angola, Kisama was a region comprised of the jurisdictions of different leaders, all of whom had the title *Kisama*, and the chief of them was known as *kafuxi*."[15]

Lopes's first claim, that Andalaquituxe was killed by bandeirante Fernão Carrilho, appears to be extrapolation from one or more versions of the anonymous "Relação" that provides no additional information about the mocambo or its leader beyond that which I cited above.[16] Lopes's second entry, about the mountains of Cafuxi, rests on the research of Brandão; he merely converted leagues to kilometers. Likewise, he accepted the contention of all before him that *kituxi* and "Kafuxi" are equivalent terms. What Lopes added here, in his claim that the land south of the Kwanza River was called Kafuxi, rather than Kisama, however, is simultaneously in harmony with and contradictory to Angolan materials.

It is certainly true that, during the sixteenth and seventeenth centuries, Portuguese sources in Angola often confounded "Kafuxi" and "Kisama," and seamlessly slipped between defining each as a person, a population, and a place. For example, on February 23, 1693, as the bandeirantes attacked Palmares, the Portuguese governor in Luanda responded to a petition from "Sova Dom Pedro da Crux Cafuchy Cambary" for baptism and vassalage for himself and his "principal woman." While Dom Pedro petitioned as an individual, the political and diplomatic culture of the time meant that his baptism served to render all of his subjects Portuguese vassals as well.[17] In his affirmative response, the governor repeatedly mentioned Kisama as a territory over which Kafuxi Ambari ruled. However, thirteen months later, an inquiry by the Conselho Ultramarino (Overseas Council) into the diplomatic progress made by the Portuguese following Kafuxi Ambari's baptism referred not to Soba Kafuxi Ambari but rather to "sova Quiçama."[18] These sources, which are contemporary with those concerning the destruction of Palmares, reveal that while the Portuguese were aware that Kafuxi Ambari was but one soba in geographical Kisama, his power and prestige, combined with their imprecision, led to him appearing in the records as soba Kisama at times. Lopes must be familiar with at least some seventeenth-century Angolan sources, as he cites António de Oliveira de Cadornega, or rather João Pereira Bastos citing Cadornega, about the seventeenth-century belief throughout the region that the mother of Saint Benedict had been enslaved in Kisama as a young girl.[19] Though Lopes seems to rely on secondary sources for his information, it is possible that his conflation of and confusion between "Kafuxi" and "Kisama" derives from at least an echo of the language of the primary sources.

Even such a generous interpretation of Lopes's second entry, however, makes his third entry, in which he defines Kisama itself, more perplexing. There are simply no known documents or secondary sources that refer to a sixteenth- (or even seventeenth-, eighteenth-, or nineteenth-) century ruler named Kisama in Palmares or elsewhere in Brazil. As I discussed earlier, while the Portuguese did at times conflate "Kisama" with "Kafuxi Ambari" or other leaders in the region, neither of these were political titles of leadership. The Portuguese referred to sobas such as Langere, Kapakasa, and Kamona Kasonga by name regularly, and while they may have called them sobas *in* or *of* Kisama, the notion that they were all called Kisama is false. There is simply no basis in either Angolan or Brazilian sources for Lopes's entry on Kisama. And while Lopes does not intend for his work to be critiqued through academic standards, my above assessment is intended to illustrate the ways in which the unacknowledged circulation of the Kisama meme has shaped both scholarly and popular notions of the past not only in Angola but also in Brazil.

To summarize, the simple statement in the anonymous "Relação" of 1678 about a mocambo and leader named Andalaquituxe was uncritically transformed into Ndala Kafuxi first by Severiano, then by Brandão, the first scholar to discern its African origins and to conflate it with mountains called Caxefe. Carneiro simply echoed Brandão's claims, while Kent was the first to associate Kafuxi with Kisama in the context of Palmares based on information from Jan Vansina. Kent, however, did not draw from the Kisama meme, or interrogate what the presence of Kisama identities in Palmares might mean. By the early twenty-first century, Lopes inferred a narrative for Andalaquituxe's demise from the "Relação," conflated "Kafuxi" with "Kisama," and invented a leader named Kisama in Palmares and a political culture within Kisama unsubstantiated by any kind of evidence, though it reflects a distant echo and adaptation of the Kisama meme.

The utility of such an exhaustive discussion of the permutations of scholars' interpretations of a single term in a single document is twofold. First, as historian Flávio dos Santos Gomes notes, until the last few years, most who wrote about Palmares consulted the archival documents published by Ernesto Ennes, Edison Carneiro, and Décio Freitas. Some, as late as the 1970s, still defended the story invented by Sebastião de Rocha Pita in the 1720s that Zumbi and his followers committed suicide rather than be captured and reenslaved or killed. With a more recent interest in pursuing new sources that may well reveal previously unknown dimensions of Palmares's history, including the extensive documents in the archives at the Universidade de Coimbra that are unavailable in Brazil, and the involvement of scholars who can bring an understanding of Palmares's history from a broader Africanist perspective, there is reason to be hopeful that the next generation of historical writing can avoid merely reproducing the paradigms of past generations of scholars.[20]

In the case of Andalaquituxe and Palmares, it is possible to step outside of these existing scholarly narratives to find tantalizing hints of dynamic African political logics in the forests of Pernambuco and Alagoas. The key to discerning this layer of Palmares's history—hidden in plain sight—lies in the term "Andalaquituxe" itself and in the existing evidence on the political development of Palmares, interrogated through the intellectual history of particular African political practices. First, it is important to note that in Angolan materials, from the sixteenth through the twentieth centuries, with all of the many orthographic variations, Kafuxi is simply never rendered as *kituxe*. Furthermore, *kituxi* is itself a Kimbundu word that conveys important dimensions of the historical antecedents of Palmares's fugitive politics.

Crime and Punishment, Life and Debt: *Angola Kituxi*

Far from an obscure term in Kimbundu or in European knowledge of Kimbundu, *kituxi* in fact appears in the first written text in the language. More than thirty years before the anonymous author of the "Relação" described the community and leader Andalaquituxe, two Catholic priests, Francisco Paccónio and António Couto, published the first bilingual text in Portuguese and Kimbundu: a catechism.[21] Intended for the use of priests within long-established and ever-expanding missions in Angola, this tract provides a fascinating glimpse into Kimbundu vocabulary and grammar—and European efforts to find a correspondence between the semantic worlds of Kimbundu speakers and the Catholic church—in the mid-seventeenth century.[22] Among the more culturally laden terms that the priests were compelled to translate were the ever-ubiquitous "sin" and "sinner." For example, Paccónio and Couto render "original, mortal, and venial sin" as "[c]uim ne amoxi mo agimbululà o *quituxi* quia luvuàlu, ne *quituxi* quia cufuà *quituxi* quialengulucà."[23]

In glossing "sin" as kituxi, the priests appropriated an earlier, general sense of kituxi, as "crime." The word carries this meaning in Kimbundu and Umbundu, as well as Cokwe, whose speakers borrowed the term from Kimbundu; Kikongo terms for "crime" come from different roots.[24] Broadly speaking, throughout West Central Africa, deeper social notions of criminality are linked to selfishness: criminals act in ways that violate prevailing social norms of reciprocity, and those who behave aberrantly risk being accused of practicing witchcraft.[25] In addition to the more mundane forms of criminality, like theft or overt violence, witches might make another person mentally or physically ill, barren, or suddenly destitute. Utilizing a variety of divination techniques and ordeals, an *nganga* could determine the guilt or innocence of the accused. Witches always succumbed to ordeal or were identified effectively through divination, while the innocent were vindicated, as in the case of the *ndua* poison ordeal in Kasanje, as discussed in chapter 6. Giovanni Antonio Cavazzi describes another similar judicial process, the *mbulungo* ordeal, in which the accused was given either snake meat, fruit pulp, or juice made from certain plants, and "after having made his imprecations, becomes dizzy, shakes like a paralytic and can no longer stand. And if someone out of compassion doesn't give him the counter venom, after a few days he dies or, if he survives, he becomes crazy and incapable of taking care of himself."[26] Such a response, to those watching the public ordeal, proved the accused's guilt.

Of course, by the time Cavazzi observed this practice, West Central Africans had lived, died, endured, fled from, and fought against the trans-Atlantic slave trade for more than a century. In response to the new extremes of malevolence, West Central Africans modified and adapted older practices and forged new strategies for mitigating the threats of violence and unequal wealth to their communities' well-being.[27] According to Cadornega, in mid-seventeenth-century Angola, criminality was already linked to the trans-Atlantic slave trade, as local leaders adapted earlier oracular and divination practices to procure an ever-expanding network of captives and to extract resources from those who had access to goods and currency through their engagement in the trade.[28] Cavazzi confirms Cadornega's observations about the influence of the trans-

Atlantic economy on local judicial institutions, which he characterizes as entirely corrupt and extractive. He describes a case he witnessed in 1660 when two men manipulated the outcome of a poisoning ordeal by paying the nganga administering it twelve Roman escudos, "which is no small thing in these regions."[29]

While the trans-Atlantic slave trade led to an alteration of both notions of criminality and of strategies for mitigating it, it also encouraged the association of "debt" with "crime." As itinerant traders intensified their presence throughout Angola's interior in the eighteenth century, the (literal and figurative) shackles of debt followed in their wake.[30] Indeed, by the nineteenth century, authorities in Luanda complained about the prevalent practice of local men selling themselves and/or their dependents to settle their debts. Even neighbors and associates of debtors were at risk of being captured and sold by those intent on recuperating their losses. Significantly, the Kimbundu term used to signify the debt that had to be repaid—in currency, goods, or human beings—was *kituxi*. For example, "In 1853 an African woman named Maria 'said she was a free woman who had been given by her uncle Antônio Damião to a black man named Manoel to pay a fine [*quituxi*] in Hari [Ambaca].' According to Maria, Manoel then went on to sell her."[31] In this case, the kituxi in question was related to a criminal fine, but other accounts of Portuguese entanglement in local judicial processes in nineteenth-century Angola show the degree to which issues of debt pervaded society and had come to occupy the same semantic field as criminality. While Portuguese colonial observers complained that "no law of civilized people is applicable" to Angolan legal categories, they nevertheless noted how kituxi, along with *upanda* (adultery), dominated local court proceedings in the mid-nineteenth century.[32]

The term kituxi, then, serves as a useful index of shifting concepts of antisociality and power in West Central Africa across three centuries. In the seventeenth-century period of extensive political change throughout the region, kituxi appears to have referred to crime itself, even as the trans-Atlantic slave trade shaped the contours of perceptions of criminality. By the nineteenth century, however, kituxi not only meant "crime," or the "sin" that European missionaries attempted to conflate with local notions of criminality, but also "debt," either incurred through criminal activity or debt that then became criminalized. These changes reflect the increasing relevance of material capital in intellectual cultures dominated by notions of social capital, and also reveal the degree to which the slave trade reoriented judicial and social practices. As Mariana Candido argues powerfully in the case of eighteenth- and nineteenth-century Benguela, it is essential to understand judicial and financial means of enslavement as part of a broader structure of violence directed toward African people.[33] That this term was borrowed into Cokwe from Kimbundu, too, illustrates the social networks through which these concepts traveled in Angola's interior. While kituxi appears to have still meant only "crime" and not yet "debt" or "fine" in the seventeenth century, because the judicial institutions of Angolan communities were bent and contorted through engagement with the trans-Atlantic slave trade, it is impossible to distinguish between local senses of criminality and the processes that pushed thousands of adults and children into captivity and across the Atlantic.[34] "Andalaki-tuxe," then, is not the "Village of Kafuxi (Ambari)," but rather "Crime Village" or, more speculatively for the period, "Debt Village." Why would Palmarinxs name this mocambo after such terms used to describe social aberration, and why would the brother of Zumbi live in a place marked by such a stigmatizing moniker?[35] Unfortunately, the 1678 "Relação" does not provide any additional details about this mocambo beyond its name, the relation of its leader to Zumbi, and its location. However, given the relationship of judicial practices to the lived experiences of bondsmen and women in the Americas, including those who fled to Palmares, such a name invokes the legal and political paths many had traveled before.

Traitors, Poison Oracles, and Judicial Process beyond the State: Political Dissent and the Undoing and Redoing of Palmares

Given its prominence as a source for scholars investigating Palmares, it is important to remember that the "Relação" was written in 1678 and does not necessarily reflect the earlier political geography of the area. The period of Dutch occupation, from 1630 to 1654, seems to have been the era of the most dramatic population growth for Palmares, likely due to the synchronicity between revolutionary ideologies circulating throughout West Central Africa and the disruptions to the normal levels of Portuguese surveillance and control due to the conflict with the Dutch.[36] By 1642, the Palmarinxs had already abandoned their primary settlement due to the unhealthy climate of the area in which it was located and had constructed a new Great Palmares, distinguished at that time from Little Palmares, each itself a confederation of a major settlement and smaller mocambos.[37] Already, within Great Palmares at least, there is evidence of social inequality among the residents. Not only did those who interacted with the Dutch speak unequivocally of a king, but Captain Johan Blaer also "encountered a black man covered in boubas [skin legions caused by the infectious disease *Treponema pertenue*, or yaws] accompanied by an elderly brasiliense [an indigenous woman], slave of the daughter of the king."[38] This type of social inequality reflects not only similar institutions in Angola, including in Kisama, but also parallel practices within Limón.

From the 1630s period until the late 1670s, there certainly seems to have been a strong centralizing political impulse among the Palmarinxs; as Robert Nelson Anderson explains, Palmares can hardly be considered a "republican" polity, as Kent imagines, given the explicitly monarchical nature of the political system described in the "Relação."[39] The anonymous chronicler describes how "all acknowledge themselves obedient to one called *Ganga Zumba*, which means Great Lord; he is King and Lord over all the rest[,] those born in Palmares, as well as those from outside; he has a palace, Houses for his family, and is attended by guards and officials that Royal Houses usually have."[40] This was the same Ngana Zumba who, as king of Palmares, negotiated a peace treaty with the Portuguese in 1678. As Sílvia Hunold Lara notes, Ngana Zumba and the Portuguese negotiated the treaty according to well-trodden scripts developed over one hundred years of colonialism in West Central Africa. Ngana Zumba and his followers agreed to relocate to Cucaú, where they would be guaranteed their freedom in exchange for refusing to harbor any future maroons.[41]

The reaction to this treaty within Palmares constitutes one of the most polemical moments in Palmares's history, and illustrates the degree to which Ngana Zumba's representation of highly effective centralized power was aspirational rather than reflective of the fragmented political practices of these thousands of fugitives. While Ngana Zumba and his followers relocated, Zumbi continued to fight against the Portuguese. According to the only known contemporary source to comment on the event, the Portuguese staff-sergeant Manuel Lopes, the governor Aires de Souza de Castro ordered him to communicate to Zumbi that, in spite of his refusing the terms of the treaty, he would (again) be pardoned by the

Portuguese, if only he would join "his uncle Ganazona to live in the same liberty which all of his family enjoys ... [Zumbi's, and other leaders'] betrayal combined [with the fact] that many of our slaves have been captured and carried off [has caused] a lack of the promised peace for them[.] All of this has been discovered by others [who are] more reliable and by Ganazona and for more justification of this truth they poisoned their king Ganazumba in order to better commit their treachery."[42]

Many scholars and activists have simply inverted the valence of Lopes's remarks, asserting that it was in fact Ngana Zumba who was the traitor for negotiating with the Portuguese and that Zumbi carried the original revolutionary ideology of Palmares forward.[43] It is clear that, in the late 1670s, there was no widespread consensus on the terms of the treaty within the large, diverse Palmares community, given the sizeable faction committed to poisoning the king and, later, to following Zumbi in his continued martial activities against the Portuguese.[44]

While Lopes obviously had no access to the internal debates and contestations around the meaning of the treaty for different factions within Palmares, given the role of poison in judicial proceedings throughout West Central Africa, it is possible that Ngana Zumba's murder was less a unilateral act of stealth and more a communal equation of illegitimate political authority with witchcraft. Even if we doubt the specificity of Lopes's account and believe instead that the opposition murdered Ngana Zumba by means other than poison, the fact that Zumbi's faction continued to reject the terms of the treaty reveals the depth of this political chasm within Palmares. Just as in the conflicts in the lands of Langere, Palmarinxs did not agree on the ways in which alliances with the Portuguese or others affected political legitimacy. Without details about the political institutions that underwrote the decision to poison Ngana Zumba, whose very name suggests a ritual authority whose craft could be interpreted as either pro- or antisocial, given the political winds, we can only speculate about the idioms through which Zumbi and others carried out their judgment. For those who had suffered the devastation wrought by the consolidation of Kasanje in the mid-seventeenth century, monarchy would not have been an attractive option. Instead, non-state politics of the kind practiced in Kisama—where authority was primarily local or only situationally, rather than institutionally, broader, fugitives were welcomed and incorporated into an ever-evolving maroon society, and both defensive and offensive violence was legitimate so long as practiced in protection of the community—would have been a more compelling political model.

I argue that support for my assertion that even with the trappings of state, Palmares was rooted in fugitive modernities deriving from Kisama and elsewhere within the region, can be found in a new interpretation of the term "Angola Janga." Widely cited by scholars and activists as proof of the Angolan origins of Palmares's population and cultural, social, and political institutions, this term also appears in only a single document written three years after the murder of Zumbi, glossed as "little Angola: as they called it."[45] Because Palmares has always been associated with those who came from Angola, until relatively recently, scholars accepted this interpretation of the late seventeenth-century name for Palmares as a straightforward artifact of origins. Anderson notes that "Angola Janga" probably did not mean "Little Angola," and instead suggests that it may be *ngola iadianga*, Kimbundu for "first Angola."[46] John Thornton disputes this possibility on the basis of grammar, given the lack of noun class concord in Anderson's construction.[47]

The most salient possible interpretation of this late title for the fugitive communities is "Angola Yanga," or "Fugitive Angola," or possibly "Wary Angola." In Kimbundu, *yanga* has a variety of meanings connected to apprehension and maroonage, including "from *ya*/nga = to be released (agitated) / . . . To be afraid, be suspicious, hurry up, shake up, worry / . . . From *e/yanga* = place of / to be apprehensive . . . / *Village of fugitives, always fearful; refuge of animals in the islets of riverine confluences.*"[48] *Yanga*, or *nyanga*, has related meanings in Cokwe: "hunter or fisher (professional or consecrated, person or animal) . . . / Spirit . . . of a deceased hunter ('embodied') . . . by possessing the body of a familiar and tormenting them because they desecrated the cult of their ancestor."[49] At its core, then, the term refers to the danger of pursuing and being pursued; the gloss emphasized in the original dictionary, of a village of apprehensive fugitives, is most suggestive about how this term was used by Palmarinxs at the end of the seventeenth century, the single time that it appears in the written record. This is not a name that a confident centralized political authority—one who aspired to the kind of power that the kings of Ndongo (Angola) held—would have used to describe itself. Rather, it evokes the kind of terror of being pursued, always watchful, stranded on a small island watching a rising tide—the experiences of the vast majority of unnamed Palmarinxs who lived under perpetual threat. While the use of "Angola" may well reflect the importance both of Ndongo political culture and of Angola as a region of provenance for many Palmarinxs, the qualification of "Angola" with "Janga" indexes both the experiences and strategies of Angola in a strange land. Angola Janga is perhaps the most eloquent testimony we can access about the affective reality of fugitive modernities.

Conclusions

In Kisama, the dialogical relationship between insiders invested in promoting a certain vision of Kisama in order to attract more fugitives and outsiders who were both awed by Kafuxi Ambari's power and baffled by the multiplicity of political power between the Kwanza and Longa Rivers helped forge and reinforce the Kisama meme. What the complicated dynamics of Kisama's history can help us understand, however, are the ways in which thousands of maroons in northeastern Brazil crafted their own fugitive modernities over more than a century. In spite of never-ending assaults, Palmarinxs created at least nine large mocambos, and many smaller, that were able to ally with each other during times of need even while maintaining a degree of autonomy. Though Ngana Zumba represented himself as king of all of Palmares, Zumbi's refusal to accept the terms of his accord with the Portuguese and his administration of a judicial ordeal to Ngana Zumba shows the depth of political dissent within Palmares. Just as in Kisama, where Kafuxi Ambari at times commanded broad enough power throughout the region that the Portuguese labeled him "king," so too was Ngana Zumba's authority within Palmares subject to the will of the waves of fugitives from whom he derived his power and legitimacy. Such an assertion of political will by fugitives, whether in Angola or in the Americas, represented fugitive ideology and political praxis that the Portuguese were wise to fear in post-Brazilian independence Angola, even as they misunderstood it.

By viewing names, titles, and terms not as evidence of origins but rather as traces of political ideology, too, we are able to turn the fragments of Palmares's archive into a vibrant, complex tableau of fugitive life and ideology in the seventeenth century world. Those who had no choice but to fight impossible fights for an even more improbable dream of freedom look heroic, from the vantage point of centuries of distance. However, their own existences were marked by terror and their very survival predicated on a persistent wary vigilance. Those living Angola Janga as their quotidian reality did not struggle to recreate a statist fantasy that none of them had experienced in the turbulent worlds of seventeenth-century Africa. The political imperatives of twentieth- and twenty-first-century respectability politics were not their own. Rather, in Palmares, they enshrined a memory of the perverted mechanisms of justice through which so many were enslaved and severed from their communities. They identified with the criminality through which they were shackled, and yet reclaimed the older, socially reciprocal forms of justice as their own in order to reject a leader who sought accommodation with the slave masters. When we ask questions of the evidence that transcend origins, Andalaquituche and Angola Janga transform from static cartographic vectors into multidimensional impressions of a world at once inconceivable and all too familiar.

CHAPTER 6

"The Ashes of Revolutionary Fires Burn Hot"

Brazilian and Angolan Nationalism and the "Colonial" and "Postcolonial" Life of the Kisama Meme, c. 1700–Present

Following the Brazilian declaration of independence in 1822, the Portuguese became obsessed with a putative conspiracy among elite slave traders in Benguela to throw off the Portuguese imperial yoke and join Brazil. Scholars have written much about the transnational, almost preternaturally corporate nature of the slave traders and their connection to early nationalist movements, and many of the most prominent slave merchants in the nineteenth century, like Ana Joaquina dos Santos e Silva, had property and residences in both Angola and Brazil.[1] However, it was not only or even primarily the affinities of urban elites with Brazilian independence that concerned Portuguese colonial officials in Angola. A mere two years after Brazilian independence, the Portuguese governor of Angola, Nicolau de Abreu Castelo Branco, reported, "Already Your Majesty knows that seditious communications have passed to Benguella, and Angola [Luanda], and that the Expeditionary Battalion of Portugal has been expelled by different Forts, and Camps, and that the residents of the most important areas of this City [Luanda] are in a state of opposition to the Government." After complaining at length about the deterioration of many of the physical features and social institutions of Portuguese colonialism throughout Angola, however, Castelo Branco did not focus on the potential danger of the circulation of "seditious communications" among the literate and literary elite in Luanda and Benguela. Instead, he wrote,

> with these examples from the Authorities you can well see what must become the dominant principals of the morality of a people comprised for the most part of factionalists, and slaves, and anarchy, and the art that is needed to contain them, when already the ashes of revolutionary fires burn hot. The subversive ideas of Demagogues have arrived from all parts of the world influencing those individuals whom they inspire. In this region, this has been a time of the most disobedience, and the most force by the vassal Sovas of Dembos to resist the violence of the [Portuguese local troops], and even the blacks under Government rule have less respect, and pay less attention to our Authorities because they can sense the weakening of Royal Power, like that of the Governors, because of the revolution [Brazilian independence]. *It is believed that principally the Quissama people of the left bank of the Quanza River are rising up, those who because of their proximity create the most inconvenience for this Government, because there with the greatest ease they collect the fugitive slaves, and because they persist in not permitting communication with Novo Redondo.*[2]

Surely, as governor of Angola and heir to decades and centuries of documentary and oral historical sources about the political character of surrounding communities, Castelo Branco was aware that those living south of the Kwanza River had harbored fugitives since the early seventeenth century, and that the fractured, intractable political practices of Kisama had long been a barrier to communication between Luanda and other parts of Angola. Indeed, Kisama's resistance to the Portuguese was largely responsible for the near autonomy of Benguela merchants from Portuguese colonial rule from Luanda from the early seventeenth century well into the twentieth century.[3] Because of the strong Benguela current, it was far easier and faster for ships to travel from Portugal or Brazil first to Benguela, and then to Luanda; the journey by sea against the current from Luanda to Benguela was difficult, and yet it was the only workable route for Portuguese traders, given the danger of attempting a land passage through geographical Kisama.[4] Beyond the standard ways in which colonial officials in Africa and the Americas forever attributed any kind of resistance to the malign influence of dangerous "outsiders," how can we understand Castelo Branco's perception that Kisama, along with Ndembos, were the most incendiary loci of revolutionary fire? Furthermore, if this connection between Brazilian and Angolan nationalism and the practical politics of rebelliousness in Kisama was clear to a contemporary observer, why then has Kisama remained largely absent from nationalist narratives on both sides of the Atlantic?

Because politics outside the state in general and Kisama's fractal, fractured fugitive modernities in particular were and are inherently unfathomable within a statist ontology, centralized states as diverse as the seventeenth-century Kingdoms of Kongo, Ndongo, and Matamba, the Portuguese imperial state in both Angola and Brazil from the sixteenth through the nineteenth centuries, imperial Brazil, republican Portugal, and finally independent Angola and Brazil, as well as scholars and activists of the African Diaspora, have been unable to fold Kisama's complicated history into a teleology of state. If the motto of modern nation-states is "Out of many, one people," then Kisama's fragmentary political culture represents a threat to this aspiration and illusion. Kisama is and always has been the nightmare of factionalism that haunts nationalists of every political persuasion.

In Angola, contradictory aspects of Kisama's history have been silenced and suppressed both from within and from without. For a society forged by thousands of fugitives and shaped in fundamentally unequal ways, historical memories that emphasize the splintered and contested aspects of history, like social inequality or internal conflict, after generations give way to more unifying mytho-politics and poetics. From the outside, Kisama's existence and enduring defiance of state power disrupts the fundamental logic through which statist thinkers organize the world. From the inside, and particularly in an era of NGO hegemony, there is much at stake in the politics of representation. "Tradition" and "ethnic culture" have always been an invented language of claim making; in an era of state abandonment, the stakes could not be higher. And for scholars and activists of the Diaspora, working as ever against the white supremacist logic that African-descended peoples in the Americas have no past, Kisama's fluidity and multiplicity look and feel unusable in a world where antecedents of empire carry much power. Thus, ironically, those both without and within the structures of state have had and continue to share overlapping interests in maintaining Kisama as a blank space, literally and figuratively. The Kisama meme straddles and troubles the intersection of these interests.

In this chapter, I trace the deployment of the Kisama meme across centuries and continents, investigating why a discourse that was already firmly established by the early seventeenth century persisted through so many changes locally in geographical Kisama, regionally in Angola, and globally as well. Kisama's first appearance in the written record, in a letter from King Mbemba a Nzinga of the Kongo to the pope in 1535, is a tacit evocation of the importance of the salt mines of Ndemba.[5] After Paulo Dias de Novais formally began colonizing Angola (the lands south of the Kingdom of Kongo) in 1575, the salt of Ndemba gained even greater importance, as the Portuguese recognized its value for purchasing bondspeople and provisions throughout the region. In the 1590s, after the Portuguese believed that they controlled Ndemba, they sought to defeat the most powerful soba in the region at the time, Kafuxi Ambari. Not only did Kafuxi Ambari rout the Portuguese and their allies, but he also briefly joined forces with the soba of Ndemba to reclaim control of the salt mines. This defeat of the Portuguese in 1594 formed the basis for Kisama's reputation for the next four centuries. Kafuxi Ambari's victory inspired other fugitives and their leaders in the region to likewise rebel, and also encouraged those fleeing from captivity and violence to seek refuge in geographic Kisama. By the second decade of the seventeenth century, fugitives from throughout the region were living in the lands of Kafuxi Ambari and other sobas in geographic Kisama, and instrumentally shaping political Kisama.

Thus, all three elements of the Kisama meme had cohered by the early seventeenth century. However, even before the transformative war of 1655–58, this meme belied the tensions within and between communities in Kisama and the changes in each over time. For example, soba Kamona Kasonga, father-in-law of and oracle to the king of Ndongo, became a vassal of Paulo Dias de Novais in 1582, largely as a strategy to secure Portuguese aid in his enduring conflicts with a neighboring soba in geographical Kisama, Muxima, who also soon became a Portuguese vassal and facilitated the construction of the only Portuguese fort south of the Kwanza in his lands in 1599. However, only nine years after swearing fealty, Kamona

Kasonga again attacked the Portuguese. Soba Langere, who in 1601 allied with the Imbangala Kalandula's band against Kafuxi Ambari, became a staunch ally of Kafuxi Ambari by 1612. By the early 1630s, there were multiple pretender soba Langere, and the succession struggles within his land illustrate the complex political changes wrought by fugitives in Kisama. During the war of 1655–58, even the redoubtable Kafuxi Ambari allied with the Imbangala, and, by the end of the seventeenth century, Kafuxi Ambari petitioned the Portuguese governor to become his vassal.[6] With all of the material and political changes in Angola and beyond over the centuries, it is well worth investigating why the Kisama meme remained static, stable, useful, and useable.

Kisama, Nationalisms, Representation, and the Long Nineteenth Century

In the eighteenth century and nineteenth centuries, Kafuxi Ambari—the central figure around whom all elements of the Kisama meme cohere— nearly vanishes from the archival record. His absence from the formulaic complaints about the "rebellious sobas of Kisama" in which he featured so regularly throughout the seventeenth century is particularly noticeable. For example, a 1735 letter to the Portuguese governor of Angola mentions the ongoing riverine raids on Portuguese traffic on the Kwanza River as well as the perpetual issue of fugitives; eleven years later, another letter from the interior to Luanda discusses the rebellions of sobas Kizua and Muxima. Neither of the authors of these reports mentions Kafuxi Ambari. In 1762, the Portuguese governor António de Vasconcellos complained of nine sobas of Kisama who notoriously harbored fugitives from slavery; Kafuxi Ambari was not among them.[7] When Kafuxi Ambari does appear in eighteenth-century Portuguese materials, he no longer carries the same gravitas as the leader whom António de Oliveira de Cadornega vividly described as the "powerful sova *Cafuchi Camabri*, whose lands stretch from the hinterlands to the sea, with abundant land and many people, who judge him to be the most powerful, as the king of this province, after the kings of Angola, to here, [and] whom all the sovas recognize and to whom they pay tribute as their king and lord."[8] Instead, he is but one of many sobas in the governor's list of mid-eighteenth-century rulers whose sovereignty had been abrogated by the Imbangala state of Kasanje.[9]

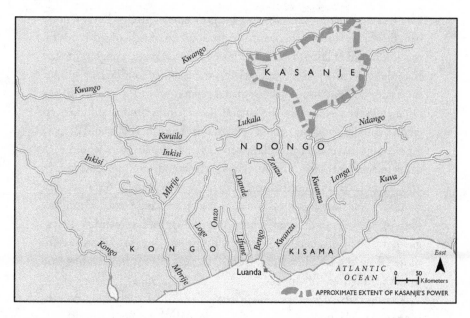

Map 6.1 — State Power in Eighteenth-Century Angola. Map by Heather Rosenfeld.

Kafuxi Ambari's inclusion in this eighteenth-century account of the role of the Kingdom of Kasanje in reconfiguring the political geography of the Angolan interior is the key to understanding why the Kisama meme developed and endured as it did. In the same critical moment in the 1620s and 1630s, when the changing political culture between the Kwanza and Longa Rivers shaped maroon communities in both Angola and the Americas, one element of another community of fugitive political practices in Angola—that of the Imbangala—was likewise shifting. During this period, some groups of Imbangala renounced their nomadic ways and founded the Kingdom of Kasanje in the Kwango River valley. Just like the Imbangala bands, this polity remained dependent on controlling the acquisition and sale of captives to the Portuguese for its survival; indeed, after the end of the trans-Atlantic slave trade in the mid-nineteenth century, Kasanje collapsed. However, Kasanje's consolidation in the 1620s and 1630s meant that for those seeking to avoid the predations of state, one major alternative had transformed itself into a threat.[10]

The eighteenth century, according to Joseph Miller, was the classical age of power and political stability in Kasanje.[11] The rulers of Kasanje, who had diplomatic relations with the Portuguese, presided over a number of *feiras*, or fairs, where merchants from the coast exchanged goods for the adults and children whom the state had procured through raiding.[12] Kasanje's power depended not only on their ability to militarily subdue their enemies, but also on the regional reputation of the efficacy of the ndua judgment. Normally, the king of Kasanje officiated at an ndua ceremony, though an nganga could also preside. The officiant would prepare a poisonous beverage from plant roots, which the litigants would each drink in equal measures. The innocent party would vomit the poison first, and the guilty party would be forced to drink increasingly poisonous substances.[13] Not only was ndua a means for reinforcing power within the state of Kasanje, but, according to one mid-eighteenth-century Portuguese traveler, ndua had become the most prominent judicial process for those "from the Libolo nation, from Quissama, from the Dembos, and from the kingdoms of Congo."[14]

Kasanje's virtual monopoly on martial and spiritual power in eighteenth-century Angola did indeed reconfigure the political geography of the region. In the mid-seventeenth century, according to Giovanni Antonio Cavazzi, *jinganga* (the plural of nganga) proficient in the use of navieza and cassumba medicines in Kisama and Libollo controlled important healing knowledge and practice sought by those from across the region.[15] During the same period, Kafuxi Ambari was renowned for commanding allegiance not only through his martial skill, but also through his ability to strike down enemies, African and Portuguese alike, with illness.[16] While it is unclear how Kafuxi Ambari's particular powers were connected to those of navieza and cassumba, if at all, these examples of regionally eminent healing medicines centered in seventeenth-century Kisama illustrate the discursive contours of political power during that period.

One hundred years later, however, these more diffuse spiritual powers relating to healing and illness had waned in importance throughout the region in comparison to the ndua oracle and its relationship to the centralized slaving state of Kasanje.[17] Kafuxi Ambari was not dead, but his power and the Kisama meme appear to have lain discursively, if not materially, dormant for much of the eighteenth century. While Kisama remained vitally important as a refuge for those fleeing the ever-mounting threats from state-sponsored violence, its power within geographies of reputation declined in the eighteenth century. Those living within geographical Kisama continued to resist incessant Portuguese incursions, to raid the ships and caravans of slave traders, and to welcome and defend fugitives throughout the eighteenth and nineteenth century. Kisama praxis did not change. However, the power of the ndua oracle and the Kasanje state altered the terrain through which politics, rumor, and reputation circulated in the region. Thus, while Kafuxi Ambari was still a soba in geographical Kisama, the ndua oracle figured far more prominently in the minds and storytelling impulses of the vulnerable, and, paradoxically, in the slave trading– and military control–centered preoccupations of the Portuguese.[18]

Thus, the only time that eighteenth-century observers render Kafuxi Ambari as a powerful, feared leader is when they are evoking the seventeenth-century Kafuxi Ambari, rather than their contemporary. Other than the Portuguese governor who listed Kafuxi Ambari among other sobas controlled by Kasanje, Portuguese Colonel Paulo Martins Pinheiro de Lacerda's "Notícias das regiões e povos de Quisama e do Mussulo, 1798" is the only eighteenth-century source I have been able to locate who even mentions Kafuxi Ambari. Lacerda describes "the great population of Cafuxe cambari, where there is a tradition, that in ancient times an Army of Portuguese were lost there in a Trap that this Barbarian set, in which all died including the leader [of the Portuguese]. All of these [sobas of Kisama] that I have named, and even this Cafuxe, were warriors, and were destroyed by an army under my command in 1784."[19]

Though Lacerda claims to have definitely subjugated Kafuxi Ambari and all of the other sobas of Kisama—a claim that appears as false as those of Manuel Cerveira Pereira and Luís Martins de Sousa Chicorro in the seventeenth century, given that Kisama continued to function as a haven for fugitives and as a political space independent of Portuguese or other state rule—he does not connect the late-eighteenth-century Kafuxi Ambari against whom he supposedly fought to any contemporary actions. Rather, he prides himself on his 1784 defeat of the Kafuxi Ambari of 1594 legend. Similarly, José Ignacio de Sousa Andrade's 1885 transcription of an account of the 1594 battle to substantiate his claim "that more than imprudent, [it is] mad to penetrate Quissama to make a war there, with the goal of conquering territory," begs the question: with accounts of fugitives in Kisama as late as the 1850s, were there no more clear and present threats from Kisama, either in the eighteenth or nineteenth centuries, that carried the same rhetorical power as Kafuxi Ambari's legendary 1594 victory?[20]

The recurrent Kafuxi Ambari, the static Kafuxi Ambari, the Kafuxi Ambari of 1594 who informs all talk and action after, compel us to reconsider, as I argued in the introduction, our understandings of personhood and of time. While liberal time and industrial time were far from hegemonic even for eighteenth- and nineteenth-century Portuguese slave traders and imperialists, here, the Portuguese archive unintentionally reflects Kisama notions of time and personhood that circulated throughout the region. This was *the* Kafuxi Ambari, the only Kafuxi Ambari, whether in 1594 or 1885, and he still represented the best hope of the vulnerable in the Jita Kwatakwata, the war of aggressive acquisition. Narration is politics. Kafuxi Ambari's subjectivity makes even the act of writing about him challenging, impossible, always partial. What tense is appropriate? It is always 1594. Kafuxi Ambari has always just crushed the Portuguese and driven them from Ndemba, erasing their presence, the memory of their presence.

The European and Euro-American missionaries, travelers, and explorer/geographers of the nineteenth and early twentieth centuries, whose accounts of the African interior global readers devoured, adopted the Kisama meme and the fixation on Kafuxi Ambari and 1594. In particular, a string of popular English-language writers, working in the standardized ethnographic genre of the time, popularized Kisama to a broader audience.[21] The first of these was the Scottish missionary David Livingstone, who traveled through Angola's interior in the mid-nineteenth century, when the Portuguese still complained of Kisama's role in harboring fugitives from Luanda. Livingstone himself never crossed the Kwanza River; instead, he based his comments about Kisama on his interactions with salt traders who came to Massangano. After mentioning that "the Quisamas (Kisamas) [are] an independent tribe, which the Portuguese have not been able to subdue," Livingstone remarks that "the few who came under my observation possessed much of the Bushman or Hottentot features."[22] Livingstone's juxtaposition of these two claims suggests that the fact of being "an independent tribe" and of resembling those whom the European colonizers labeled Bushmen or Hottentots were intimately connected. Colonizers and colonial anthropologists have long linked "Bushmen" and their supposed essential love of liberty to a more primitive stage of human social and political development.[23] Despite the fact that the people from geographical Kisama with whom Livingstone interacted were obviously engaged in commercial trade with the Portuguese and with Africans living north of the Kwanza River—just as those living in the Kalahari have long traded with Tswana speakers and other neighbors—their independence invited him to make this comparison with the quintessential example of primitiveness in the colonial lexicon.

Next, he describes Kafuxi Ambari's defeat of the Portuguese, conflating the events of 1594 with the strategies relating to water from the war of 1655–58.[24] It seems likely that Livingstone's amalgamation of two conflicts separated by six decades derives from his dependence on oral histories circulating among the Portuguese soldiers at Massangano, many of whom were Brazilian or children of local women. These soldiers would have been those most directly involved in the perennial efforts to compel the sobas of Kisama to submit to Portuguese authority and, most importantly, to cease harboring maroons. Nevertheless, even with direct experience of armed conflict with Kisama, these soldiers and colonial officials depicted the threat of Kisama through reference to the same formulaic account of Kafuxi Ambari that had been prominent since the late sixteenth century. If those who provided Livingstone with his information about Kisama were embedded within Kisama notions of subjectivity and time and strategies for narration, it is no wonder that the traveler, constricted as he was by his own white supremacist optics, perceived the people of Kisama as timeless primitives.

Later in the nineteenth century, European travelers would employ the emerging "ethnographic present" approach to accounts of Kisama that were nevertheless still rooted in the sixteenth and seventeenth centuries, demonstrating the undeniable power of the Kisama meme and the intellectual repertoire of Kisama fugitive modernities. Price, who delivered a paper at a meeting of the Anthropological Institute of Great Britain and Ireland based on the notes and observations of Charles Hamilton, evokes both the salt and the ferocity components of the Kisama meme. Perhaps because his approach was ethnographic and not historical, he did not discuss the presence of fugitives from slavery in Kisama. However, he remarks that "the Quissamas are very proud towards other tribes, and the traveler never observed a Quissama deign to address an Ambonda [non–Kisama Kimbundu speaker]. The latter would say to him, Why don't you speak to me? The Quissama man would reply: I cannot, you have masters, and slaves are beneath us. They even refuse to trade with them."[25]

While this appears to be an instance of imagined dialogue, Hamilton/ Price nevertheless drew from a pervasive discourse employed by those both within and without Kisama to distinguish themselves from their neighbors. Given the historical and demographic realities of life between the Kwanza and Longa Rivers, Hamilton/Price's imagined speaker was himself likely only a generation or two removed from slavery. However, this discourse is reminiscent of the ways in which maroon groups throughout the Americas often explicitly and deliberately distinguish themselves from their nonmaroon African-descended neighbors by commenting on their own status as self-liberated.[26] By becoming Kisama, even through the conditions of social inequality that existed at least in the early seventeenth century, fugitives could distance themselves from the status of slave.

The essential structure of accounts of Kisama thus remained grounded in the three-part meme established by the early seventeenth century, even in the face of massive political, social, and cultural movements within Kisama as well as in the region and globally. If these European travelers remained oblivious to locally driven changes, they were certainly aware of broader global shifts, such as the more rigorous British suppression of the trans-Atlantic slave trade or the introduction of steamships to the Kwanza River in the middle of the century and its impact on trade in the interior.[27] They did not mention these changes because the genre conventions of travel writing and ethnography mandated a static representation, and because the preexisting meme prevailed both in the previous accounts to which they had access, such as Battell, Cavazzi, and Cadornega, and within local oral traditions, among both Africans and Portuguese. However, even those Portuguese military figures who directly fought against leaders from Kisama in the eighteenth and nineteenth centuries, like Lacerda and Andrade—even after the Berlin Conference—continued to articulate the essential danger of Kisama by reference to the sixteenth and seventeenth centuries.

As I have argued, the Kisama meme and its focus on the sixteenth and early seventeenth centuries endured through eighteenth- and nineteenth-century Angola because of the relative degree to which its power waned in relation to the Kingdom of Kasanje. However, with the end of the trans-Atlantic slave trade in the mid-nineteenth century, Kasanje's power began to decline, and Kisama began to rise to greater prominence within the region. While the centralized Kasanje had been in a better position to benefit from an economy centered on the slave trade, the fragmented polities of Kisama were more suited to participate in the nineteenth-century extractive trade in ivory, wax, and rubber. Thus, around the beginning of the twentieth century, a Kafuxi Ambari not completely bound to the seventeenth century once again emerges from the Portuguese archival record, and, for nearly the first time since the seventeenth century, Portuguese military officers were apparently able to identify the immediate dimensions of their conflict with Kafuxi Ambari. The forward march of capital did not destroy the long-standing power of the Kisama meme, but Euro-capitalist interests did introduce into the archive perspectives on early twentieth-century Kisama unbound from the Kisama meme.

In 1911, two years into an ineffective campaign to "pacify" Kisama, Portuguese Lieutenant Alberto da Silva Pais wrote of the continued mortality that he faced in his attempts to subjugate Kafuxi Ambari. Frustrated by the ways in which Kafuxi Ambari's ongoing success against the Portuguese inspired his neighbors to revolt, Pais recommended an "intuitive and radical solution, leaving open the path to passive defense, [as the land is] unimportant and absolutely sterile from the point of view of colonization. What will follow will flow naturally from our [Portuguese] attitude. Faithful villages will return to us definitively."[28] Here, Pais broke from the Kisama meme by describing the nature of his conflict with Kafuxi Ambari *in 1911*. However, even Pais's logic for abandoning the attempts to defeat Kafuxi Ambari was at least partially shaped by historical memory of the seventeenth century and the enduring ways that Kisama defied all attempts at conquest.

A Fragmented Past, a Monolithic Future:
The MPLA and Kisama

Mid-twentieth-century Angolan nationalists affiliated with the MPLA (Movimento Popular de Libertação de Angola, or the Popular Movement for the Liberation of Angola, which was one of the primary parties that fought to liberate Angola from Portugal and has been the ruling party of the nation since independence in 1975) conjured the Kisama meme to support their contention that fragmentary politics and ominous "factionalism" had been and continued to represent the greatest threat to victory against the Portuguese and a barrier to achieving independence. Writing in the bloody milieu of the independence struggle, the MPLA's ethnological and historical working group, Grupo de Trabalho História e Etnologia, published the official *História de Angola* in Algeria in 1965. The authors intended that the *História de Angola* function as a critical element of nationalist instruction and consciousness raising, arguing, "It is necessary that a revolutionary knows the history of his country. Many revolutionaries of our time study the great battles of ancient times in order to learn methods of fighting (tactics) that will be very useful in the revolutionary wars of our time."[29] Given this imperative, one would expect that the authors would emphasize the martial strategies that allowed for Kafuxi Ambari to defeat the Portuguese and their allies in 1594. For a group engaged in multifront guerilla struggles against a better-armed adversary, what could be more inspiring or relevant? However, rather than appropriating the legacy of Kafuxi Ambari and the Kisama meme as heroic inspiration, the authors of *História de Angola* chose instead to use the Kisama meme as a cautionary tale regarding factionalism.

The authors divide history into three main epochs, following a chronotypology familiar to any student of mid-twentieth century leftist movements—prehistory, protohistory, and history—and within the history epoch, they further distinguish between the precolonial and colonial ages, along with the post-1940 "contemporary" age of anticolonial struggle. Within the precolonial phase, the authors describe Kisama as

FREE STATES OF KISSAMA / South of the Kwanza River was the region of Kissama. In this region there were numerous small sobados or Independent States. They didn't pay tribute to anyone and passed all of their time fighting against Congo, Ndongo and the Portuguese to defend their liberty. In Kissama they mine bars of salt. These bars were a kind of money with which they traded in the Highlands of Bié. Because of the Salt, Kissama was a very important region that all wanted to dominate. These Free States of Kissama never knew how to fight all together or to form a Single State. Because of this they were often defeated, principally by the Portuguese. Only their love of Liberty compelled them to revolt constantly against their oppressors. Some of the Free States of Kissama were the following: MUXIMA, KITANGOMBE, KIZUA, NGOLA KIKAITO, KAFUXE.[30]

While the authors return to Kisama a few times later in the text, such as mentioning the alliance of some of the sobas of Kisama with Njinga, this is their only substantive discussion of Kisama. Kafuxi Ambari is relegated to final place in an unelaborated list of sobas, and the dynamic history of Kisama is reduced to an admonition about political factionalism. In this rendering, Kisama resistance is essential(ist), instinctive, not political. This MPLA passage is jarringly reminiscent of Castelo Branco's assessment of the political dangers emanating from Kisama in the 1820s with which I opened this chapter. However, while Castelo Branco found Kisama dangerously subversive, the MPLA characterized them as tragically, but inevitably, doomed to failure, a relic of a preconscious approach. Through this narrative, again, the people of Kisama are endowed with an innate—and unthinking—love of freedom and with a shocking lack of political awareness. Their very absence of unified statehood made these "Free States of Kissama" unviable candidates for Angolan nationalist mythmaking. Kisama, so far from any models of political modernity employed by African kingdoms, European colonists, or African nationalists, can be laudable only in qualified ways and only in a distant, undemanding, and inherently moribund past. The Kisama in this text has no possible future, and any who likewise embrace fragmentation are equally doomed to the refuse heaps of history.

In many ways, these discourses mimic the twentieth-century appropriations of maroon history by nonmaroon nationalists and artists throughout the Americas, and, in particular, in Jamaica. After fighting against first the Spanish and then the British for nearly a century, the two major groups of Maroons on the island signed a treaty with the British in 1739.[31] In exchange for their own freedom, they agreed to serve as bounty hunters for other maroons and to aid the British in quelling rebellions. While the terms of the treaty were always a point of contention within Maroon communities, and it is by no means clear that they consistently upheld the bargain, there is nevertheless a pervasive discourse within non–Maroon society in Jamaica that while the pre-1739 Maroons, and in particular the leaders Kojo and Nanny, who is an official Jamaican national hero, were heroic and admirable, the post-1739 Maroons are traitors.[32] As Ken Bilby notes, non–Maroon discourse about the Maroons tend to polarize between admiring pretreaty Maroon "'strength' and 'spirit' that allowed the heroic Maroons to resist enslavement and reclaim their freedom and humanity" and disdaining posttreaty "primitiveness and backwardness; isolationism . . . and, most importantly, an apparent inability to seize, and remain faithful to, the larger ideological significance of their struggle."[33]

The MPLA narrative functions in just this manner, further omitting even a specific discussion of Kafuxi Ambari's 1594 victory against the Portuguese and denying him a place in a pantheon of national heroes.

The authors of the 1965 *História de Angola* did not omit a specific engagement with Kafuxi Ambari because they were ignorant of his importance. To the contrary, this is nearly a textbook example of Michel-Rolph Trouillot's notion of silencing. Indeed, MPLA militants and authors were aware of the enduring power of Kafuxi Ambari's memory in Kisama and beyond, and appear to have perceived it as antithetical to their vision of Angolan nationalism. Perhaps the most famous literary work of the revolutionary period, Pepetela's *As aventuras de Ngunga*, features a Kafuxi figure.[34] Pepetela wrote this novel in 1972 specifically to raise consciousness and promote literacy on the eastern front during the struggle for independence. He designed it for an audience to whom it would be read aloud in military or education camps, and its structure reflects this imperative. In Pepetela's narrative, Kafuxi is a traditional authority, ruling over a number of villages with the permission of the MPLA guerillas, whom he agreed to support with food. Kafuxi initially harbors Ngunga, the peripatetic orphan child hero of the story. However, Ngunga quickly realizes that Kafuxi only adopted him in order to put him to work in his fields to produce an agricultural surplus, which he then withholds from the desperate guerillas. The disillusioned Ngunga brings the hidden food to the hungry fighters and then leaves Kafuxi. Later, when he recounts his experiences to his teacher and questions why such a corrupt leader cannot be replaced, União (Union)—the only sympathetic adult in the narrative—explains, "Kafuxi is the elder there. . . . No one has the courage to remove him from the Presidency. Already in the time of the tugas [Portuguese] he was the chief of the people. But don't think it is only he [who is corrupt]."[35]

While Pepetela represents all adults save the teacher União as dishonest, arguing none too subtly that only the younger generation could build the nation, his choice to use the name Kafuxi to represent the illogic and corruption of "traditional" rule is no coincidence. Though by the time Pepetela wrote, the last soba named Kafuxi Ambari had been dead for fifty years, his reputation and his subjectivity were still vibrant and strong enough—and inspirational enough, even far outside of Kisama, near the Zambian border, in the Cokwe-speaking communities from which his name had come more than half a millennium earlier—that using him as a symbol of treacherous, doomed "traditional" authority could still resonate with the young people who were Pepetela's intended audience. The only adult who isn't a villain or traitor, the teacher União, or Union, is the antithesis of a "traditional" authority that evokes a disunified politics. While the historical Kafuxi Ambari long abjured participation in the flows of capital, as the enduring Portuguese complaints about his role in not only personally rejecting trade with slave merchants, but also in heading a constituency of others within geographical Kisama to do the same, in this skillful agitprop, Pepetela joins factionalism, tradition, and selfish, greedy capitalism as the enemy of the young, the future. These are of course the signal enmities in mid-twentieth-century leftist narrative, and there is no question that *As aventuras* was tremendously effective as a tool of mobilization and consciousness raising. It did, however, contribute to exiling Kisama history from inclusion within the revolutionary imagination of the Angolan state.

By contrast, the MPLA loves nothing better than casting itself as heir to a heroic Njinga. After centuries of representation by European writers and artists as a barbaric and deviant other, the MPLA has made Njinga into the "mother of the nation," featuring them prominently not only in the *História de Angola* and all historical school texts, including a recently commissioned graphic novel, but also in party-sponsored novels, plays, a film, and the famous statue at a busy roundabout in Luanda, Kinaxixi, where wedding parties and couples gather to take pictures. Linda Heywood details the ways in which Njinga's legacy is central to the MPLA's claims to legitimacy and also to Black politics in Brazil.[36] Njinga's statist machinations will always be a favored fairy tale of the states for whom Kafuxi Ambari will forever represent a threat.

But what of the relationship of those in present-day geographical Kisama to the historical legacy of Kafuxi Ambari? If nationalists have found Kisama useful as a cautionary tale or archetypical villain, how have actors within Kisama itself drawn from the same set of circulating discourses, and from the Kisama meme, to make claims in a nominally "postconflict" (2002) society in which life, by every measure, continues to be more and more difficult? What is the value of the Kisama meme in a time without food, water, access to education, or any kind of political voice in the closed nation? Intriguingly, in the last decade, the Kisama meme in general and Kafuxi Ambari in particular have enjoyed a resurgence of popularity among a Protestant- and MPLA-affiliated, missionary-educated segment of the population in the southeastern corner of geographical

Kisama, Luandos. According to Dionísio Gonçalves, a former resident of Luandos who is now the adjunct administrator of the municipality of Kisama and who belongs to this demographic, Protestant missions in the region after World War II gave children access to literacy and other skills unavailable to those in other parts of Kisama. Thus, many of the people of Kisama who have had professional success and access to the MPLA since independence have come from Luandos.[37] Even today, the primary school in Muxima offers only the first four years of schooling. Controversially, this school is named after Kafuxi Ambari, in spite of being located on the lands of soba Muxima, who had had a long, enduring conflict with Kafuxi Ambari. In Luandos, however, the school offers nine grades.

In 2004, a group of well-connected people from Luandos, many of whom live and work in Luanda, founded CNAL (Clube dos Nativos e Amigos de Luandos, or the Club for Natives and Friends of Luandos). It would be misleading to label this a nongovernmental organization, since the founders and many of the members are deeply involved with the MPLA. One of CNAL's goals is to promote the "restoration of the traditional popular festivals" of Luandos, which, according to the group, occur on the weekend before the 13th of September each year—conveniently close to the annual pilgrimage to the church of Our Lady of Muxima. According to Serafim Quintino, one of the founders of CNAL, in 2004, as they were working to popularize the festival, the group "discovered the tomb of the King of Kissama . . . the same Cafuxi to whom Cavazzi refers as the father of 36 children and the priest of a satanic religion."[38]

Largely due to the material, social, and political capital of CNAL members, this group has been successful in promoting this festival. People from all over Kisama come to dance, socialize, and compete in soccer tournaments, and CNAL also deliberately popularizes it as an important moment for *muxiluandos* (those who were born in Luandos) to leave their lucrative, if stressful, lives in Luanda and reconnect with their homeland. Not coincidentally, CNAL also invites European and American missionaries to attend the festival. Promoting these connections has given CNAL the resources to construct some improved concrete homes (rather than the standard wattle and daub materials) and to repair roads in the area.[39]

As has been the case throughout much of Africa, these missionary/ charitable connections have encouraged local people to narrate their own past in particular ways, emphasizing powerful rulers of centralized kingdoms. Though Kafuxi Ambari, as a "priest of a satanic religion," would hardly seem to be the appropriate figure for crafting such a narrative, CNAL's appeal to Cavazzi's documentation represents a curious path of historical memory and consciousness. First, despite the fact that there was a Kafuxi Ambari in Luandos until he died in 1916—within the lifetime of grandparents of people still living in the region—it is the early seventeenth-century Kafuxi Ambari that CNAL evokes.[40] Second, CNAL does not represent this seventeenth-century Kafuxi Ambari as a figure who had long endured in oral tradition, but rather as someone who was famous, familiar, or even known through his appearance in the chronicles of a contemporary Italian priest. Third, the sudden appearance of a seventeenth-century grave in a well-trodden area of Luandos at the propitious moment that CNAL members were trying to promote a renaissance of a likely invented tradition places this "discovery" firmly within the discursive framework of Christian miracles.

By suggesting that Kafuxi Ambari's tomb is of recent vintage and that the "traditional festivals" are a strategic invention, I do not intend to imply that they are unimportant or inauthentic. Rather, I argue that the resonance between the Kisama meme and the epistemologies of state has promoted its endurance through every step of political and social change in Angola. Kisama was, after all, largely formed *through* the Kisama meme, in the sense that the reputation of Kafuxi Ambari and other sobas in the early seventeenth century encouraged fugitives to expect sanctuary in the lands between the Kwanza and Longa Rivers. However, the Kisama meme was always the public face of Kisama, and belied its far more complex, and contested, private faces. These same tensions are evident in the ways in which Kisama has been evoked and silenced in Brazil.

Racial State Imperatives in Brazil and Post-1988 Blackness

The effusive twentieth-century regionalist and anthropological/sociological echo chamber engagement with Palmares that I critiqued so extensively in the previous chapter is part of a critical moment in the histories of Latin American and Caribbean nationalism more broadly. Throughout the region, elites mobilized an ostensible, ambiguously cultural/biological "creoleness," i.e., *mestizaje/mestiçagem*, to articulate a political distinction from the colonial metropole and a right to self-determination.[41] This is an early and iconic iteration of what Greg Tate adeptly identified as white appropriation of "everything but the burden" from Blackness, a way of commandeering symbolic capital without taking on political struggle.[42] In the case of Brazil, most (in)famously, this movement reached its apogee with the publication of sociologist Gilberto Freyre's *Casa-grande e senzala* in 1933.[43] Freyre sought to distance Brazil from an incapacitating belief that modernity was purely and solely European. In Freyre's initial articulation, Brazil lacked the virulent racism of North America because of the predilection of Portuguese men for miscegenation with Amerindian and African women; indeed, Freyre went further, arguing that Portuguese men provided a willing sadism to the inherently masochistic tendencies of indigenous and African women. In Freyre's nostalgic, romanticized, eroticized conception of the Brazilian nation as modeled on the casa grande, there is little space for Black or indigenous men. Black and indigenous women, and particularly mulattas, serve as the objects of desire for Portuguese men; their purpose is to fulfill the sexual and physical needs of white men. Black and indigenous men recede into the background, serving only as unseen—and more importantly unvoiced—labor. Freyre's argument that miscegenation produced the Brazilian nation is definitively unidirectional; white women appear in Freyre's work frequently enough to evince jealousy over their husbands' attractions to Black and indigenous women, but not often enough to exhibit desire toward Black or indigenous men. In the world that Freyre constructs, white masculinity is constructed in no small part through the sexual conquest of Black and indigenous women, while Black masculinity is conspicuously absent. Mulatt*as* proliferate to serve the sexual needs of white men, and mulatt*os* seemingly don't exist at all.[44] It should go without saying at this point that Freyre's efforts to empower white Brazilian politics was very much at the expense of and on the backs of Black and indigenous Brazilians.

Within this same complicated political geography of race, gender, and sexual desire, practitioners of African-associated combat arts, like capoeira, and ritual practices, like Candomblé, became critical elements of Brazilian national culture. T. J. Desch Obi has written at length about the transformations of capoeira in the early twentieth century from a criminal-associated praxis of the Black working class to a respectability oriented, sanctioned, institutional *martial art* with its own nationalist mythology.[45] James Lorand Matory has likewise illuminated how, far from representing an essentialist, primordial, unbroken line of transmission, elite Black Bahians and merchants in Lagos worked together to forge a notion of tradition that served both their own interests and, ultimately, those of the Brazilian state.[46] For a small number of artists and entrepreneurs, there was money to be made from a particular performance of Blackness. For the Black majority without access to land or capital—the Brazilian majority—there was no money to be made at all. This was as true in 1917 as it is in 2018. Nevertheless, it has become something of an axiomatic truism for any scholar of Brazil that Freyre's lusotropicalist ideologies and the notion of Brazil as culturally Black/African (and here, the slippage is critical) while politically white/mestiço are hegemonic.

Palmares has always served as the focal point for Brazilian thought about the history, meaning, and nature of Blackness and African people in the nation, and even as thousands of Africans fought the Dutch and later the Portuguese for their freedom, interested chroniclers began producing a veritable cannon of writing about Palmares.[47] While from the late seventeenth century on, chroniclers and historians have included Palmares in their narratives of Brazilian history, until the early twentieth century, Palmares narratives largely served to emphasize the bravery of the Paulista bandeirante frontier fighters. In essence, then, this was a kind of regionalism that predated discourses normally considered "nationalist." Tales of bandeirante/glory, however, have an enduring presence in Brazil; as sociologist Jessita Maria Nogueira Moutinho notes, Paulista identity, based on an "ideology affirming the ethnic, economic, and political superiority of those from the State of São Paulo relative to the rest of Brazilians, surges in all periods of crisis and reformation of central power."[48]

The role of bandeirantes in defeating both the "external" enemy of the seventeenth century (the Dutch) as well as the tenuously "internal" enemy of both indigenous and Black communities in the forests has long been central to Brazilian nationalist narratives. Beginning in the early twentieth century, however, the new regionalist scholars who focused on the African past and its role in the contemporary cultures of the northeast began revising the role of Palmares in Brazil's historical narrative.[49] For these new regionalists, like Nina Rodrigues and Edison Carneiro, African cultural practices in the Brazilian northeast were critical aspects of Brazil's national character. These early and mid-twentieth-century scholars sought to create a vision of Palmares and the African past that linked the seventeenth-century struggles by the enslaved for liberty with the racial and political issues of their times. While Freyre, like other nationalists throughout Latin America, addressed prevailing Eurocentric notions of modernity by glorifying the putatively prevalent mestiçagem of Brazil, Carneiro and others focused on what was particularly, uniquely, and, in their interpretation, entirely, African within Brazil's past and present.

Scholars would again begin prolific production of studies on Palmares following the end of the military dictatorship in 1985 and the eventual ratification of the postdictatorship constitution in 1988.[50] During the constitutional negotiation process, groups advocating for the rights of thousands of landless, dispossessed peasants and wealthy land owner/corporate advocates compromised on a clause guaranteeing collective land titles to "remnants of quilombo communities."[51] Within the context of the widespread poverty and land alienation affecting rural Brazil, the impetus to self-define as a "remnant" community is incredibly strong. In 1994, the Brazilian Anthropological Association (ABA) offered a definition of "quilombo" that officially broadened it to its more widely acknowledged meaning to include any black communities that had developed practices for maintaining their own identity, which the ABA characterized as resistance. These communities were to have a sense of ethnic identity, defined as a self-ascriptive process. This placed communities in the position of performing a particular kind of Blackness for material benefit and political gain.[52]

For example, during my 2010 fieldwork in Bacabal, a maroon community on the fluvial island of Marajó in the Amazon River in the northern province of Pará, I asked residents about a form of local martial arts (*luta marajoana*) that I had seen mentioned in a pamphlet in the archives in Belém, the provincial capital, as a local form of capoeira.[53] They told me that this was not an art practiced in Bacabal but rather by cowboys (*vaqueiros*) on neighboring cattle ranches; unlike capoeira, which is a striking-and-dodging style of combat, the luta marajoana is a form of wrestling. Then, they related that some "quilombo people"—by which they meant activists with the quilombo group in Belém—had visited the local school the previous year to teach the children capoeira, so that they could perform it for a festival celebrating their "local cultural traditions." When I mentioned that I had been practicing capoeira for a few years, some of the schoolchildren hastily organized a *roda* (the circle within which capoeira is performed) to test my skills. My initial astonishment at urban activists coming to this remote community—where according to the type of prevailing national discourse that Bilby explains above, supposedly pure African traditions had ostensibly been preserved in a pristine form since the time of slavery—to instruct the children on how to appropriately perform their Black/quilombolo identities was reinforced by the song the children sang for our impromptu *roda*. Repeating a song they had been taught by the visiting activists, the children sang, "Tem dendê, tem dendê / É Bacabal que tem dendê!" ([It] has dendê, [it] has dendê / It's Bacabal that has dendê). In Brazil, people associate *dendê*, or red palm oil, with Candomblé and affiliated culinary practices in the northeast, and the term works as a kind of synecdoche for the type of cultural Africanity mapped onto the northeast and associated with Yoruba-ness.[54] Indeed, in the original song, it is Bahia, the region of the northeast, that functions as the locus classicus of Blackness in Brazil, that has the dendê, not Bacabal. Incidentally, no one produces or cooks with red palm oil in Bacabal itself. These imported "traditions," however, are vital to demonstrating Bacabal's legitimacy as a quilombo on an island where cattle ranchers continue to encroach upon more and more land.[55] This song, then, serves as a kind of semantic map for the reimagining and policing of cultural Blackness in post-1988 Brazil.

How, specifically, does this relate to the uses and abuses of the Kisama meme? Under both the Vargas regime and the military dictatorship, Kisama remained marginal to the normative discourses about the African Diaspora in Brazil. In the previous chapters, I've detailed the ways in which the trans-Atlantically circulating Kisama meme shaped Kisama's interpolation into the scholarship on Palmares, but finding these references was indeed like finding needles in a haystack, and there is no evidence to suggest that conversations about Kisama entered into more mainstream discourse. If Palmares and a reified vision of the northeast are the simulacra of Blackness in Brazil, what does it mean that Kisama is absent from this conversation? Even quilombo claimants in Quissamã, the community in northern Rio de Janeiro whose foundational story opens this book, engage the history of those who fled the intensive slavery and mechanized sugar production in the region in the nineteenth century without making any direct or particular claims to a link with the politics and culture of Kisama.

As politically unwieldy as Kisama is to an Angolan nationalism forever preoccupied with the dangers of factionalism, Kisama is even more problematic to a Brazilian national project. For white elites, Africa is the source of apolitical culture, not politics. Within this paradigm, Kisama has little to offer. There are no signature, brightly costumed masquerades, no royalist ritual practices, no distinct language, no intelligible, commodifiable symbols of authority or identity. For Black activists, Kisama represents the same conundrum. While Kafuxi Ambari could well serve as a model of rebelliousness, of revolutionary politics, of a refusal to engage with exploitive market economies—a model that has clear resonance for many Black communities in present-day Brazil—the very statelessness of his political orientation represents an insurmountable challenge to activist discourses that remain centered on making claims on the state. Kafuxi Ambari and Kisama remain antithetical, unthinkable, within state hegemonies. Fugitive modernities do not serve states.

Fugitive Modernities in
the Neoliberal Afterlife of
the Nation-State

I am writing the final words of this book in a superficially very different—and fundamentally all-too-familiar—world from the one in which I wrote the first draft of this project as a graduate seminar paper some ten years ago. The ruling party in Angola is the same, in spite of a new president. As Dog Murras's decade-old popular song reminds us, it's a beautiful Angola for everyone except Angolans.[1] Oil and diamond money continue to bloat the pockets of the members of the inside circle of the regime and of foreigners, leaving most of the country, including those who fought for the MPLA in the endless war, with nothing. *Nothing* in Angola is literal, and lethal. Isabel do Santos, the daughter of José Eduardo dos Santos ("Zedu"), president from 1979–2017, is one of the richest women in the world; most Angolans live off of less than two dollars a day. Zedu's nearly forty years of rule were almost as long as the life expectancy for a child born in Angola today.

While Zedu leaving office is tremendously important, it is also not the point. Those who use Jita Kwatakwata as a historical reference know well the material differences in life from the sixteenth century to the twentieth, but these changes did not alter the basic topographies of power and violence, and it is this landscape that such a capacious category of time and experience encapsulates. So, too, in today's Angola.

The new president, João Lourenço, finally sacked Zedu's children from the head of the Angolan sovereign wealth fund and national petroleum company. What will this mean for the people of Angola? It takes only a cursory perusal of the Panama Papers or even mainstream news to understand a reality that continues to evade well-fed liberals worldwide.[2] This is not corruption. This is not aberration. This is how state power entangled with capital works, has always worked. Jita Kwatakwata—the war of aggressive acquisition—captures the roots and branches of Eurocentric, statist modernity perfectly, and the revolutionary conflagration that promised to burn this pernicious structure to the ground have long since been doused. Who in today's Angola can call another *camarada* (comrade) without choking on the toxic ash of the incinerated promise of that kind of horizontal community in the smoking shadow of the towering hierarchy of state power? *A luta continua* (the struggle continues), to be sure.

This is a story about Angola, but it is far from a particularly Angolan story, then or now.

The workers' party that governed Brazil when I started writing has been deposed by a coup, and Brazil is once again ruled by those non-elected individuals who express overt enmity to the poor. The new president, Michel Temer, has promised to cut the popular subsidies for poor and working-class Brazilians, and funding for education and health care. He is moving to privatize all that can be privatized, to sell all that can be sold, to usurp all that can be taken from those from whom taking has been the very foundation of the state. Unsurprisingly, this promises to devastate Black communities who have faced militarized aggression even during the populist regime. The government's planned solution to Brazilian economic woes appears to be, to move again on the backs of the nation's most vulnerable.

While the police throughout Brazil, and in Rio de Janeiro in particular, have executed Black residents of the favelas with impunity for decades, the recent military takeover of state police came merely weeks before the police murdered Marielle Franco. Marielle Franco, favela resident, Black, queer, outspoken; a member of the city council, but aware, always, that the politics that matter are in the everyday work of favela residents. She condemned state murder of her community members daily, and for this, the Brazilian state murdered her. Shortly thereafter, the Rio police also filled the body of Carlos Alexandre Pereira Maria, another Black activist who fought against the military takeover of poor, Black communities, and a witness set to testify about Franco's murder, with bullets. Our dead tell no tales. What sense can we, the living, make?

In the erstwhile New Kingdom of Grenada, the ground has shifted, too. When I began this project, Venezuela was deep in the Bolivarian Revolution, transforming oil profits into substantial gains in terms of literacy, health care, housing, employment, education, and food security for the nation's poor, including the substantial number of Black Venezuelans. Hugo Chávez is dead now. He was no stranger to coup attempts, but his successor, Nicolás Maduro, has inherited a far more troubled economy, and the largesse of earlier years has faded. The price, as ever, is being paid by those least able to afford it.

Fidel Castro is dead, and the vultures of transnational capital circle ever closer over Havana's skies. It's not the afterlife of slavery so much as its incessant rebirth.

Barbuda no longer has a living human population, and the national government from Antigua is already planning to reallocate the land of the children of slaves and fugitives to the corporations of the children of slave masters.

Puerto Rico has now become a blank spot on the map, no light visible from the night sky as three and a half million colonial subjects die below, quickly, slowly, surely.

I began writing and researching this as the United States shifted to a political campaign focused on the rhetoric of hope and change, even as leftists remained wary. A decade later, and the wariness, at once so apparently cynical, now seems prescient. In the United States, the military spending of the Bush years transferred to police departments, who have been using their tactical equipment to escalate attacks against Black communities and individuals. The year 2008 damaged many, but none more than Blacks and Latinxs, who have fewer resources with which to recover. The state is as strong as ever, deposing governments and assassinating individuals with robots across the world, maintaining secret prisons, and glorifying in a symbolic politics of representation. More than ever, many in my community acknowledge that we were never meant to be citizens here. Our exclusion isn't a problem. It is part of the design. We, the multiply dispossessed, chant "Viva Puerto Rico Libre!," but what does that mean? We chant "Black Lives Matter!," but to whom? Not to the state, nor for the agents of state power and capital, who not only kill us regularly and with impunity, but then profit, continue to profit, stay profiting for charging us with culpability in our own murders.

What *can* independence, freedom, Black lives mattering, mean in an age of neoliberal capital?

The answers to these questions are not particular to my block, or my neighborhood, or even this country. These are, ultimately, the same questions with which those abandoned and betrayed by national politics—by design, from the beginning—across the globe are asking. By centering states, state histories, state paradigms, state notions of personhood and time, we recur again and again to the same bloody horizon.

Fugitive modernities and the history of Kisama do not tell a bloodless story, nor promise a gilded future. Kisama's survival was, after all, always predicated on the exercise of violence. This is far from unique, and is a common feature of every revolution. However, Kisama refused to adopt an idiom of violence, to reify warriors as the models of political and social belonging. For all who have wondered what happens after the revolution, why Castro in 1959 was not Castro in 1980, Neto in 1975 was not Neto in 1977, Mugabe in 1980 was not Mugabe in 2008, and so on, the answer may lie in a closer study of Kisama, and of other nonstate societies like Kisama. We know how states try and usually fail to handle or ignore social inequality. We would be well served to know how nonstate societies wrestle with these essential questions of power.

I have traced the dynamic relationship between the counterstate politics of Kisama, the attraction and incorporation of fugitives into decentralized societies, and the uneven development of fugitive modernities within Kisama, in dialogue not only with the slaving and imperial interests of Kongo, Ndongo, Matamba, Kasanje, the Portuguese, and the Dutch, but also with other fugitive modernities, such as those of Kasanze and the Imbangala. From Kafuxi Ambari's decisive defeat of the Portuguese in 1594 onward, Kisama's enemies, African and European alike, understood Kisama as a dual threat. While Kisama's resistance materially harmed imperial and slaving interests, and its role as a haven for fugitives was detrimental to the slaving economy, as the Portuguese recognized, perhaps the most significant threat posed by Kisama was the psychological and discursive power of its ongoing victories. From the seventeenth-century Portuguese preoccupation with the fact that the resistance of Kisama "publicize[s] to the neighboring nations that the arms of Your Majesty do not conquer, because theirs [those of the people of Kisama] are the strongest," and that the inhabitants of Kisama "glorify in a certain independence," to the post-Brazilian independence assertion that Kisama was the most dangerous node of resistance in Angola at a time when the "ashes of revolutionary fires burn hot," Kisama represented the enduring possibility of life outside of the increasingly synonymous tyrannies of state and slave-trading powers.[3]

Like all of its neighbors to the north, south, and east, Kisama society was marked by divisions between newcomers and old-timers, the powerful and the dependent. What distinguished Kisama from these likewise unequal neighboring societies, however, was the centrality of fugitives in shaping political will. While in contemporary Ndongo, leaders were consolidating their centralized rule by using royal bondsmen and women as agents of their interests, in Kisama, a class of dependent newcomers themselves exercised a decisive role in determining the contours of political legitimacy, rejecting the authority of leaders whose interests seemed inimical to the well-being of fugitives.[4] Fugitives initially fled to Kisama because Kafuxi Ambari's powerful martial and spiritual skills attracted those who were weak and vulnerable, and sought defense from the predatory raids and actions of centralized states and Imbangala alike. They remained in geographical Kisama and continued to flee there for centuries because the people of Kisama defended the interests of their fugitive dependents, to such an extent that António de Oliveira de Cadornega cited defense of recent fugitives as the "motive of these powerful Sobas of Quissama to make this revolution."[5]

Not only did this revolutionary reputation spread far beyond the Kwanza and Longa Rivers in Angola, attracting an endless stream of maroons well into the nineteenth century, but it also traveled across the Atlantic in the experiences and imaginations of the millions of West Central Africans who arrived in the Americas in chains. In particular, the ideology developing within Kisama during the 1620s and 1630s, when fugitives began to assert their political will in shaping the exercise of political authority, had ramifications far beyond Angola. Indeed, in the testimonies of maroons from the palenque Limón outside of Cartagena, New Kingdom of Grenada, it is possible to discern continuities in discourses about the relationship between violence, community, and political legitimacy. While the Limoneses who testified identified some of their comrades as Kisama, we do not have the same name specificity in our evidence from the Brazilian quilombo Palmares. Nevertheless, the profound disagreement between

Ngana Zumba and Zumbi over the legitimacy of an authority marked by accommodation with the Portuguese reflects similar disputes in Kisama, particularly during the war of 1655–58. Despite the ways in which Kisama political practice was characterized by dissent and dispute on either side of the Atlantic, however, the one-dimensional Kisama meme has dominated both scholarly and popular representations of Kisama. From Portuguese army officers in the eighteenth, nineteenth, and twentieth centuries to Angolan nationalist writers of the revolution, discourses about Kisama remained firmly rooted in the salt, war, and the fugitive dynamics of the early seventeenth century. By disaggregating Kisama histories from the Kisama meme, however, we draw closer to an understanding of the ways in which fugitive modernities develop, change, and spread across landscapes, oceans, cultures, and time.

Kisama's history has not remained at the margins of both popular and scholarly discourse because it is unimportant. Rather, Kisama's relegation to the margins reflects the very challenge that its existence—as a martially rebellious region, as a politically fragmented and autonomous society, and as a set of political ideologies and tools that traversed both the rugged terrain of Angola's interior and the treacherous waves of the Atlantic Ocean—represents to states and empires. Gilroy usefully reminds us that any notion of modernity that fails to account for the transnational practices of Black intellectuals navigating the varied terrains of disenfranchisement and violence within and between many different nation states is inadequate. But imagining that Black intellectuals are only or even primarily those who write is just as substantive a conceptual failure. I have argued that any scheme of modernity and political development that fails to account for the intellectual and political dynamism in the diffuse and diverse political entities that rejected institutionalized centralization not only misses more than half of the story, but also distorts the history of states themselves. Why else would the common mythology of state evoke the danger from the barbaric hordes at the border?

The notion of fugitive modernities disrupts the neat teleological arguments of states, and forces us to ask questions that transcend anachronism. By insisting on a view of fugitive modernities in the plural, we can examine important differences between, for example, Kisama politics and ideologies and practices among Imbangala groups in early seventeenth-century Angola on a level deeper than "cultural difference." While the people who became Kisama and those who became Imbangala may have spoken mutually intelligible languages and shared broad cosmological notions, they held radically divergent conceptions of political legitimacy and the relationship of violence to just authority. Their languages may have been mutually intelligible, but their organizing social idioms were far less so. Unpredictably, however, the Imbangala transposed their radical rejection of widespread notions of social reciprocity and kinship onto an emerging state by the mid-seventeenth century. Kasanje thrived from capturing and selling its neighbors, while sobas within Kisama expanded their power by attracting and incorporating fugitives.

In the turbulent world of the seventeenth century, those who participated in crafting fugitive modernities—in Kisama, in Limón or Palmares, or in the thousands of maroon communities across Africa and the Americas, not to mention maritime maroons—responded to the increasingly brutal, dangerous conditions wrought by the cooperation, competition, and contestation between European, African, and indigenous American states by forging viable political alternatives. These fugitive societies at times incorporated technologies and practices of the state, but always in service of defending autonomy. Despite his frequent and shifting alliances within and beyond Kisama and his sporadic subjugation of his neighbors, after all, Kafuxi Ambari never formed a kingdom; indeed, while he was reputed to be in line of succession for leadership of Ndongo, Kafuxi Ambari remained committed to nonstate politics in a land dominated by the presence of maroons.

Employing the concept of fugitive modernities for our interrogation of the relationship between African intellectual and political practices and the meaning of such universalizing terms as modernity requires reimagining the kinds of questions we ask of history. In effect, it challenges us to suspend our assurance in the vectors of human society and instead broaden our notions of what was possible in the past; more importantly, perhaps, it compels us to imagine futures not woven by the inevitable threads of state. Instead of searching for narratives to explain the accretion of power, we can begin to listen to the fragmented ideologies that underwrote what we all too often dismiss as mere survival. Fugitive modernities forges a space for rigorous, translocal, transnational studies of "the aspirations that fueled flight and the yearning for freedom . . . these shared dreams that might open a common road to a future in which the longings and disappointed hopes of captives, slaves, and fugitives might be realized."[6] While states have shown themselves remarkably adept at appropriating the legacies of resistance, the political developments worldwide over the last few years show that hegemony is never absolute, and that even in the twenty-first century, those resisting unjust power do not necessarily aspire to reform or restaff the state.

These dreams of freedom. These prayers for liberty. These hopes, these imaginations, in the *musseques* of Luanda and the *favelas* of Rio, in my own hood, in every prison. They must be unmoored from the machinery of state and capital.

NOTES

Introduction

1   As is true for historical transcriptions of words in African languages by European interlocutors, orthographic representations vary wildly. Kisama can appear as Quissama, Quisama, Quiçama, Quissamã, Quisyma, and other forms. This is also the case for the name Kafuxi Ambari (Cafushe, Cafuchy, Cafuxe, Cafuxhe Cambare, Kafuxi kya Mbari), and *soba* (*sóva, sova*), and many others. Unless quoting an original source, in which case I use the orthography as it appears in the text, I write "Kisama," "Kafuxi Ambari," and "soba" in accordance not only with the most recent conventions of Kimbundu orthography but also to reflect the most current pronunciation within geographical Kisama and the Kimbundu-speaking world more broadly. This can obscure important grammatical relationships, however, and, where important, I explain these.

2   Miguel Ayres Maldonado and Jozé de Castilho Pinto Pinto, "Descripção que faz o Capitão Miguel Ayres Maldonado e o Capitão Jozé de Castilho Pinto e seus compaheiros dos trabalhos e fadigas das suas vidas, que tiveram nas conquistas da capitania do Rio de Janeiro e São Vicente, com a gentilidade e com os piratas n'esta costa," *Revista Trimensal do Instituo Histórico e Geographico Brazileiro* 56 (1893): 379.

3   "Relação da costa de Angola e Congo pelo ex-governador Fernão de Sousa," February 21, 1632, *Monumenta Missionaria Africana: África Occidental*, ed. Antonio Brásio, 10 vols. (Lisbon: Agência Geral do Ultramar Divisão de Publicações e Biblioteca, 1962), 8:121 (hereafter cited as *MMA*).

   Soba is a Kimbundu term meaning "local leader," and speakers usually imbue it with both governmental and ritual authority. The Portuguese appropriated the term and used it throughout Angola to mean "lord," or, later, "chief," even in regions where neither the concept of "chief" in general nor "soba" in particular initially had any meaning. In present-day geographical Kisama, people use the term *soba*, and the Portuguese sources use it to refer to authority figures in Kisama from the late sixteenth century on, but it is impossible to know if that was the term people within Kisama used during that period, or if not, when it was adopted. Because of its presence in archival sources, oral histories and memories, and political culture in present-day geographical Kisama, I use the term throughout this manuscript with the understanding that it is a fractured echo distorted through a colonial chamber. Moreover, while the Kimbundu plural of *soba* is *jisoba*, I have chosen to use *sobas* to cohere to present-day use in Kisama. Throughout this text, I eschew linguistic prescriptivism and the highly gendered and classed politics of propriety and authentic usage in favor of orthography that reflects living language. For a discussion of the comparative and historical linguistic history of the term soba, see Jan Vansina, *How Societies Are Born: Governance in West Central Africa before 1600* (Charlottesville: University of Virginia Press, 2004), 163–67.

4 See Michel-Rolph Trouillot, *Silencing the Past: Power and the Production of History* (Boston: Beacon Press, 1995).

5 *Illmatic* refers to Nas's debut album, and *Time is Illmatic* to the documentary about its making. My intellectual world has been very much shaped by both this album, released during my childhood, and the paradigms of time that it evokes. Illmatic is a moral episteme of time and being, one that contrasts with the teleological Whiggishness of Eurocentric historicity and instead conceives of the value of being in terms of relationships to community and creation. See Nas, *Illmatic* (New York: Columbia Records, 1994); *Time is Illmatic*, dir. One9, New York: Tribeca Film Institute, 2014.

Johannes Fabian and Matti Bunzl, *Time and the Other: How Anthropology Makes Its Object* (New York: Columbia University Press, 2002).

6 Clifton Crais and Pamela Scully, *Sara Baartman and the Hottentot Venus: A Ghost Story and a Biography* (reprint; Princeton University Press, 2010), 5. While they articulate Baartman's circulation in the late twentieth and early twenty-first century as "speaking from beyond the grave," Crais and Scully also tell a story of Baartman that suggests an enduring subjectivity.

7 For an instructive example from eighteenth-century Jamaica, see Jessica A. Krug, "Social Dismemberment, Social (Re)membering: Obeah Idioms, Kromanti Identities and the Trans-Atlantic Politics of Memory, c. 1675–Present," *Slavery & Abolition* 35, no. 4 (2014): 537–58.

8 For a discussion of the convergence of Atlantic history and microhistorical methods and approaches, see Lara Putnam, "To Study the Fragments/Whole: Microhistory and the Atlantic World," *Journal of Social History* 39, no. 3 (2006): 615–30; Roquinaldo Ferreira, *Atlantic Microhistory: Slaving, Transatlantic Networks, and Cultural Exchange in Angola (ca. 1700–ca. 1830)* (New York: Cambridge University Press, 2011), 5–7. For an elaboration of reputational geographies, see David Parker and Christian Karner, "Reputational Geographies and Urban Social Cohesion," *Ethnic and Racial Studies* 33, no. 8 (2010): 1451–70. The seminal work on the entanglement of oral and written sources is Alessandro Portelli, *The Death of*

Luigi Trastulli, and Other Stories: Form and Meaning in Oral History (Albany: State University of New York Press, 2001).

9 I refer to the territories between the Kwanza and Longa Rivers as "geographical Kisama," in contrast to the evolving, nonspatially-bound repertoire of political orientations and social practices that delineate Kisama political identities and reputations. Throughout this work, I will distinguish between the two overlapping but noncongruent senses of the term, specifying where I mean geographical Kisama, and leaving "Kisama" unmarked to connote the political/reputation sense.

10 Joseph Miller, "Imbangala Lineage Slavery," in *Slavery in Africa: Historical and Anthropological Perspectives*, ed. Suzanne Miers and Igor Kopytoff (Madison: University of Wisconsin Press, 1977), 208–9.

11 I use the past tense here because after centuries of Portuguese interference and decades of state dictates, the always already invented traditions of local rule now function as apparatuses of state interest.

12 There are but two exceptions: the response to Kafuxi Ambari's apparent petition for baptism, and the record of Kafuxi Ambari's death. "Cópia da carta ao Soba Cafuchi, que pede o baptismo," February 23, 1693, in Brásio, *MMA*, 14:279–81. For the death of Kafuxi Ambari in 1916, see "Carta de Frederico Augusto Esteves, Capitania Mor da Quissama, ao Chefe da Secretaria Militar do Distrito do Cuanza," August 1, 1916, 2/2/45/7, Muxima, Arquivo Histórico Militar, Lisbon, Portugal (hereafter cited as *AHM*).

13 Benedict Anderson, *Imagined Communities: Reflections on the Origin and Spread of Nationalism*, rev. ed. (London: Verso, 1998).

14 For an illuminating look at the entanglement of conjure, capital, and modernity, see Andrew Zimmerman, "Guinea Sam Nightingale and Magic Marx: Conjure and Communism in Civil War Missouri" (forthcoming).

15 For a discussion of political and moral chronotopes in hip hop, see Jessica Krug, "'Amadou Diallo, Reggae Music Knows Your Name': Popular Music, Historical Memory, and Black Identity in New York City in the Wake of Amadou Diallo's Murder," in *Remembering Africa: Memory, Public History, and Representations of the Past: Africa and Its Diasporas*, ed. Audra Diptee and David Vincent Trotman (Trenton, NJ: Africa World Press, 2012), 291–308.

16 Trouillot, *Silencing the Past*; Ann Laura Stoler, *Along the Archival Grain: Thinking through Colonial Ontologies* (Princeton, NJ: Princeton University Press, 2008); Luise White, "Hodgepodge Historiography: Documents, Itineraries, and the Absence of Archives," *History in Africa* 42, no. 309–18 (2015): 309–18; Luise White, *Speaking with Vampires: Rumor and History in Colonial Africa* (Berkeley: University of California Press, 2009); Nancy Rose Hunt, "An Acoustic Register, Tenacious Images, and Congolese Scenes of Rape and Repetition," *Cultural Anthropology* 23, no. 2 (2008): 220–53; Neil Kodesh, "History from the Healer's Shrine: Genre, Historical Imagination, and Early Ganda History," *Comparative Studies in Society and History* 49, no. 3 (2007): 527–52.

17 Saidiya Hartman, "Venus in Two Acts," *Small Axe* 12, no. 2 (2008): 14.

18 After having these conversations about the politics of sources and narrative for a number of years, Greg Childs brilliantly crystalized the disciplinary relationship between historians and slave catcher in Greg Childs, "Insanity, the Historian, and the Slave Catcher: 'Capturing' Black Voices," in *Black Perspectives*, African American Intellectual History Society, February 15, 2015, http://www.aaihs.org/insanity-the-historian-and-the-slave-catcher-capturing-black-voices/.

19 While in many maroon societies, historical narratives center on the struggles through which the ancestors freed themselves from slavery, there are competing narratives within many of these same communities, including the Angolars in São Tomé and the Maroons in Jamaica, of being descended from those who survived the wreckage of slave ships. This trope is a way of disavowing a connection to the experiences of enslavement.

20 This raises important questions about the political underpinnings of a proliferation of scholarship that fixates on a freedom that leaves a thick archival trace. See, for example, Rebecca J. Scott, *Freedom Papers: An Atlantic Odyssey in the Age of Emancipation*, ed. Jean M. Hébrard (Cambridge, MA: Harvard University Press, 2012).

21 For an important conversation about the politics of history as romance or tragedy, albeit from a limited and singular perspective on modernity, see David Scott, *Conscripts of Modernity: The Tragedy of Colonial Enlightenment* (Durham, NC: Duke University Press, 2005).

22 Marisa J. Fuentes, *Dispossessed Lives: Enslaved Women, Violence, and the Archive* (Philadelphia: University of Pennsylvania Press, 2016), 5.

23 Aisha K. Finch, *Rethinking Slave Rebellion in Cuba: La Escalera and the Insurgencies of 1841–1844* (Chapel Hill: University of North Carolina Press, 2015), 2–3.

24 David Eltis, *Atlas of the Transatlantic Slave Trade*, ed. David Richardson (New Haven, CT: Yale University Press, 2010), 90; Mariana Candido, *An African Slaving Port and the Atlantic World: Benguela and Its Hinterland* (New York: Cambridge University Press, 2013), 152.

25 Aurora Ferreira, *A Kisama em Angola do século XVI ao início do século XX: Autonomia, ocupação e resistência* (Luanda: Kilombelombe, 2012).

26 Even in the present day, it is nearly impossible to arrive at a reasonable estimate of the population of Angola as a whole, or of Kisama in particular. In 2014, the Angolan government undertook the first census since independence. The last census prior to this was undertaken by the Portuguese in 1970, five years prior to independence; many Angolans avoided being counted for fear of being detained by the colonial government. According to the Instituto Nacional de Estatística (National Statistical Institute), the preliminary census registers 25,086 inhabitants of geographical Kisama today. Instituto Nacional de Estatística, Censo 2014, http://censo.ine.gov.ao/xportal/xmain?xpid=censo2014&xpgid

=provincias&provincias-generic-detail_qry=BOUI=10505458&actualmenu =10505458, last accessed April 15, 2018. Ferreria cites different nineteenth- and twentieth-century estimates of Kisama's population. Among these are the colonial district official in Massangano's estimate of the population in the northern part of the region as 9,350 to 10,350 in 1847. In the same period, German explorer Laszlo Magyar estimated that approximately 25,000 people lived in Kisama. By the 1920s, Ernst Wilhelm Mattenklodt cited Portuguese sources who claimed that in the proceeding thirty years, only 10,000 of the original 30,000 to 40,000 inhabitants of Kisama survived a particularly virulent outbreak of sleeping sickness. In the mid twentieth century, an ecologist estimated that approximately 6,000 people lived in the region. A. Ferreira, *A Kisama em Angola*, 69–72.

27 See, for example, Joseph Miller, "The Significance of Drought, Disease and Famine in the Agriculturally Marginal Zones of West-Central Africa," *Journal of African History* 23 (1982): 17–61; and Jill Dias, "Famine and Disease in the History of Angola c. 1830–1930," *Journal of African History* 22 (1981): 349–78.

28 For example, in 1588, an anonymous Portuguese source reported an extremely severe drought in part of Kisama, which I will discuss at greater length in chapter 2. See "Estado religioso e politico de Angola," in Brásio, *MMA*, 3:375–76.

29 For a detailed critique of this process in an East African context, see Jan Bender Shetler, *Imagining Serengeti: A History of Landscape Memory in Tanzania from Earliest Times to the Present* (Athens: Ohio University Press, 2007).

30 Linda Heywood, "Slavery and Its Transformations in the Kingdom of Kongo: 1491–1800," *Journal of African History* 50 (2009): 1–22; Linda Heywood and John Thornton, *Central Africans, Atlantic Creoles, and the Making of the Foundation of the Americas, 1585–1660* (New York: Cambridge University Press, 2007), 1–22; Linda M. Heywood, *Njinga of Angola: Africa's Warrior Queen* (Cambridge, MA: Harvard University Press, 2017); John Thornton, "The Origins and Early History of the Kingdom of Kongo, c. 1350–1550," *International Journal of African Historical Studies* 34, no. 1 (2001): 89–120; Joseph Miller, *Kings and Kinsmen: Early Mbundu States in Angola* (Oxford: Clarendon Press, 1976); Joseph Miller, *Way of Death: Merchant Capitalism and the Angolan Slave Trade, 1730–1830* (Madison: University of Wisconsin Press, 1988); Roquinaldo Ferreira, *Cross-Cultural Exchange in the Atlantic World: Angola and Brazil during the Era of the Slave Trade* (New York: Cambridge University Press, 2012); Vanessa Oliveira, "The Gendered Dimension of Trade: Female Traders in Nineteenth-Century Luanda," *Portuguese Studies Review* 23, no. 2 (2015): 93–121. Important exceptions include Mariana Candido, "Jagas e sobas no 'Reino de Benguela': Vassalagem e criação de novas categorias políticas e sociais no contexto da expansão portuguesa na África durante os séculos XVI e XVII," in *África: Histórias Conectadas*, ed. Alexandre Vieira Ribeiro, Alexsander de Almeida Gebara, and Marina Berthet (Niterói: Programa de Pós-graduação em História da Universidade Federal Fluminense, 2015), 41–77; T. J. Desch Obi, *Fighting for Honor: The History of African Martial*

Art Traditions in the Atlantic World (Columbia: University of South Carolina Press, 2008); Roquinaldo Ferreira, "Slave Flights and Runaway Communities in Angola (17th–19th Centuries)," *Revista Anos 90* 21, no. 40 (2015): 65–90; and Beatrix Heintze, *Asilo ameaçado: Oportunidades e consequências da fuga de escravos em Angola no século XVII* (Luanda: Museu Nacional da Escravatura, 1995).

31 Beatrix Heintze, "Beiträge zur Geschichte und Kultur der Kisama (Angola)," *Paideuma* 16 (1970): 159–86; Beatrix Heintze, "Historical Notes on the Kisama of Angola," *Journal of African History* 13, no. 3 (1972): 407–18; A. Ferreira, *A Kisama em Angola*. Ferreira in particular relies on Miller for nearly all of her perspective on reading earlier archives, resulting in a narrative that essentially replicates all of the overdetermined structuralist conceptual limitations of Miller, *Kings and Kinsmen*.

32 Prefeitura de Quissamã, http://www.quissama.rj.gov.br/index.php?option=com_content&view=article&id=17128&Itemid=528, last accessed April 15, 2018.

33 For an incisive critique of the politics of the origins and development of African Diasporic Studies as a field, see James Lorand Matory, *Black Atlantic Religion: Tradition, Transnationalism, and Matriarchy in the Afro-Brazilian Candomblé* (Princeton: Princeton University Press, 2005), 10–16.

34 Mariza de Carvalho Soares, *Devotos da cor: Identidade étnica, religiosidade e escravidão no Rio de Janeiro, século XVIII* (Rio de Janeiro: Civilização Brasileira, 2000); Mariza de Carvalho Soares, "A 'nação' que se tem e a 'terra' de onde se vem: Categorias de inserção social de africanos no Império português, século XVIII," *Estudos Afro-Asiáticos* 26, no. 2 (2004): 303–30; Luis Nicolau Parés, *A formação do candomblé: História e ritual da nação jeje na Bahia* (Campinas: Editora Unicamp, 2006); James Sweet, "Mistaken Identities?: Olaudah Equiano, Domingos Álvares, and the Methodological Challenges of Studying the African Diaspora," *American Historical Review* 114, no. 2 (2009): 279–306; James Sweet, *Domingos Álvares, African Healing, and the Intellectual History of the Atlantic World* (Chapel Hill: University of North Carolina Press, 2011).

35 Pablo Gómez, *The Experiential Caribbean: Creating Knowledge and Healing in the Early Modern Atlantic* (Chapel Hill: University of North Carolina Press, 2017), 34; Candido, "Jagas e sobas."

36 Krug, "Social Dismemberment, Social (Re)membering."

37 Matory, *Black Atlantic Religion*; James Lorand Matory, *Sex and the Empire That Is No More: Gender and the Politics of Metaphor in Oyo Yoruba Religion* (Minneapolis: University of Minnesota Press, 1994).

38 Vincent Brown, *The Reaper's Garden: Death and Power in the World of Atlantic Slavery* (Cambridge, MA: Harvard University Press, 2008), 7.

39 For details on the experience of capture and march toward the coast in Angola, see Miller, *Way of Death*.

40 Nearly every historian who writes about Angola during the age of the trans-Atlantic slave trade writes about the Jaga, or Imbangala. The debates concerning

Jaga historiography are vast and deep, and contend with questions as varied as origins, cultural practices, and the veracity of the widespread claims in contemporary European sources that the Jaga practiced anthropophagy. See Jan Vansina, "More on the Invasions of Kongo and Angola by the Jaga and the Lunda," *Journal of African History* 7 (1966): 421–29; Miller, "Imbangala," 549–74; Miller, "Requiem for the 'Jaga,'" *Cahiers d'études africaines* 13 (1973): 121–49; John Thornton, "A Resurrection for the Jaga," *Cahiers d'études africaines* 18 (1978): 223–31; and Beatrix Heintze, "The Extraordinary Journey of the Jaga through the Centuries: Critical Approaches to Precolonial Angolan Historical Sources," *History in Africa* 34 (2007): 67–101. For a critical examination of Andrew Battell, the seminal source for all who write about the Imbangala, see Jared Staller, "Rivalry and Allegory: Reflections on Andrew Battell's Jaga Materials Printed by Samuel Purchas from 1613 to 1625," *History in Africa* 43 (2016): 7–28. For an analysis of the Jaga as products of Portuguese imperial spatiopolitical imagination, see Candido, "Jagas e sobas." For our purposes here, it is important to recognize Imbangala society as a rejection of kin-based descent in favor of a society bound by a newly forged warrior ethos in the wake of burgeoning regional violence. In chapter 3, I will explore the difference between Imbangala and Kisama responses to these conditions at length.

41 James C. Scott, *The Art of Not Being Governed: An Anarchist History of Upland Southeast Asia* (New Haven: Yale University Press, 2009), 328.

42 J. C. Scott, *Art of Not Being Governed*, 8.

43 For a detailed discussion of the relationship of oral traditions of voluntary confederation and military conquest in early Kongo to the politics of the sixteenth-, seventeenth-, and eighteenth-century state, see Thornton, "Origins and Early History," 89–120. For a discussion of an ecologically, politically, and linguistically similar shatter zone in Angola, where there is suggestive evidence for the deeper antiquity of the practice of flight, see Jan Vansina's discussion of the area around the lower Okavango River in southern Angola, Vansina, *How Societies Are Born*, 182–86.

44 Although I believed that I had coined the term "fugitive modernities," as I completed my doctoral dissertation in 2012, I discovered that it appears in South African literary scholar David Attwell's *Rewriting Modernity* (2005). Attwell, however, engages fugitivity primarily through an existential/cultural production lens, rather than through a material, political approach. He explains, "I suggested that the investment in modernity on the part of South Africa's black writers had a 'fugitive' quality, that it produced something like 'fugitive modernities.' By this, I meant that such investment was never complete or unguarded. It always involved an element of counter-humanism; it always sought, in other words, to define itself outside of received, colonial versions of authority. Fugitiveness, in this sense, has less to do with flight—as in, for example, the fugitive slave culture of nineteenth-century African-American experience—than with the fugitiveness of

being in-and-out simultaneously." David Attwell, *Rewriting Modernity: Studies in Black South African Literary History* (Athens: Ohio University Press, 2006), 23–24. Atwell and others, including Homi Bhabha and John Comaroff, cannot unhinge modernity from coloniality, and thus their sense of fugitivity remains irrevocably linked to elite, literate interlocutors of states and colonial regimes. See Homi Bhabha, ed. *Nation and Narration* (London: Routledge, 1990); John Comaroff and Jean Comaroff, *Christianity, Colonialism, and Consciousness in South Africa*, vol. 1 of *Of Revelation and Revolutio* (Chicago: University of Chicago Press, 1991). My own sense of fugitive modernities is thus distinct from that of Attwell and emerges most directly from the traces of seventeenth-century fugitive discourse I discuss in chapter 5.

45 For further elaboration of these ideas, see Eric Wolf, *Europe and the People without History* (Berkeley: University of California Press, 1983); Stephan Palmié, *Wizards and Scientists: Explorations in Afro-Cuban Modernity and Tradition* (Durham, NC: Duke University Press, 2002); and Frederick Cooper, *Colonialism in Question: Theory, Knowledge, History* (Berkeley: University of California Press, 2005).

46 Many of these arguments were first posited by the anthropologist Johannes Fabian in Johannes Fabian, *Remembering the Present: Painting and Popular History in Zaire* (Berkeley: University of California Press, 1996); and Fabian and Bunzl, *Time and the Other*.

47 See, for example, Ella Shohat, "Notes on the 'Post-Colonial,'" *Social Text*, no. 31/32 (1992): 99–113; Frederick Cooper, "Conflict and Connection: Rethinking Colonial African History," *American Historical Review* 99, no. 5 (1994): 1516–45; T. O. Ranger and Richard P. Werbner, *Postcolonial Identities in Africa* (Atlantic Highlands, NJ: Zed Books, 1996); Cooper, *Colonialism in Question*.

48 Aijaz Ahmad, "The Politics of Literary Postcoloniality," *Race & Class* 36, no. 3 (January 1, 1995): 6–7, cited in Rita Abrahamsen, "African Studies and the Postcolonial Challenge," *African Affairs* 102, no. 407 (2003): 193.

49 Ludo de Witte, *The Assassination of Lumumba* (New York: Verso, 2001), 6.

50 "Carta do Rei do Congo a Paulo III," 21 February 21, 1535, cited in Brásio, *MMA*, 2:38; Linda Heywood, "Letter from Queen Ana Njinga to the Governor General of Angola, December 13, 1655," in Kathryn McKnight and Leo Garofalo, *Afro-Latino Voices: Narratives from the Early Modern Ibero-Atlantic World, 1550–1812* (Indianapolis: Hackett Publishers, 2009), 47; letter text translated by Luis Madureira.

Most scholars, writers, artists, activists, and everyday people who talk about Njinga refer to "Queen Njinga" and use feminine pronouns, "she" and "her." However, it is important to note that for much of Njinga's adult life, they deliberately and conscientiously gendered themselves as masculine. Taking seriously the work of scholars of gender and sexuality and of trans and genderqueer and gender nonconforming activists, as well as Njinga's own actions, I refer to their royal personage throughout this text either by name or with the gender-neutral pronoun "they." It is not necessary to reify biological sex as social or political identity to understand Njinga through a lens of feminism. Rescuing the legacy of Njinga from centuries of Eurocentric abuse and use to demonize Black womanhood does not require a retrograde gender essentialism as a corrective. For a fascinating discussion of Njinga's gender practices and politics, and appropriation and afterlife, see Heywood, *Njinga of Angola*.

51 Candido, *African Slaving Port*, 43.

52 By far the most thoroughly researched and rigorously argued of the creolist studies are Heywood and Thornton, *Central Africans, Atlantic Creoles*; and Toby Green, *The Rise of the Trans-Atlantic Slave Trade in Western Africa, 1300–1589* (New York: Cambridge University Press, 2014). For an insightful critique of creolist scholarship, see T. J. Desch Obi, "The Jogo de Capoeira and the Fallacy of 'Creole' Cultural Forms," *African and Black Diaspora: An International Journal* 5, no. 2 (2012): 211–28.

53 Jason Young, *Rituals of Resistance: African Atlantic Religion in Kongo and the Lowcountry South in the Era of Slavery* (Baton Rouge: Louisiana State University Press, 2007), 16. Earlier, Mariza de Carvalho Soares critiqued the culturalist roots of much of the scholarship of the African Diaspora, noting, "Culturalist authors begin from the presupposition that an ethnic group is defined in terms of cultural traits that operate in society, as discrete entities that can be subtracted or added, without this affecting the relations that comprise the unity of the group ... these retentions assume a quasi-ontological existence, without considering the conditions and the transformations through which segments of the 'transplanted' ethnic groups pass, violently, from one continent to another"; Soares, *Devotos da cor*, 114–15.

54 The archaeological, linguistic, and oral data from the Kavango River delta in southern Angola support this contention. While there is suggestive evidence that Kisama also functioned as such a refuge for those fleeing Kongo and Ndongo before the sixteenth century, until comparable linguistic and archaeological studies are conducted in geographical Kisama, it is impossible to detail this history conclusively. Vansina, *How Societies Are Born*, 182–86. It is also important to note that much of Scott's argument rests on the particular forms of economic extraction and violence associated with societies organized around paddy-based rice cultivation. Because the agriculture labor regimes and political culture of West Central African states differed greatly from those of Southeast Asia, the contours of state practice and resistance also differed.

55 Cooper, *Colonialism in Question*, 113–49.

56 Jan Vansina, *Paths in the Rainforests: Toward a History of Political Tradition in Equatorial Africa* (Madison: University of Wisconsin Press, 1990).

57 Sweet, *Domingos Álvares*; Brown, *Reaper's Garden*; "Social Death and Political Life in the Study of Slavery," *American Historical Review* 24, no. 5 (2009): 1231–49; Matory, *Sex and the Empire*.

58 See Neil Kodesh, *Beyond the Royal Gaze: Clanship and Public Healing in Buganda* (Charlottesville: University of Virginia Press, 2010); and Dipesh Chakrabarty, *Provincializing Europe: Postcolonial Thought and Historical Difference* (Princeton, NJ: Princeton University Press, 2000).

Chapter 1. Kafuxi Ambari and the People without State's History

1 Kodesh, "History from the Healer's Shrine," 527–52.
2 According to Beatrix Heintze, fugitives from as far away as Luanda fled to Kisama throughout the seventeenth century. When combined with the regular flight of those whom the Portuguese purchased from many inland markets and congregated at the forts in Muxima, Massangano, and Cambambe, this means that Kisama developed a far-flung reputation as a safe haven. See Heintze, *Asilo ameaçado*.
3 Report of José Ignácio de Sousa Andrade, January 13, 1885, Sala 1L, Caixa 6/790, Doc. 227, Arquivo Histórico Ultramarino, Lisbon, Portugal (hereafter cited as AHU).
4 For a discussion of the connected histories of dislocation, social dismemberment, and rupture south of geographical Kisama, see Candido, *African Slaving Port*.
5 Heintze, "Historical Notes," 412–14; Paes Brandão, "Diário da marcha do chefe do Concelho de Libolo, tenente Paes Brandão, a região de Quibala," *Portugal em África* 11 no. 123 (1904) 407–8; A. Ferreira, *A Kisama em Angola*, 88–89. While Miller mentions Kafuxi Ambari as an *ngola* title in *Kings and Kinsmen*, he does not discuss Kisama at length in *Way of Death*, beyond mentioning the importance of Kisama as a "maroon colony" and also the role that salt from Ndemba played in the regional economy. As I argue in chapter 6, this may be because in *Way of Death*, Miller is concerned with the eighteenth and nineteenth centuries, when Kafuxi Ambari faded from the archival record. See Miller, *Kings and Kinsmen*; and Miller, *Way of Death*.
6 This challenge has been taken up in different ways by many scholars of Africa and the African Diaspora in recent years, ranging from more individualistic to more collective. See, for example, Finch, *Rethinking Slave Rebellion in Cuba*; Benjamin N. Lawrance, *Amistad's Orphans: An Atlantic Story of Children, Slavery, and Smuggling* (New Haven, CT: Yale University Press, 2014); and João José Reis, *Domingos Sodré, um sacerdote africano: Escravidão, liberdade, e candomblé na Bahia do século XIX* (São Paulo: Companhia das Letras, 2008); Sweet, *Domingos Álvares*.
7 Even today, Kisama's population density is roughly 2.88 people per square mile, an exceptionally low figure, even for rural areas of Angola.
8 See Dias, "Famine and Disease," 349–78.
9 Based on what he admits is "sparse linguistic evidence," Jan Vansina speculates that "the society of the proto-Njila speakers [including the ancestors of those

living in sixteenth-century geographical Kisama] had become less structured than earlier Bantu-speaking societies to its north had been through the loss of formal overarching institutions concerning both leadership and political territory. If this impression is borne out by future research, then one can certainly attribute this loss of formal complexity to an increased influence of the foraging way of life on horticulturalists as a result of the emergence of proto-Njila speakers into new environments so different from their familiar equatorial rain forests." Vansina, *How Societies Are Born*, 52. Vansina's postulations here regarding proto-Njila speakers belies the notion of a teleological progression from more nomadic, foraging-based subsistence strategies to settled, nomadic ones. We should not assume that in geographical Kisama or elsewhere agriculture was the normative, desired subsistence strategy or that foraging, hunting, and other practices represented strategies of last resort.

10 Within present-day Kisama, Kimbundu speakers use both *nganga* and *kimbanda* to refer to ritual authorities.

11 Referring to these entities as "spirits" can elide the ways in which they in fact represent enduring subjectivities that interact with and order the world of human subjects, though they are not themselves physically embodied.

12 "Estado religioso e politico de Angola," in Brásio, *MMA*, 3:375–76. It is interesting to note that in this account, Kafuxi Ambari does not himself have the power to bring rain, but must rely on another authority. Unfortunately, there is no indication in any subsequent archival source if this bifurcated authority remained the same as Kafuxi Ambari's reputation grew, or if he in time came to monopolize rain-making powers as well. For a discussion of the relationship of rainmaking to political power in a Tanzanian context, see Steven Feierman, *Peasant Intellectuals: Anthropology and History in Tanzania* (Madison: University of Wisconsin Press, 1990).

13 In their discussion on the historical ramifications of drought, disease, and crop failure in West Central Africa, both Jill Dias and Joseph Miller mention the correlation of warfare and raiding with drought and crop failure. See Dias, "Famine and Disease"; and Miller, "Significance of Drought," 17–61. For discussion of raiding during times of drought in areas to the south of geographical Kisama, see also Obi, *Fighting for Honor*, 20.

14 "Estado religioso e politico de Angola," in Brásio, *MMA*, 3:375–76.

15 Dias, "Famine and Disease," 355; J. J. Monteiro, *Angola and the River Congo*, 2 vols. (London: Cass, 1968 [1875]), 103–4.

16 "Carta do Rei do Congo a Paulo III," in Brásio, *MMA*, 2:38.

17 David Livingstone, *Missionary Travels and Researches in South Africa: Including a Sketch of Sixteen Years' Residence in the Interior of Africa* (New York: Harper and Brothers, 1858), 246. Archaeological investigation in the region is necessary to ascertain the exact antiquity of rock salt mining and trade in the region; as yet, none has been conducted.

18 "Carta da doação a Paulo Dias de Novais," September 19, 1571, in Brásio, *MMA*, 3:36.

19 Pero Rodrigues, "História da residência dos padres da Companhia de Jesus em Angola, e cousas tocantes ao reino, e conquista," January 5, 1594, in Brásio, *MMA*, 4:571. For the seventeenth and eighteenth centuries, see Miller, *Way of Death*, 57, 182, 255. For the nineteenth century, see Dias, "Famine and Disease," 355. By the first decade of the seventeenth century, the Portuguese were forced to concede that these famed silver mines of Cambambe, which motivated so much of the Portuguese interest in Angola's interior in the later sixteenth century, as they dreamed of controlling mines as rich as those the Spanish had conquered in the Americas, did not exist. See "Regimento a Governor Manuel Perreira," March 23, 1607, Caixa 1, Doc. 3-A, Conselho Ultramarino, AHU. Portuguese mineral lust was not confined to Kisama. Indeed, fantasies of controlling nonexistent copper mines in Benguela were central to the Portuguese project of conquest in seventeenth-century Benguela. See Candido, *African Slaving Port*, 47–48.

A *peça*, short for *peça da Índia*, was a measurement of cloth which Portuguese slave traders calibrated to the value of one young, healthy African over a certain height. Thus, when working within the archives of imperial violence, it is critical to remember that even the most seemingly straightforward articulations of the commodification of African people carry with them the evidence of the inherent entanglement between slavery, capitalism, and Euromodernities. For more on the terms with which Portuguese calculated the value of bondspeople, see Daniel Domingues Da Silva, "The Atlantic Slave Trade from Angola: A Port-By-Port Estimate of Slaves Embarked, 1701–1867," *The International Journal of African Historical Studies* 46, no. 1 (2013): 105–22.

20 Resident of Ngalinda, interview by author, Muxima, Angola, July 22, 2010. In his efforts at gathering and understanding local history, António Sondoka has also heard people throughout Kisama, including in Ndemba, relate this as common knowledge.

21 Rodrigues, "História," in Brásio, *MMA*, 4:571.

22 Original text from 1594 transcribed in, "Report of Capitão José Ignacio de Sousa Andrade," December 15, 1885, Sala 1L, Caixa 790, Doc. 227, AHU.

23 For the importance of cavalry for Portuguese military operations in Angola in the seventeenth and eighteenth centuries, see Roquinaldo Ferreira, "The Supply and Development of Horses in Angolan Wafare (17th and 18th Centuries)," in *Angola on the Move: Transport Routes, Communications, and History*, ed. Beatrix Heintze and Achim Von Oppen (Frankfurt: Lembeck, 2008), 41–51.

24 Rodrigues, "História," in Brásio, *MMA*, 4:576.

25 Transcription by Capitão José Ignacio de Sousa Andrade.

26 Rodrigues, "História," in Brásio, *MMA*, 4:576–77.

27 Transcription by Capitão José Ignacio de Sousa Andrade.

28 Rodrigues, "História," in Brásio, *MMA*, 4:576–77.

29 "Relção da costa da África," 51–1X-25, f. 17, Biblioteca da Ajuda, Lisbon (hereafter cited as BdA).

30 António Sondoka, interview by author, Muxima, Angola, July 28, 2010.

31 Miller, *Kings and Kinsmen*.

32 Transcription by Capitão José Ignacio de Sousa Andrade.

33 António de Oliveira de Cadornega, *História geral das guerras angolanas*, 3 vols. (Lisbon: Agência Geral do Ultramar, 1972 [1680]), 1:69.

34 For a discussion of the colonial gaze and invention of political titles in other Angolan contexts, see Candido, "Jagas e sobas."

35 Cadornega, *História geral das guerras angolanas*, 2:114.

36 "Catalogo dos governadores de Angola," in *Ensaios sobre a statistica das possessoes portuguezas na África occidental e oriental, na Asia occidental, na China e na Oceania escriptos de ordem do Governo de S. M. D. Maria II*, ed. José Joaquim Lopès de Lima, 3 vols. (Lisbon: Imprensa Nacional, 1784), 3:xxi.

37 Steven Feierman, "Change in African Therapeutic Systems," *Social Science and Medicine* 13, no. 4 (1979): 277–84.

38 Cadornega, *História geral das guerras angolanas*, 1:71.

39 Rodrigues, "História," in Brásio, *MMA*, 4:566–75. José Joaquim Lopès de Lima, *Ensaios sobre a statistica das possessoes portuguezas na África occidental e oriental, na Asia occidental, na China, e na Oceania escriptos de ordem do governo de S. M. D. Maria II*, 3 vols. (Lisbon: Imprensa Nacional, 1844), 3:xxi.

40 Andrew Battell, *The Strange Adventures of Andrew Battell of Leigh, in Angola and the Adjoining Regions* (London: The Hakluyt Society, 1901 [1625]), 27.

41 "Notícia de Paulo Martins Pinheiro de Lacerda, coronel de infantaria da Província de Quissamã, em Angola, a respeito do exército enviado para punir os gentios dessa mesma província pelos furtos e mortes cometidos contra os moradores de Luanda e das margens do rio Cuanza," 1798, África/Angola, DL32,12.01, C791, 9v., Instituto Histórico e Geográfico Brasileiro, Rio de Janeiro (hereafter cited as IHGB).

42 Report of José Ignácio de Sousa Andrade, January 13, 1885, Sala 1L, Caixa 6/790, Doc. 227, AHU.

43 Rodrigues, "História," in Brásio, *MMA*, 4:550–51.

44 Cadornega, *História geral das guerras angolanas*, 1:81.

45 For a critical discussion of the intersections of combat, honor, and masculinities in West Central Africa and among West Central Africans and their descendants in the Americas, see Obi, *Fighting for Honor*.

46 Battell, *Strange Adventures of Andrew Battell*, 28.

47 Cadornega, *História geral das guerras angolanas*, 2:93.

48 Vansina, *How Societies Are Born*, 199.

49 Cadornega, *História geral das guerras angolanas*, 1:69–70.

50 Fernão Guerreiro, "Missão dos Jesuítas em Angola," 1602–3, in Brásio, *MMA*, 5:53.

51 John Thornton, "Legitimacy and Political Power: Queen Njinga, 1624–1663," *Journal of African History* 32 (1991): 25–40.

52 The ability of leaders to keep those over whom they ruled safe from capture and enslavement became a crucial factor in political legitimacy and in societies throughout Africa during the era of the trans-Atlantic slave trade. See, for example, Heywood, "Slavery and Its Transformations," 1–22. For a fascinating comparative study of the connections between protection from enslavement and political legitimacy in West Africa, see Jennifer Lofkrantz, "Protecting Freeborn Muslims: The Sokoto Caliphate's Attempts to Prevent Illegal Enslavement and Its Acceptance of the Strategy of Ransoming," *Slavery and Abolition* 32, no. 1 (2011): 109–27.

53 Unfortunately, there are no ethnographic materials describing spiritual beliefs and practices of Kisama in this period in any detail. While perhaps some of the same complexes of belief present north of the Kwanza River in Ndongo and south of the Longa River in the central highlands may have also been a part of Kisama society, it would be unwise to assume such unity. It seems likely, however, that these dramatic changes in the political landscape were accompanied by an alteration of the spiritual landscape as well. For an intriguing examination of the connection between militarization, masculinization, and ritual practice in Oyo, see Matory, *Sex and the Empire*. For a discussion of the ways that anthropological and historical obsessions with lineage and kinship in Africa spring from and recreate problematic racist notions about Africa and a compelling argument that lineage theory is a Western myth, see Wyatt Macgaffey, "Changing Representations in Central African History," *Journal of African History* 46, no. 2 (2005): 189–207.

54 Guerreiro, "Missão," in Brásio, *MMA*, 5:54.

55 "Catalogo dos governadores de Angola," 93.

56 Beatrix Heintze, "The Angolan Vassal Tributes of the 17th Century," *Revista de História Económica e Social* 6 (1980): 57–78.

57 The original archival records are in the Biblioteca Pública de Évora in Évora, Portugal, and fully transcribed and published in facsimile in Aida Freudenthal and Selma Pantoja, *Livro dos baculamentos: Que os sobas deste reino de Angola pagam a sua majestade, 1630* (Luanda: Arquivo Nacional de Angola, Ministério da Cultura, 2013).

58 Miller, *Way of Death*, 189–90.

59 "Carta de André Velho da Fonseca a El-Rei," February 28, 1612, in Brásio, *MMA*, 4:65.

60 Contrast this, however, with the ways in which those rejecting state politics in Upper Guinea became deeply embedded within the trans-Atlantic slave trade, exchanging captives for the iron necessary for the cultivation of wet rice. See Walter Hawthorne, *Planting Rice and Harvesting Slaves: Transformations along the Guinea-Bissau Coast, 1400–1900* (Portsmouth, NH: Heinemann, 2003).

61 "Carta de Bento Banho Cardoso," August 10, 1611, Caixa 1, Doc. 16, AHU. Contrast this with the situation in the late eighteenth century, when Portuguese

colonel Paulo Martins Pinheiro de Lacerda described Kisama as "populated with many blacks, all heathens, and where many whites, and other merchants, come to buy slaves." "Notícia de Paulo Martins Pinheiro de Lacerda," IV, IHGB.

62 "Letter by the Governor of Benguela to the King of Portugal, Benguela, February 21, 1631," 51–1X-21, f. 18, BdA.

63 Battell, *Strange Adventures of Andrew Battell*, 27.

64 "Relação da costa de Angola e Congo pelo ex-governador Fernão de Sousa," February 21, 1632, in Brásio, *MMA*, 8:125, 29.

65 Fernão de Sousa, "O extensor relatório de governador a seus filhos," 1625–30, in Heintze, *Fontes para a história*, 1:285.

66 A. Ferreira, *A Kisama em Angola*, 202.

67 "Carta do Padre Baltasar Barreira para O Padre Sebastião de Morais," January 31, 1582, in Brásio, *MMA*, 3:208–11.

68 A. Ferreira, *A Kisama em Angola*.

69 John Thornton, "Letter from Queen Ana Njinga to the Governor General of Angola, December 13, 1655," in McKnight and Garofalo, *Afro-Latino Voices*, 47; text translated by Luis Madureira. I open chapter 3 with this moment.

70 Citing the Italian Capuchin Cannecattim, who compiled a dictionary and linguistic observations of Kimbundu based on his time as a missionary in the region during the nineteenth century, Joseph Miller argues that Kisama was an Umbundu-speaking (Guthrie R10) rather than Kimbundu-speaking (Guthrie H21) region until the late eighteenth century. Undoubtedly, as Miller argues and I discuss in the next chapter, changes to the cultural and linguistic environment of Kisama did occur as a result of the increasing numbers of fugitives who fled to Kisama. However, to be true, Miller's argument would have to explain why the Umbundu-speaking inhabitants of Kisama either completely shifted language or were overwhelmed or eliminated in the (relatively, in the world of languages) short period of two centuries. See Bernardo Maria de Cannecatim, *Colleccaõ de observacaõs grammaticas sobre a lingua Bunda ou Angolense e diccionario abreviado da lingua Congueza (aque acresce uma quarta columna que contém os termos da lingua Bunda identicos ou similhantes à lingua Congueza)* (Lisbon: Imprensa Nacional, 1859); Miller, *Kings and Kinsmen*, 39. In her study of the development of the Kimbundu language, Carolyn Vieira-Martinez argues that Kisama emerged as a distinct dialect of Kimbundu by 1300. Carolyn Vieira-Martinez, "Building Kimbundu: Language Community Reconsidered in West Central Africa, c. 1500–1750" (PhD diss., University of California–Los Angeles, 2006), 186–87. An article by two Brazilian linguists and one Angolan linguist in 2011 posits Kisama as the most lexically similar dialect to the Kimbundu spoken in Malanje. However, their analysis is based on a word list collected from a single informant, long a resident in Luanda. Indeed, their word lists and phonetics both suggest significant issues with their data. See Maria Fátima Lima de Sousa, Vatomene Kukanda, and Joane Lima Santiago, "A posição lexical do Songo dentro

do Gruop H20 (Kimbundu *strictu sensu*, Sama, Bolo, e Songo)," *Papia* 21, no. 2 (2011): 303–14.

71 Jan Vansina, personal communication with author, March 6, 2011.

72 Resident of Cacumba (anonymous by interviewee's request), interview by author, Cacumba, Angola, July 15, 2010. Resident of Kisama, (anonymous by interviewee's request), interview by author, Ndemba Chio, Angola, July 18, 2010. António Sondoka, interview by author, Muxima, Angola, August 2, 2010. Resident of Mumbondo (anonymous by interviewee's request), interview by author, Mumbondo, Angola, August 10, 2010.

73 According to John Thornton, place names beginning with Ki- are common in KiKongo. John Thornton, personal communication with author, January 7, 2011.

74 Jan Vansina, personal communication with author, March 6, 2011.

75 "Carta do Rei do Congo a Paulo III," in Brásio, *MMA*, 2:38.

76 A. E. Horton, *A Dictionary of Luvale* (El Monte, CA: Lithographed by Rahn Bros., 1953), 127, 280, 315. David Schoenbrun helpfully brought these glosses to my attention.

77 Adriano C. Barbosa, *Dicionário cokwe-português* (Coimbra: Universidade de Coimbra, 1989), 479.

78 Horton, *Dictionary of Luvale*, 37.

79 The complexity of linguistic practices in Kisama begs for a new framework of linguistics that applies the same tools that scholars have devised for analyzing "creole" languages. Kisama shows every sign of having long been a contact language, though, as Vansina notes, there is a deep history of language contact and borrowing throughout the region. However, linguists traditionally reserve the term "creole" for analysis of languages formed through contact between an Indo-European and non-Indo-European language—the same epistemological pitfall that characterizes historical scholarship on Atlantic creoles. See Vansina, *How Societies Are Born*, 53.

Chapter 2. Fugitive Politics and Legitimacy, c. 1620–55

1 Consulta do Conselho Ultramarino, "Exame das cartas do Governador de Angola acerca do estado da Provincia, guerra da Quiçama e do Congo," July 13, 1655, in Brásio, *MMA*, 9:498–99. Njinga shaped much of the political, social, and military landscape of the region from the 1620s on. However, centering Njinga in historical narratives, long a favored approach of ruling party elites in Angola and their imperial predecessors, reifies a statist approach. Here, I reinterrogate this period in Angolan history from the perspective of the history of Kisama and other fugitive societies, including Njinga where relevant.

2 "Carta do Irmão Antóio Mendes ao Padre Geral," May 9, 1563, in Brásio, *MMA*, 2:495; Candido, *African Slaving Port*, 33.

3 For a discussion of the notion of social dismemberment and political beheading, see Krug, "Social Dismemberment, Social (Re)membering."

4 "Carta de D. Diogo rei do Congo, queixando-se a D. João III do mau procedimento dos padres e mais vassallos portuguezes que estavam n'aqulle reino, e pedindo-lhe confirmasse a carta d'elrei D. Manuel, da qual remettia o traslado," January 28, 1549, in Levy Maria Jordão, *História do Congo: Obra posthuma do Visconde de Paiva Manso, socio effectivo da Academia real das sciencias de Lisboa* (Lisbon: Academia Real das Sciencias, 1877), 92.

5 Heintze, *Asilo ameaçado*. My claim here concerning relative instability is, of course, predicated on archival sources that were more preoccupied with the macropolitics of the Dutch-Portuguese conflict and its local iterations.

6 Query of Voyages: The Trans-Atlantic Slave Trade Database, www.slavevoyages .org, accessed April 13, 2018.

7 David Wheat, "The First Great Waves: African Provenance Zones for the Transatlantic Slave Trade to Cartagena de Indias, 1570–1640," *Journal of African History* 52, no. 1 (2011): 1–22.

8 Antonio Bezerra Fajardo, "Lembrança das couzas que se há de declarar a sua Mg.de tocantes ao Reyno de Angola," February 24, 1624, f. 29, 51-IX-25, BdA.

9 "História política de Angola, 1622–1623," in Brásio, *MMA*, 7:78.

10 "Copia da rellação que foy ao secretario de estado Francisco de Lucena," January 30, 1627, f. 236, 51–1X-20, BdA.

11 "Letter by the Governor of Benguela to the King of Portugal, Benguela, February 21, 1631," 51–1X-21, BdA; Report by the Camara of Luanda to the King of Portugal, June 20, 1633, Caixa 3, Doc. 5, AHU.

12 Papers of Fernão de Sousa, 51–1X-20, f. 208, BdA.

13 For an insightful examination of the sources and narratives for the foundation of the Kingdom of Kongo, see Thornton, "Origins and Early History," 89–120.

14 Pero Rodrigues, "História da residência dos padres da Companhia de Jesus em Angola, e cousas tocantes ao reino, e conquista," January 5, 1594, in Brásio, *MMA*, 4:571. According to Rodrigues, the Portuguese eventually rescued the remainder. For an overview of Kasanze, see Joseph Miller, "A Note on Kasanze and the Portuguese," *Canadian Journal of African Studies / Revue canadienne des études africaines* 6, no. 1 (1972): 43–56. Miller's important sketch of Kasanze history, repeated endlessly and uncritically in four decades of secondary scholarship, includes a number of assumptions and methodologically questionable conclusions.

15 Miller, "Note on Kasanze and the Portuguese." Miller's conclusions here are based most compellingly on Kasanze's geographic position on the coast, between the Portuguese and the captive men, women, and children whom the king of Ndongo and others would have sold. More problematically, Miller argues that those who were transported to mid-sixteenth-century São Tomé must have been Kimbundu

speakers because the descendants of a slave ship wreck in 1544 still spoke Kimbundu years later. This shipwreck is part of the mythos of the origins of the Angolar community in São Tomé, and, more broadly, part of a global idiom through which maroon communities deny the enslavement of their ancestors by claiming descent from shipwrecked people. Maroon communities in Jamaica, Puerto Rico, and Saint Vincent likewise make this claim. For a thorough, detailed discussion of the sources and political machinations of various origin myths of São Tomé's Angolar community, see Gerhard Seibert, "Tenreiro, Amador e os Angolares ou a reinvenção da história da Ilha de São Tomé," *Revista de Estudos AntiUtilitaristas e PosColoniais* 2, no. 2 (March 25, 2013): 21–39.

16 Jan Vansina, *Kingdoms of the Savanna* (Madison: University of Wisconsin Press, 2011), 61.

17 Battell, *Strange Adventures of Andrew Battell*, 40. For an extensive history of the role of maize cultivation in Africa, see James McCann, *Maize and Grace: Africa's Encounter with a New World Crop, 1500–2000* (Cambridge, MA: Harvard University Press, 2005).

18 "Carta de João Correia de Sousa ao Marquês de Frecilha," June 3, 1622, in Brásio, *MMA*, 7:18.

19 "Carta de João Correia de Sousa ao Marquês de Frecilha," June 3, 1622, in Brásio, *MMA*, 7:18. De Sousa's understanding of Kasanze's political structure and history was clearly flawed. In the same paragraph he describes the supposedly eternal and absolute obedience of Kasanze to Kongo and Mbamba and an account of Paulo Dias de Novais's conflict with Kasanze that imputes the motive to Kasanze's inherent enmity against the Portuguese and not to the Portuguese acting on behalf of Kongo against a rebellious subject polity.

20 Cadornega, *História geral das guerras angolanas*, 1:101. Alfredo de Albuquerque Felner, *Angola: Apontamentos sôbre a ocupaccio do estabelecimento dos portugueses no Congo, Angola e Benguela; Extraídos de documentos históricos* (Coimbra, Portugal: Imprensa da Universidade, 1933), 212–13.

21 "Carta de João Correia de Sousa ao Marquês de Frecilha," June 3, 1622, in Brásio, *MMA*, 7:17.

22 Cadornega, *História geral das guerras angolanas*, 1:101.

23 "Carta de João Correia de Sousa ao Marquês de Frecilha," June 3, 1622, in Brásio, *MMA*, 7:17.

24 Iberian combat in this era included within its arsenals both closed formation strategies and open formation strategies that were part of Moorish martial heritage. T. J. Desch Obi, personal communication, June 18, 2016. "Carta de João Correia de Sousa ao Marquês de Frecilha," June 3, 1622, in Brásio, *MMA*, 7:19–20. De Sousa records the amount of brush each commander was required to clear as "fifty *varas*." I have used Brásio's assessment that one *vara* is equivalent to 1.1 meters to calculate present-day equivalents.

25 Brásio, *MMA*, 7:20–24.

26 Heywood and Thornton, *Central Africans, Atlantic Creoles*, 137.

27 Heywood and Thornton, *Central Africans, Atlantic Creoles*, 138–40.

28 The Portuguese authorization of Nzenza's war against Kafuxi Ambari was necessary in order to satisfy the formal legal conditions for a "just war" and "legitimately acquired slaves." See Emilia Viotti da Costa, "The Portuguese-African Slave Trade: A Lesson in Colonialism," *Latin American Perspectives* 12 (1985): 41–61. Fernão de Sousa, "O extenso relátorio do governador a seus filhos," 1625–1630, in Beatrix Heintze, *Fontes para a história de Angola do século XVII*, 2 vols. (Stuttgart: Franz Steiner Verlag Wiesbaden, 1988), 1:226.

29 "Letter of Governor Sousa Chicorro to King of Portugal, November 22, 1658," in Brásio, *MMA*, 12:179–80. Jan Vansina, "Histoire du manioc en Afrique centrale avant 1850," *Paideuma* 43 (1997): 259–62.

30 Joseph Miller deracinates the "Jaga" who invaded Kongo in the sixteenth century from the "Jaga" who ravaged many parts of Angola in the late sixteenth and seventeenth centuries. See Miller, "Requiem for the 'Jaga.'" John Thornton recognizes Miller's contribution in this respect but problematizes his understanding of the invasions of Kongo. See Thornton, "Resurrection for the Jaga."

31 Thornton, "Resurrection for the Jaga," 226.

32 Thornton, "Legitimacy and Political Power," 32.

33 Report of Camara de Luanda officials to Lisbon, June 20, 1633, Caixa 3, Doc. 5, AHU.

34 Battell, *Strange Adventures of Andrew Battell*, 30. Miller notes, however, that "felling palm trees to obtain the edible pulp turns up repeatedly as a desperation tactic to avoid starvation," an argument belied, however, by the fact that "Battell also noted ample provisions in the Imbangala camp." Miller, "Significance of Drought," 40.

35 See John Janzen, *Lemba, 1650–1930: A Drum of Affliction in Africa and the New World* (New York: Garland, 1982). This appears less a survival strategy and more a particular and marvelously spectacular choreography of violence, designed to engender fear in enemies and observers.

36 For a riveting discussion of mimesis, violence, ritual, and colonialism in a different context, see Michael Taussig, *Mimesis and Alterity: A Particular History of the Senses* (New York: Routledge, 1993). John Thornton, "Angola e as origens de Palmares," in *Mocambos de Palmares: Histórias e fontes (séculos XVI–XIX)*, ed. Flávio dos Santos Gomes (Rio de Janeiro: 7Letras, 2010), 55.

37 Vansina, *How Societies Are Born*, 199.

38 Cadornega, *História geral das guerras angolanas*, 2:90–91.

39 Cadornega, *História geral das guerras angolanas*, 2:381.

40 The document from which this account is derived, 51–1X-20, f. 264–5, BdA, is undated and comes from materials governor Fernão de Sousa wrote for his sons between 1624–1630, according to Heintze. I consulted the original document in the Biblioteca da Ajuda, but also viewed Heintze's notes on her transcription of

parts of the archival source in order to better date the document. Heintze, *Fontes para a história*, 1:217. I have arrived at the 1629 or 1630 date by assuming that the account could have been written no later than 1630 per Heintze, and no earlier than 1629 due to de Sousa's mention of Portuguese official Dionísio Soares de Albergaria, who did not arrive in Angola until 1629. See Heintze, *Fontes para a história*, 1:67. In the document, the term de Sousa uses is *gingo*, translated by Beatrix Heintze as "the potential candidate for a title and political function, for example the mani in the region of Luanda or the soba of the Mbundus." Heintze, *Fontes para a história* 1:117–18. While it is unclear from de Sousa's account, it seems that the previous Langere had been expelled from his own lands by his people, thus precipitating a succession struggle.

41 Here I use "pretender" to refer to the man who sought investment as Langere at the hands of the Portuguese. I do not mean to imply a personal opinion on his political legitimacy.

42 See Heintze, *Fontes para a história*, 1:126–27. Drawing from the documents to which Heintze refers in her glossary, however, Thornton adds that imbare were also the specially trained, professional, free and bonded soldiers of the Kingdom of Ndongo. See John Thornton, "The Art of War in Angola, 1575–1680," *Comparative Studies in Society and History* 30 (1988): 362. T. J. Desch Obi agrees with Thornton's view, defining *imbare* as "groups of professional soldiers ... in the northern region of West Central Africa." T. J. Desch Obi, "'Koup Tet': A Machete-Wielding View of the Haitian Revolution," in *Activating the Past: History and Memory in the Black Atlantic World*, ed. Andrew Apter and Lauren Derby (Newcastle upon Tyne, UK: Cambridge Scholars, 2010), 248. In an article on Ambaca society and the slave trade in the eighteenth and nineteenth centuries, Jan Vansina quotes Cadornega and various dictionaries to define *imbare* as "African mobile traders ... , a term which in an earlier age was reserved for 'workers [for the Portuguese] who pay a tithe from their harvest, just as if they were chiefs.'" Jan Vansina, "Ambaca Society and the Slave Trade c. 1760–1845," *Journal of African History* 46, no. 1 (2005): 9. In the context of this argument, I follow Heintze's definition which seems the most consistent with de Sousa's meaning in all of his writings, though I acknowledge that a sociolinguistic study of the changing meanings and slippery applications of *kimbare* throughout Angolan would likely shift our understanding of what de Sousa meant to convey.

43 51–1X-20, f. 264 v, BdA.

44 Combe Riaquina was a vassal soba in Libolo. I have chosen to reproduce the word "Riaquina" here as it appears in the original text, despite the fact that there is no "r" phoneme in present-day Kimbundu. Given the gulf between orthography and speech acts, and change over time, it is difficult to know what sounds these archival traces truly represent.

45 51–1X-20, f. 264 v, BdA.

46 51–1X-20, f. 264 v, BdA.

47 See Miller, "Imbangala Lineage Slavery," in *Slavery in Africa: Historical and Anthropological Perspectives,* ed. Suzanne Miers and Igor Kopytoff (Madison, University of Wisconsin Press, 1977), 231. Heintze relates the term *quizico* as derived from the ethnonym Anzico (Tio), which refers to those around the Malebo Pool, but nevertheless identifies it with a subservient status. See Heintze, *Fontes para a história,* 1:127. John Thornton disagrees with this etymology, pointing to how its use confirms its application to those in a position of subservience. John Thornton, personal communication, June 1, 2011. For linguistic and semantic reasons, I agree with Thornton's and Miller's positions. Indeed, early seventeenth-century Jesuit priest Pierre du Jarric refers to ijiko as "those who strictly speaking are the serfs and slaves . . . who are like an attachment to the patrimony of the Lord thereof, and devolve to the successor of the estate, like other patrimonial goods." Pierre du Jarric, *Histoire des choses plvs memorables advenves tant ez Indes Orientales, que autres païs de la descouuerte des Portugais, en l'establissement et progrez de la foy chrestienne, et catholique: Et principalement de ce que les religieux de la Compagnie de Iesvs y ont faict, et enduré pour la mesme fin; depuis qu'ils y sont entrez jusques à l'an 1600,* 3 vols., (Bordeaux: S. Milanges, 1614), 2:79.

48 Miller, "Imbangala Lineage Slavery," 211; Heintze, *Fontes para a história,* 1 :115.

49 Vansina, *How Societies Are Born,* 203.

50 Miller, *Kings and Kinsmen,* 232–35; Heywood and Thornton, *Central Africans, Atlantic Creoles,* 133.

51 António da Silva Maia, *Dicionário complementar: Português-Kimbundu-Kikongo* (Cucujães: Tipografia das Missões, 1961), 266.

52 Cadornega, *História geral das guerras angolanas,* 2:93.

53 See Heywood and Thornton, *Central Africans, Atlantic Creoles,* 75–79.

54 John Thornton, personal communication, June 1, 2011.

55 Roquinaldo Ferreira, "Dos sertões ao Atlântico: Tráfico ilegal de escravos e comércio lícito em Angola, 1830–1860" (master's thesis, Universidade Federal do Rio de Janeiro, 1996), 86–87. I do not mean to imply that the political forms of the early seventeenth century would remain static through the nineteenth century, or indeed that the broader regional and global contexts remained stable over three centuries. In the nineteenth century, for example, the decline of the trans-Atlantic slave trade and the subsequent increase in the number of Africans held in bondage locally would reconfigure the material imperatives for maroonage in the region. See R. Ferreira, *Cross-Cultural Exchange.*

56 For example, one family that was instrumental in fighting against the Portuguese in their early twentieth-century iterations of scorched earth campaigns designed to force people off of the land in order to convert it to a game park has a surname that alludes to the ability to move around game without being detected. According to family members and others from the same region, the members of this family have been "renowned elephant hunters" since the Jita Kwatakwata.

57 Obi, *Fighting for Honor,* 21.

58 Battell, *Strange Adventures of Andrew Battell*, 28.

59 Cadornega, *História geral das guerras angolanas*, 1:170.

60 "Petition by Captain-General P. Barreiros to the Governor of Angola for More Troops, Massangano," August 21, 1656, Caixa 6, Doc. 67, AHU.

61 Unfortunately, I have located no direct descriptions in an Angolan context of the tactics through which armed people in fishing canoes attacked two-masted seagoing ships on the river.

62 "Carta Régia para o governador geral de Angola," November 23, 1735, cód. 546, fls. 92v.-93, AHU.

Chapter 3. Gender, Food, and Politics in the War of 1655–58

1 Linda Heywood, "Letter from Queen Ana Njinga to the Governor General of Angola, December 13, 1655," in McKnight and Garofalo, *Afro-Latino Voices*, 47; letter text translated by Luis Madureira.

2 "Carta de Diogo Gomes Morales," October 20, 1648, Caixa 4, Doc. 11, AHU.

3 "Rellação que Bertholameu Pays de Bulbão fez a vs Mag," September 17, 1655, Caixa 5, Doc. 28, AHU.

4 On October 6, 1650, Portuguese governor Salvador Correia de Sá erroneously claimed in a letter to the king of Portugal that "the province of Quissama made an accord with us and is pacified." "Salvador Correia au roi," October 6, 1650, Luanda, in Louis Jadin, *L'ancien Congo et l'Angola, 1639–1655: D'après les archives romaines, portugaises, néerlandaises et espagnoles*, 3 vols. (Brussels: Institut Historique Belge de Rome, 1975), 3:1265. The Dutch were in geographic Kisama itself by 1644. See Lisbon, July 14, 1644, Caixa 5, Doc. 33, AHU; and "Les maîtres de camp, gouverneurs de Pernambouc, à João IV, ET pour copie au comte de Vidigueira," in Jadin, *L'ancien Congo*, 2:865–66.

5 "Carta de Luís Martins de Sousa Chicorro," September 16, 1653, Caixa 6, Doc. 92, AHU.

6 The sobas of Ndembos, a region between Kongo and Ndongo that likewise attracted fugitives, did, however, engage in this kind of letter-writing exchange. As in the case of Kasanze, this reveals the multiplicity of fugitive political forms in seventeenth-century Angola and the widespread hegemonic nature of Kongo political culture.

7 For a detailed examination of the intricate diplomatic and military relationship between Njinga, the Dutch, and the Portuguese, see Heywood, *Njinga of Angola*.

8 The fragmentary nature of politics also characterized the region around Benguela. While the Portuguese attempted to render Benguela a coherent, legible political entity ("the Kingdom of Benguela"), this always reflected imperial imagination rather than reality. It is important to note, however, that in spite of the region's decentralized political forms, its geography of reputation was not the same as Kisama's. See Candido, *African Slaving Port*; Candido, "Jagas e sobas."

9 Heywood and Thornton, *Central Africans, Atlantic Creoles*, 157.

10 Janzen, *Lemba*; Sweet, *Domingos Álvares*; Gómez, *Experiential Caribbean*.

11 Giovanni Antonio Cavazzi, *Descrição histórica dos três reinos do Congo, Matamba, e Angola*, 3 vols. (Lisbon: Junta de Investigações do Ultramar, 1965 [1665]), 2:210. For a discussion of *xinguila*, see James Sweet, *Recreating Africa: Culture, Kinship, and Religion in the African-Portuguese World, 1441–1770* (Chapel Hill: University of North Carolina Press, 2003), 140–42.

12 "Catalogo dos governadores de Angola," 3: xxi. For a discussion of this event, see chapter 1. For an exploration of the connection between political change and spirit mediumship in the context of the Great Lakes, see Kodesh, *Beyond the Royal Gaze*.

13 All too often, "Atlantic" is coded language for a specific set of entanglements with capitalism and colonialism that leave a particular type of archival trace. Indeed, what single conceptual framework can be said to make Sweet's Domingos Álvares, Wilson-Fall's Madagascar-descended historical actors, or Ferreira's or Candido's traders all Atlantic subjects? See Sweet, *Domingos Álvares*; Wendy Wilson-Fall, *Memories of Madagascar and Slavery in the Black Atlantic* (Athens: Ohio University Press, 2015); R. Ferreira, *Cross-Cultural Exchange*; Candido, *African Slaving Port*.

14 Cavazzi, *Descrição histórica*, 2:215.

15 See Carlo M. Cipolla, *Fighting the Plague in Seventeenth-Century Italy* (Madison: University of Wisconsin Press, 1981).

16 Mark Eppinger et al., "Genome Sequence of the Deep-Rooted *Yersinia pestis* Strain Angola Reveals New Insights into the Evolution and Pangenome of the Plague Bacterium," *Journal of Bacteriology* 192, no. 6 (2010): 1685–99; Maria A. Spyrou et al., "Historical *Y. pestis* Genomes Reveal the European Black Death as the Source of Ancient and Modern Plague Pandemics," *Cell Host & Microbe* 19, no. 6 (June 8, 2016): 874–81.

17 For a suggestive discussion of the political centrality of priests of Sakpata, a *vodoun* (deity) of smallpox, in the Bight of Benin in resisting Dahomean expansion in the eighteenth century, see Sweet, *Domingos Álvares*, 20–25.

18 This pattern is nearly universal in so-called "cults of affliction" or "drums of affliction" across Africa and the African Diaspora. See, for example, Janzen, *Lemba*; Kodesh, *Beyond the Royal Gaze*.

19 Miller, "Significance of Drought," 44.

20 "Letter by Governor Sousa Chicorro to the King," August 3, 1656, Caixa 6, Doc. 59, AHU.

21 Candido, however, reminds us to not conflate the experiences of invading soldiers or those caused by invading soldiers with that of local populations. Candido, *African Slaving Port*, 77.

22 There is a rich Africanist literature on social health and healing and the notion of violence and colonialism itself as illness. Among others, see John Janzen and

Steven Feierman, *The Social Basis of Health and Healing in Africa* (Berkeley: University of California Press, 1992); Gwyn Prins, "But What Was the Disease? The Present State of Health and Healing in African Studies," *Past & Present*, no. 124 (1989): 159–79; Feierman, *Peasant Intellectuals*.

23 Cadornega, *História geral das guerras angolanas*, 2:90.

24 Cadornega, *História geral das guerras angolanas*, 2:93.

25 For an overview of Portuguese and African military tactics in seventeenth century Angola, see Thornton, "Art of War in Angola." Thornton deemphasizes the importance of cavalry for Portuguese forces in seventeenth-century Angola. For a discussion of the importance of horses, see R. Ferreira, "Supply and Development of Horses."

26 Cadornega, *História geral das guerras angolanas*, 2:93.

27 Cadornega, *História geral das guerras angolanas*, 2:94.

28 Cadornega, *História geral das guerras angolanas*, 2:94. Intriguingly, the Jamaican maroons famously used the same tactic of forcing a single-file assault on their stronghold in the Cockpit Country on the western part of the island in the early eighteenth century. See Robert Charles Dallas, *The History of the Maroons: From their Origin to the Establishment of Their Chief Tribe at Sierra Leone*, 2 vols., vol. 1 (New York: Cambridge University Press, 2010), 41–42.

29 Cadornega, *História geral das guerras angolanas*, 2:96.

30 "Carta de João Correia de Sousa ao Marquês de Frecilha," June 3, 1622, in Brásio, *MMA*, 7:17.

31 Iberian combat repertoires in this era included within its arsenals both closed formation strategies and open formation strategies that were part of Moorish martial heritage. T. J. Desch Obi, personal communication, June 18, 2016.

32 "Carta de João Correia de Sousa ao Marquês de Frecilha," June 3, 1622, in Brásio, *MMA*, 7:19–20. De Sousa records the amount of brush each commander was required to clear as "fifty *varas*." I have used Brásio's assessment that one *vara* is equivalent to 1.1 meters to calculate present-day equivalents.

33 Cadornega, *História geral das guerras angolanas*, 1:191–93.

34 Cadornega, *História geral das guerras angolanas*, 2:96–97.

35 "Assento que fizeram os oficiais da camara em 6 de janeiro de 1652," cód. 6, fls. 105v.–106v., Biblioteca Municipal de Luanda, Luanda, Angola.

36 Thornton, "Art of War in Angola."

37 Cadornega, *História geral das guerras angolanas*, 2:103.

38 Cadornega, *História geral das guerras angolanas*, 2:103.

39 Cadornega, *História geral das guerras angolanas*, 2:104.

40 Cadornega, *História geral das guerras angolanas*, 2:104–5.

41 Thornton, "Art of War in Angola."

42 António Sondoka, interview by author, Muxima, Kisama, Angola, July 25, 2010.

43 Miller, *Way of Death*, 123.

44 Livingstone, *Missionary Travels*, 441.

45 Cadornega, *História geral das guerras angolanas*, 2:105.

46 Cavazzi, *Descrição histórica*, 2:119.

47 Cavazzi, *Descrição histórica*, 2:119.

48 Cadornega, *História geral das guerras angolanas*, 3:248–49.

49 Cadornega, *História geral das guerras angolanas*, 2:111.

50 This is, of course, a somewhat speculative conclusion. European sources documenting that women were critical to agricultural production during the seventeenth century abound. While Vanessa Oliveira and others have articulated the importance of women merchants in later Angolan history, and they may well have been active in markets during this period as well, that does not mean that they were not primarily agricultural producers during the seventeenth century. The scant evidence for seventeenth-century Kisama participation in markets unfortunately includes nothing that allows us to discern gendered topographies of labor. See Vanessa Oliveira, "Gendered Dimension of Trade."

51 Aurora da Fonseca Ferreira, "La Kisama (en Angola) du XVIe au début du XXe siècle" (PhD diss., École des hautes études en sciences sociales, 2000), xlii–iii.

52 Heywood and Thornton, *Central Africans, Atlantic Creoles*, 157.

53 It was only in the 1730s that Luso-African residents of Massangano were able to take control of the trade out of the hands of independent merchants from Kisama. See Miller, *Way of Death*, 255, 560. In addition to its many economic functions, Cavazzi reports that Kisama rock salt was also "very useful for domestic uses and in medicine, as it is diuretic. Thus, it is sold in the markets in large quantities." Cavazzi, *Descrição histórica*, 1:22.

54 According to Heintze, *cassuea* is a term whose "origin and exact meaning [she has] not succeeded in clarifying, [and] appears various times in sources on Angola of the seventeenth century to mean a type of punishment, undefined.... Perhaps it also designates a certain type of slave. It is also applied in a figurative sense ... meaning 'rebel.'" Heintze, *Fontes para a história*, 1:116.

55 Papers of Governor Fernão de Sousa, 51–1X-20, f. 264 v.—f. 265, BdA.

56 For a comprehensive examination of the life of maize in Africa, see McCann, *Maize and Grace*.

57 Miller, *Way of Death*, 103. For more on the importance of manioc to the seventeenth-century slave trade, see Luiz Felipe de Alencastro, *O trato dos viventes: Formação do Brasil no Atlântico Sul* (São Paulo: Companhia Das Letras, 2000), 251–56.

58 Vansina, "Histoire du manioc," 260. While here I focus on the uniqueness of Kisama's early commercial cultivation of manioc and maize, it is important to consider that in Kisama and in other parts of West and West Central Africa, these crops may have helped sustain fugitive communities as part of a strategy of what James C. Scott calls "escape agriculture." Scott writes, "The logic of escape agriculture and the friction of appropriation apply not only to a technical complex as a whole, such as shifting cultivation, but to particular crops as well. Of course,

the overall resistance of swiddening to state appropriation lies both in its hilly location and dispersal and in the very botanical diversity it represents." For Scott, crops like sweet potatoes, maize, and especially manioc stand in contrast to the padi-cultivated rice favored by states in Southeast Asia; they require far less labor to cultivate, can be intercropped successfully, and, in the case of sweet potatoes and manioc, can be left underground and can thus both be abandoned and then returned to and also are resistant to enemy burning or seizure. J. C. Scott, *Art of Not Being Governed*, 195–207. While in the case of Kisama and in other parts of West Central Africa, the possibility of leaving manioc untended for up to two years in the ground certainly made it an attractive crop for those who had to flee and return. Maize, manioc, and sweet potatoes did not come to replace a grain like rice as a staple, but rather intersected with yams, plantains, and millet as the major subsistence crops. In other words, because of the preexisting agricultural repertoires and strategies throughout the region, which overall favored shifting cultivation, the labor regimes involved in growing these American cultigens may have represented less of a change than they did in Southeast Asia.

59 See Adam Jones, "Decompiling Dapper: A Preliminary Search for Evidence," *History in Africa* 17 (1990): 171–209; and Olfert Dapper, *Description de l'Afrique . . . avec des cartes et des figures en taille-douce . . . traduite du Flamand [A Translation of "Naukeurige beschrijvinge der Afrikaensche gewesten van Egypten" and "Naukeurige beschrijvinge der Afrikaensche eilanden" by Two Separate Translators]* (Amsterdam: Wolfgang, 1686), 374. Here, "millet" could mean either millet (*eleusine coracana*) or maize (*zea mays*), as seventeenth-century sources are notoriously poor at distinguishing between the two. It seems most likely, however, that here, *milho* typically means millet, though below we see evidence of both being cultivated together in geographic Kisama. For a comparative discussion of the evidence in sixteenth-century east Africa, see Paul E. H. Hair, "Milho, Meixoeira and Other Foodstuffs of the Sofala Garrison, 1505–1525 (Milho, meixoeira et autres aliments de la garnison de Sofala, 1505–1525)," *Cahiers d'études africaines* 17, no. 66/67 (1977): 353–63.

60 Dapper, *Description de l'Afrique*, 374. The contrast in food security is, of course, due to no essential characteristic of any people. However, the diversity of subsistence practices that flourished in the notoriously arid region of geographical Kisama may have helped those living there be less vulnerable to fluctuations in the climate.

61 Dapper, *Description de l'Afrique*, 366.

62 "Carta de André Velho da Fonseca a El-Rei," February 28, 1612, in Brásio, *MMA*, 6:65.

63 Cavazzi, *Descrição histórica*, 1:22.

64 Cavazzi, *Descrição histórica*, 1:22.

65 Dapper, *Description de l'Afrique*, 374.

66 Here, Candido and I both disagree vehemently with Joseph Miller, whose arguments about the relationship of climate to politics in West Central Africa down-

play the impact of Portuguese violence in favor of environmentally deterministic arguments. See Miller, "Significance of Drought"; Candido, *African Slaving Port*, 77.

67 Cadornega, *História geral das guerras angolanas*, 2:95–96.

68 Cadornega, *História geral das guerras angolanas* 2:110.

69 Cadornega, *História geral das guerras angolanas* 2:111.

70 "Letter by Governor Sousa Chicorro to the King of Portugal, Luanda, June 19, 1656," Caixa 6, Doc. 54, AHU.

71 "Letter by Governor Sousa Chicorro to the King of Portugal, Luanda, June 19, 1656," Caixa 6, Doc. 54, AHU.

72 Cadornega, *História geral das guerras angolanas*, 2:102–3.

73 Cadornega, *História geral das guerras angolanas* 2:90.

74 According to Cadornega, however, the envoys who had been sent to negotiate peace with the Portuguese and who had agreed to these terms never returned. He speculates that the envoys were intended only to postpone the Portuguese invasion of their territories. Cadornega, *História geral das guerras angolanas*, 2:90.

75 Cadornega, *História geral das guerras angolanas*, 2:113–14.

76 If earlier evidence is any indication, however, it is likely that there were far more enslaved people on board these Rio de la Plata–bound ships, and that the captains' claims about storms were a ploy to evade taxation regimes and other imperial regulations. See Kara D. Schultz, "'The Kingdom of Angola Is Not Very Far from Here': The South Atlantic Slave Port of Buenos Aires, 1585–1640," *Slavery & Abolition* 36, no. 3 (2015): 424–44.

77 Query of Trans-Atlantic Slave Trade Database.

Chapter 4. (Mis)Taken Identities

1 Here, I use Kathryn McKnight's calculation of distance. Kathryn McKnight, "Confronted Rituals: Spanish Colonial and Angolan 'Maroon' Executions in Cartagena de Indias (1634)," *Journal of Colonialism and Colonial History* 5 (2004): 1–23. While I later dispute some of McKnight's interpretations of evidence from Limón, her narrative in this article and in later work of the ritual killings is excellent. I am further grateful to McKnight for providing me with her exemplary transcriptions of the massive collection of testimonies and evidence concerning the palenque Limón. See also McKnight and Garofalo, *Afro-Latino Voices*.

2 "Papeles tocantes a la Alteracion de los Negros Zimarrones, y Castigos que en ellos hizo el Governador de Cartagena causados en el Año de 1634," Patronato 234, ramo 7, bloque 2, Archivo General de Indias, Seville (hereafter cited as AGI). All testimonies hereafter come from this same *legajo*, which will be abbreviated as AGI 234/7, after which I will note the name of witness or witnesses who testified. Gaspar Angola, Juan Criollo de la Margarita, and Sebastian Angola.

3 AGI 234/7, "Papeles tocantes," Sargento Miguel Antunes, Francisco Julian de Piña, and Juan Ortíz.

4 AGI 234/7, "Papeles tocantes," Juan Criollo de la Margarita, Catalina Angola, and Francisca Criolla.

5 AGI 234/7, "Papeles tocantes," Francisco de la Fuente and Juan de la Mar.

6 AGI 234/7, "Papeles tocantes," Gaspar Angola, Lázaro Angola, Jacinto Angola, and Juan Angola. "Perico" is of course a common nickname for "Pedro," so my focus here is on the difference not in the first name but rather in the last.

7 AGI 234/7, "Papeles tocantes," Pedro Angola (testimony) and Pedro Angola (sentence).

8 Cadornega, *História geral das guerras angolanas*, 2:381.

9 David Wheat, *Atlantic Africa and the Spanish Caribbean, 1570–1640* (Chapel Hill: Published for the Omohundro Institute of Early American History and Culture, Williamsburg, Virginia, by the University of North Carolina Press, 2016).

10 Cavazzi, *Descrição histórica*, 1:22. Nicolau de Abreu Castelo Branco, "Oficio do Governador de Angola," October 19, 1825, Caixa 149 A, AHU.

11 Many scholars of the African Diaspora have faced this challenge by working with ecclesiastical sources. Marriage and baptismal records, for example, provide an unparalleled source for discerning family relationships and community bonds, while the records of *cofradias*, or lay organizations affiliated with churches, can shed light on the social organization and politics in Diasporic locations. Inquisition records, too, can allow us to glimpse details about the individual lives and ideas and experiences of enslaved people, with all of the obvious caveats about employing sources generated through such extreme torture. The danger of relying on these sources—on any archive—is the logical fallacy of conflating the world that it is possible to reconstruct through these sources with the world as it was. Many scholars radically overstate the degree to which the church was important in the lives of enslaved people, simply because they are working with church sources. For an important methodological caution, see R. Ferreira, *Cross-Cultural Exchange*.

12 Resident of Cabo Ledo (anonymous by interviewee's request), interview by author, Cacumba, Angola, July 16, 2010. While it is difficult to date these memories, I suspect that they may reflect the realities of smuggling in the post-1836 (Portuguese abolition of the slave trade) world.

13 Sweet, *Domingos Álvares*, 16. See also Soares, *Devotos da cor*; and Parés, *A formação do candomblé*. Parés's construction of ethnicity and metaethnicity derives from the formulation of Jesús Guanche Pérez ("Contribución al estudio del poblamiento africano en Cuba," *África: Revista do centro de estudos africanos* 18–19 [1996]: 119–38), who borrowed the idea from the Soviet theorist Yulián Vladimirovich Bromlei, *Etnografía teórica* (Moscow: Editorial Nauka, 1986). Thus, the politics animating this theoretical intervention are rooted in Soviet imperialism in Central Asia.

14 Nearly all scholars of the African Diaspora today disavow primordialist views of ethnicity and acknowledge the fluidity of terms of identity in the Diaspora. While some ascribe greater or less agency to colonial agents in assigning names and meanings to the identities of enslaved people, nearly all scholars remain preoccupied with the narrative of origins that Parés critiques so thoroughly. See Parés, *A formação do candomblé*. As I've argued elsewhere, I believe that these supposed terms of identity circulated as claims of political orientation, separate from physical geography. This is in no small part what animates the geographies of reputation. See Krug, "Social Dismemberment, Social (Re)membering."

15 McKnight and Garofalo, *Afro-Latino Voices*, 67.

16 Rodrigues, "História," in Brásio, *MMA*, 4:566–75. Lopès de Lima, *Ensaios sobre a statistica*, 3: xxi.

17 Of those who testified, thirteen were executed by the Spanish: Antón Angola, Gaspar Angola, Francisco Angola, Pedro Angola, Juan Criollo de la Margarita, Lorenzo Criollo, Sebastián Anchico, Domingo Anchico, Juan Angola, Francisco de la Fuente, Lázaro Angola, Juan de la Mar, and Sebastián de Angola Cachorro. The six others, Juan Carabalí, Jacinto Angola, Juan Angola, two different women named Catalina Angola, and Francisca Criolla, were sentenced to exile.

18 AGI 234/7, "Papeles tocantes," Juan de Sotomayor.

19 For a detailed discussion of these killings, see McKnight, "Confronted Rituals."

20 McKnight, "Confronted Rituals."

21 AGI 234/7, "Papeles tocantes," Sebastian Anchico. Sebastian Anchico claimed that this attack was motivated by romantic jealousy.

22 McKnight, "Confronted Rituals."

23 McKnight, "Confronted Rituals."

24 This is all contained in AGI 234/7, "Papeles tocantes."

25 Perico Quisama testified under the name "Pedro Angola." I will discuss his testimony and the meaning of the various, inconsistent ways in which he is named, below. Throughout the Americas, European claims to have "destroyed" maroon communities were rarely true. In most cases, including in the (in)famous supposed destruction of Palmares in Brazil in 1695, "the survivors did what other maroons before and after had done when required to—they melted into the hinterlands to coalesce into new and more remote settlements and begin their free lives anew." See Jane Landers, "Leadership and Authority in Maroon Settlements in Spanish America and Brazil," in *Africa and the Americas: Interconnections during the Slave Trade*, ed. José Curto and Renée Soulodre-La France (Trenton: Africa World Press, 2005), 181. Juan de la Mar notes that, at the time of his testimony, Luis Quisama was in jail. AGI 234/7, "Papeles tocantes," Juan de la Mar.

26 In addition to these seven who are described as "Kisama" by their peers, there is one man whom Lázaro Angola intriguingly calls "Kafuxi" (rendered "Capuche" and "Capiche"). According to Lázaro Angola, Kafuxi participated in an attack against a Spanish farm as well as against the indigenous community at Chambacú.

Kafuxi had fled from his master, Captain Baquesel. Unfortunately, these are all of the details that we have about this tantalizingly named resident of Limón, who is never described outright as "Kisama." AGI 234/7, "Papeles tocantes," Lázaro Angola.

27 For a stimulating discussion of the continuities of rupture in the Atlantic world, see James Sidbury and Jorge Cañizares-Esguerra, "Mapping Ethnogenesis in the Early Modern Atlantic," *William and Mary Quarterly* 68, no. 2 (2011): 181–208. See also the responses, especially James Sweet, "The Quiet Violence of Ethnogenesis," *William and Mary Quarterly* 68, no. 2 (2011): 209–14.

28 Wheat, "First Great Waves," 1–22.

29 AGI, "Carta de Miguel Diez de Armendáriz al Rey," July 24, 1545, Patronato 27, AGI, cited in María del Carmen Borrego Plá, *Cartagena de Indias en el siglo XVI* (Seville, Spain: Escuela de Estudios Hispano-Americanos, Consejo Superior de Investigaciones Científicas, 1983), 430–31.

30 "Cedula que manda que no se proceda contra los negros que de su voluntad bolvieren de paz, y a servier a sus amos, estando alçados," September 7, 1540, cited in *Cedulario indiano*, ed. Diego de Encinas and Alfonso García Gallo (Madrid: Ediciones Cultura Hispánica, 1946), 394.

31 For a review of maroonage in Panamá throughout the sixteenth century, see Ruth Pike, "Black Rebels: The Cimarrons of Sixteenth-Century Panama," *Americas* 64, no. 2 (2007): 243–66; and Jean-Pierre Tardieu, *Cimarrones de Panamá: La forja de una identidad afroamericana en el siglo XVI* (Madrid: Iberoamericana, 2009). For a discussion of their relationship with pirates, see Kris E. Lane, *Pillaging the Empire: Piracy in the Americas, 1500–1750* (Armonk, NY: M. E. Sharpe, 1998).

32 Ortega Valencia to the King Nombre de Dios, February 22, 1573, Panama 11, AGI, cited in *Documents Concerning English Voyages to the Spanish Main, 1569–1580*, ed. Irene Aloha Wright (London: Hakluyt Society, 1932), 46–47.

33 Cristóbal Monte, Nombre de Dios, May 1573, Patronato 267, AGI, cited in *Documents Concerning English Voyages*, 60.

34 John Oxenham, deposition made at Rincóncholon, October 20, 1577, Panama 41, AGI , cited in *Documents Concerning English Voyages*, 170–77.

35 Oxenham testifies that after the conflict with the Spanish, the maroon "leaders ordered them [the other maroons] to give them nothing . . . . They lived on bananas which they picked in the groves, and occasionally a kind-hearted negro gave them a little maize." *Documents Concerning English Voyages*, 176.

36 "Carta escrita por Pedro de Ortega, general de Bayano [Vallano] a su mejestad, y a esta real audiencia," August 30, 1580, Panama, AGI, cited in *Indios y negros en Panamá en los siglos XVI y XVII: Selecciones de los documentos del Archivo General de Indias*, ed. Carol F. Jopling (South Woodstock, VT: Plumsock Mesoamerican Studies, 1994), 359.

37 Heywood and Thornton, *Central Africans, Atlantic Creoles*, 58.

38 Enriqueta Vila Vilar, "The Large-Scale Introduction of Africans into Veracruz and Cartagena," in *Comparative Perspectives on Slavery in New World Plantation*

Societies, ed. Vera D. Rubin and Arthur Tuden (New York: New York Academy of Sciences, 1977), 276.

39 Borrego Plá, *Cartagena de Indias*, 432.

40 AGI, "Carta de Licenciado Mejía al Rey," August 4, 1575, Santa Fe, 187, AGI.

41 For a perspective on the financial impact of the continued conflicts with maroon groups in the seventeenth century, see Enriqueta Vila Vilar, "Cimarronaje en Panamá y Cartagena: El costo de una guerrila en el siglo XVII," *Cahiers du monde hispanique et luso-brésilien* 49 (1987): 77–92.

42 Query of the Trans-Atlantic Slave Trade Database.

43 For a pointed critique of the Trans-Atlantic Slave Trade Database, and in particular its notable gaps in relation to sixteenth-century West Africa, see Green, *Rise of the Trans-Atlantic Slave Trade*, 7–9.

44 Query of Trans-Atlantic Slave Trade Database.

45 Wheat, "First Great Waves," 4.

46 For a discussion of this legislation, see Vila Vilar, "Cimarronaje."

47 "Carta de Gerónimo de Suazo al Rey," February 16, 1603, in Roberto Arrazola, *Palenque: Primer pueblo libre de América* (Cartagena, Columbia: Ediciones Hernández, 1970), 35. For the revolt and subsequent maroonage of Africans enslaved in the gold mines of Zaragoza, see María Cristina Navarrete, "Cimarrones y palenques en las provincias al norte del Nuevo Reino de Grenada, siglo XVII," *Fronteras de la historia* 6 (2001): 97–122. Vila Vilar identifies "Acla cove[,] between Portobelo and Cartagena[, as the] place where . . . the maroons from both places would meet." Vila Vilar, "Cimarronaje," 82.

48 De la Fuente testified that he could not hope to avoid detection by the Spanish after he fled because his facial brands made his identity obvious. See AGI 234/7, "Papeles tocantes," Francisco de la Fuente (el Morisco). Although in sixteenth-century Seville, slave masters frequently branded the faces of those whom they owned, enslaved Moors more commonly suffered this violence than did enslaved Africans from further south. See Ruth Pike, "Sevillian Society in the Sixteenth Century: Slaves and Freedmen," *Hispanic American Historical Review* 47, no. 3 (1967): 244–59. The branding marks on the faces of royal galley slaves, however, were distinctive and readily recognizable. See David Wheat, "Mediterranean Slavery, New World Transformations: Galley Slaves in the Spanish Caribbean, 1578–1635," *Slavery & Abolition* 31, no. 3 (2010): 327–44.

49 AGI 234/7, "Papeles tocantes," Francisco de la Fuente (el Morisco).

50 AGI 234/7, "Papeles tocantes," Juan de la Mar.

51 AGI 234/7, "Papeles tocantes," Juan de la Mar.

52 AGI 234/7, "Papeles tocantes," Juan Criollo de la Margarita.

53 AGI 234/7, "Papeles tocantes," Francisco de la Fuente (el Morisco).

54 AGI 234/7, "Papeles tocantes," Francisco de la Fuente (el Morisco).

55 Miller, *Way of Death*, 386.

56 AGI 234/7, "Papeles tocantes," Francisco de la Fuente (el Morisco).

57 This division remains important, however, in the political discourse of some present-day maroon communities. For Jamaica, see Kenneth Bilby, *True-Born Maroons* (Gainesville: University Press of Florida, 2005).

58 AGI 234/7, "Papeles tocantes," Juan de la Mar.

59 Juan Angola refers to Queen Leonor's father as both Angola and Bondondo. Sebastian Angola also refers to him as Bondondo; Francisca Criolla calls him Domingo Angola exclusively. AGI 234/7, "Papeles tocantes," Juan Angola, Sebastian Angola, and Francisco Criolla. I have been unable to conclusively trace the meaning of "Bondondo." Following traditional approaches to Diaspora scholarship would suggest that it is best to look for places in Angola named Bondondo and to connect Domingo to one of these locations. There are, in fact, a number of towns in Angola called Ndondo—including one in the present-day province of Kwanza Norte and one in present-day Uige—that could easily suffice as putative points of origin for Domingo. However, this descriptor appears nowhere else in any of the documents connected to Limón, nor in any of other sources that scholars typically use to discern patterns relating to African identities in the Americas with which I am familiar, including Sandoval's writings, plantation records and the baptism, marriage, and death records kept by the Catholic church throughout the Iberian-colonized world. In the absence of other evidence that would link this surname to a place, I suggest that "Bondondo" might instead be a kind of nickname. If we understand Bondondo as the bu- (prefix) ndondo, then Domingo's name could have a number of other, more individual meanings. "Bondondo" could simply have referred to the fact that Domingo was a particularly dark-skinned person, as one of the meanings of ndondo in Kimbundu is "dark or very black." However, many of the other glosses of ndondo in Kimbundu are connected to the natural world: seasonally submersed land, a plant with black roots, or a small rat. It is possible that Domingo was called Bondondo because of a semantic link between watered land, plants, and particular kinds of medicine used by powerful *jimbanda* in Angola—as in the case of Kafuxi Ambari's ritual practitioner who attempted to end the drought in Kisama in 1588—and throughout its diasporas. While spiritual power was not strictly hereditary, other palenquerxs widely regarded Domingo's daughter Leonor as a powerful ritual practitioner, and it is probable that Domingo also had some type of spiritual power. Lastly, the small rat called ndondo is the subject of some important proverbs in Kimbundu focusing on the role of the vulnerable: "The 'Ndondo,' who doesn't have a father or mother, doesn't think: let's make an alliance!" It is of course impossible to say conclusively which, if any, of these possible meanings the Bondondo attached to Domingo's name carried. The most compelling possibilities—that "Bondondo" meant either the small rat of the Kimbundu proverbs or the potential ritual connotations of plants and rain-covered land—invite speculation as to the idioms through which palenquerxs and both their free and bonded contemporaries throughout the Americas understood and negotiated with the violence and rup-

ture that were their constant companions. If "Bondondo" meant the rat, then Domingo may have adopted that surname (or others may have begun calling him by that label) as a sign that he acted on the lesson of the proverb. Though if he was indeed born in freedom in the palenque, he may well have known one or both of his parents for much of his life, the palenquerxs were well aware of the alienation from kin and community that formed the backdrop for their presence in the Americas. Unlike those in the palenque who preferred to accommodate the Spanish, Domingo Bondondo may well have believed that it was unwise to make alliances from a position of vulnerability. Conversely, if "Bondondo" was meant to convey an association with ritual power, and perhaps a rain-specific medicine, then Domingo's presence in the palenque and his relationship to the queen point to ways in which the increasingly aggressive politics that Queen Leonor promoted and the ritual murders in which she participated may have been intended to heal some of the damage wrought by violence and slavery and restore fertility to the community. See João Albino Alves Manso, *Dicionário etimológico Bundo-Português: Ilustrado com muitos milhares de exemplos, entre os quais 2.000 provérbios indígenas* (Lisbon: Tipografia Silvas, 1951), 873–74. For a discussion of Angolan healing and ritual practices in the Diaspora, see Sweet, *Recreating Africa*. Manso, *Dicionário etimológico Bundo-Português*, 874. McKnight, "Confronted Rituals." Unfortunately, the meaning of "Bondondo" remains unclear, and I cannot discern why Juan Angola called Domingo both Angola and Bondondo while Sebastian Angola called him only Bondondo, and Francisca Criolla called him only Angola. Of the three, Sebastian Angola spent the longest period in the palenque at six years, and knew Domingo from the time he was taken from Piña's farm. It is entirely possible, and even probable, that he knew Domingo before his capture, as well. Juan Angola had spent less than a year inside the palenque, as he had joined only in the aftermath of the Limoneses' destruction of Diego Marquez's farm, where he had been enslaved. However, as we shall see, it is likely that he, too was familiar with many of residents of Limón, since the enslaved residents of Marquez's farm had a particularly intimate relationship with Limón. Whether or not Juan Angola knew Domingo before his arrival in Limón, however, is impossible to say. Francisca Criolla, too, had been in Limón for only a short time since the palenquerxs had taken her from the farm of Gomez Hernandez de Rivera, where she was enslaved. Since arriving in Limón, however, she had worked as a cook in the home of Magdalena, the palenque-born sister-in-law of Queen Leonor. As a member of the household of Leonor's extended family, it is likely that she knew Domingo well, at least since her arrival in Limón. AGI 234/7, Gaspar Angola, Lázaro Angola, Jacinto Angola, Juan Angola, Juan de la Mar, Sebastian Angola, and Francisca Criolla.

60 AGI 234/7, "Papeles tocantes," Gaspar Angola and Juan de la Mar. McKnight remarks that Gaspar Angola "uses the Amerindian (Chibcha) word mohana, which means shaman, to name Queen Leonor, suggesting a transculturation

that allows him to recognize a similarity between local political-spiritual practices and those he may have known in Angola." Because Chibcha was spoken
in the central highlands region surrounding present-day Bogotá, it is unlikely
that those who lived near the Caribbean coast would have adopted a term from
this language. The term does appear broadly in seventeenth-century Spanish legal
documents from the Americas, meaning that it is possible that the Spanish simply
adopted it from Chibcha or another indigenous language and applied it broadly.
For example, in 1651, the inquisitors making a case against Mateo Arará in Cartagena defined a mohan as "the same as a witch and the master of them, because
they operate through words and herbs and a pact with the devil." In other words,
it is conceivable that *mohan* represents a Spanish conceptual category articulated
through an indigenous word, rather than a meaningful category for the Limoneses. It is also possible, however, that the Spanish misappropriated an African term
for a particular kind of ritual practitioner. In the transcription of Juan de la Mar's
testimony, mohan is spelled as *mohongo*, offering an insight into the potential
etymology of the term. If we understand mohongo as *mu-hongo*, then *mohan*
could be derived from a Kimbundu name for sacred objects used to bring wealth
to its owners. See "Confronted Rituals." McKnight mistakenly attributes this use
of mohan to Anton Angola, when it in fact comes from the testimony of Gaspar
Angola. Pablo Gomez, personal communication, May 7, 2012. Inquisition case
against Mateo Arará, cited in Luz Adriana May Restrepo, "Botanica y medicina
africanas en la Nueva Granada, siglo XVII," *Historia crítica* 19 (2000): 37. Manso,
Dicionário etimológico Bundo-Português, 1:170. For more on *mohan*, see Gómez,
Experiential Caribbean, 11–12.

61 Scholars normally associate Arará-identified people with Allada, an inland
kingdom in present-day Benin. Allada was a powerful kingdom in the region
throughout the seventeenth century until it was defeated by Dahomey in 1724.
See Robin Law, *Ouidah: The Social History of a West African Slaving "Port," 1727–
1892* (Athens: Ohio University Press, 2004), 105.

62 AGI 234/7, "Papeles tocantes," Juan Criollo de la Margarita and Lorenzo Criollo.
For Tunba, see Francisco de la Fuente (el Morisco) and Juan Carabalí.

63 AGI 234/7, "Papeles tocantes," Sebastian Angola.

64 For an excellent discussion of community, morality, civic virtue, and ethnic identities, see Bruce Berman and John Lonsdale, *Unhappy Valley: Conflict in Kenya
and Africa*, 2 vols. (Athens: Ohio University Press, 1992).

65 AGI 234/7, "Papeles tocantes," Juan de la Mar.

66 "Carta de André Velho da Fonseca a El-Rei," February 28, 1612, in Brásio, *MMA*, 6:65.

67 AGI 234/7, "Papeles tocantes," Francisco de la Fuente (el Morisco).

68 AGI 234/7, "Papeles tocantes," Sebastian Anchico and Domingo Anchico. However, Manuel Angola; Lorenso Angola, who had fled from Alonso Martin; and
Lorenso Angola and Anton Angola from Monopox, former residents of Polín,
did participate in the attack on Diego Marquez's farm. See AGI 234/7, "Papeles

tocantes," Juan de la Mar. In the past it seems that the two communities had more congenial relationships despite any underlying political differences, as several high-ranking members of Limón mention amicable interactions with Polín. It is impossible to say for certain what precisely prompted the Limoneses to attack their neighbors. Both of the Anchico men mention that the goal of the raid was to obtain either more women in general or a particular woman who was the object of Juan Criollo's desires, though Francisco de la Fuente also remarks that Francisco "the Hunchback" Criollo, Manuel Congo, and Jarangongo, all of whom were enslaved by Juan de Sotomayor, told the Limoneses that the people of Polín engaged in acts of anthropophagy. AGI 234/7, "Papeles tocantes," Sebastian Anchico, Domingo Anchico, and Francisco de la Fuente (el Morisco).

69 AGI 234/7, "Papeles tocantes," Juan de la Mar.

70 AGI 234/7, "Papeles tocantes," Sebastian Angola. According to Sandoval, "Biafaras" came from the same region as Brans and Balantas in coastal Upper Guinea (present-day Guinea-Bissau). Alonso de Sandoval, *De instauranda aethiopum salute: El mundo de la esclavitud negra en America* (Bogota: Biblioteca de la Presidencia de Colombia, [1627] 1956), 61. Just as with Leonor, the trial documents contain no information about Diego and Gonzalo's mother, nor any contextual clues that might help us unpack the meaning of "Chale."

71 Brown, *Reaper's Garden*, 7–8. For a provocative analysis of the relationship between the language of ethnicity, morality, and politics, see Berman and Lonsdale, *Unhappy Valley*.

72 McKnight, "Confronted Rituals."

73 Juan de la Mar, translated in McKnight, "Confronted Rituals."

74 McKnight, "Confronted Rituals."

75 Janzen, *Lemba*, 3–4.

76 Cited in Janzen, *Lemba*, 279.

77 Janzen, *Lemba*, 291.

78 AGI 234/7, "Papeles tocantes," Juan Criollo de la Margarita.

79 AGI 234/7, "Papeles tocantes," Gaspar Angola.

80 AGI 234/7, "Papeles tocantes," Juan Criollo de la Margarita.

81 It is not enough to simply state that African identities in both Africa and the Americas were fluid. Rather, it is essential to interrogate the politics animating these fluidities. For a critique of Eurocentric epistemology in regards to African identities, see Sweet, "Mistaken Identities?"

82 See Heintze, *Asilo ameaçado*.

83 Heintze, "Historical Notes on the Kisama of Angola," 412–14; A. Ferreira, "La Kisama," 88–89; Brandão, "Diário da marcha," 407–8.

84 See chapter 3.

85 AGI 234/7, "Papeles tocantes," Juan de la Mar.

86 AGI 234/7, "Papeles tocantes," Jacinto Angola and Francisco de la Fuente (el Morisco).

87 AGI 234/7, "Papeles tocantes," Jacinto Angola.

88 AGI 234/7, "Papeles tocantes," Jacinto Angola, Lázaro Angola, Juan Carabali, Juan Angola, Catalina Angola, Juan de la Mar, and Sebastian Angola.

89 AGI 234/7, "Papeles tocantes," Jacinto Angola.

90 Thornton, "Angola e as origens de Palmares," 55.

91 AGI 234/7, "Papeles tocantes," Pedro Angola. *Catiba de mangele*, or *cativo de mangle*, according to the 1869 *American Journal of Pharmacy*, "is used in this country [Panamá] for catching flies. . . . It is also used as a coating for the bottoms of canoes and small vessels, being boiled with quick lime and applied warm." John M. Maisch, "On Some Panama Drugs," *American Journal of Pharmacy* 61, no. 18 (1869): 236–37. Though a wild-gathered product, it was valuable enough for Spanish landowners in the early seventeenth century to keep a supply and for palenquerxs to work in exchange for it, as it was an effective balm for troubling and infected sores.

92 AGI 234/7, "Papeles tocantes," Pedro Angola.

93 AGI 234/7, "Papeles tocantes," Lázaro Angola.

94 See José María Oliva Melgar and Carlos Martínez Shaw, *Sistema atlántico español: Siglos XVII–XIX* (Madrid: Marcial Pons, Ediciones de Historia, 2005).

95 Alfred Métraux, "The Concept of Soul in Haitian Vodu," *Southwestern Journal of Anthropology* 2, no. 1 (1946): 87.

96 Maureen Warner-Lewis, "African Continuities in the Rastafari Belief System," *Caribbean Quarterly* 39, no. 3–4 (1993): 115.

97 AGI 234/7, "Papeles tocantes," Francisco Julián de Piña.

98 AGI 234/7, "Papeles tocantes," Gaspar Angola and Francisco de la Fuente (el Morisco).

Chapter 5. Fugitive Angola

1 The scholarship on Palmares is vast and continues to expand. For an overview of the scholarly literature, see Robert Nelson Anderson, "The Quilombo of Palmares: A New Overview of a Maroon State in Seventeenth-Century Brazil," *Journal of Latin American Studies* 28, no. 3 (1996): 545–66; Pedro Paulo Funari and Aline Vieira de Carvalho, *Palmares, ontem e hoje* (Rio de Janeiro: Zahar, 2005). Referring to Palmares as a *quilombo* reflects much more about twentieth- and twenty-first-century Brazilian politics than it does about seventeenth-century realities, as Portuguese sources did not begin to use this Imbangala term for maroon societies more broadly until the very end of the seventeenth century. Prior to this, the Kimbundu term *mocambo* was far more common. While quilombo is to an extent anachronistic, I use it here because my arguments lie on the borderlands between history and the production of historical memories in the context of evolving, historicized politics of the present.

2 Similarly, Sílvia Hunold Lara observes that while nearly all scholars note the April 1678 treaty that Ngana Zumba signed with Portuguese governor Aires de

Souza de Castro in the course of a broader narrative arc about betrayal, they ignore the actual terms and conditions of the treaty. See Sílvia Hunold Lara, "Marronnage et pouvoir colonial: Palmares, Cucaúet les frontières de la liberté au Pernambouc à la fin du XVIIe siècle," *Annales: Histoire, Sciences Sociales* 62, no. 3 (2007): 639–62.

3 BBC News, "Legacy of Brazil's Slave Leader," September 22, 2006, http://news.bbc.co.uk/2/hi/americas/5370962.stm.

4 Sílvia Hunold Lara, "Como fé, lei, e rei: Um sobado africano em Pernambuco no século XVII," in *Mocambos de Palmares: Histórias e fontes (séculos XVI–XIX)*, ed. Flávio dos Santos Gomes (Rio de Janeiro: 7Letras, 2010), 100–101.

5 For an important critique of the politics animating the enduring Herskovitsian nature of Diasporic scholarship, see Matory, *Black Atlantic Religion*; Palmié, *Wizards and Scientists*.

6 Bandeirantes were the infamous São Paulo based colonial shock troops who not only enslaved indigenous people and attacked maroon communities, but also expanded the region of Portuguese imperial domination.

7 "Relação das guerras feitas aos Palmares de Pernambuco no tempo do governador dom Pedro de Almeida de 1675 a 1678 (M. S. offerecido pelo Exm. Sr. Conselheiro Drummond)," *Revista do Instituto Histórico e Geográfico Brasileiro* 22 (1859 [1678]): 304; emphasis in italics in the transcribed text; emphasis in bold mine. The version of the text published in the *Revista* comes from the Biblioteca de Évora. Two others, found in the Biblioteca Nacional and the Arquivo Histórico Ultramarino in Lisbon, are published in Décio Freitas, *República de Palmares: Pesquisa e comentários em documentos históricos do século XVII* (Maceió: Edufal: Ideário Comunicação e Cultura, 2004), 19–48. See Thornton, "Angola e as origens de Palmares," 59n9.

8 Severiano described his investigations along the Bolivian border and throughout Mato Grosso in João Severiano da Fonseca, *Viagem ao redor do Brasil, 1875–1878* (Rio de Janeiro: Typ. de Pinheiro, 1880). His claim about the meaning of "Kafuxi," however, is, according to Alfredo Brandão, made in *Origem de alguns nomes patronímicos da provincia das Alagoas* (Maceió: Revista do IAGA, 1876). The only copy of this text on record is in the Zentralbibliothek in Zurich, Switzerland, and I have therefore been unable to consult the original and cannot account for how Severiano glosses the *Andala* portion of the toponym. My knowledge of Severiano's claim comes from Brandão's citation. See Alfredo Brandão, *Viçosa de Alagoas: O municipio e a cidade (notas historicas, geographicas, e archeologicas)* (Recife: Imprensa Industrial, 1914), 25n12; emphasis in the original.

9 Brandão, *Viçosa de Alagoas*, 24–25.

10 Cited in Brandão, *Viçosa de Alagoas*, 257.

11 Edison Carneiro, *O quilombo do Palmares, 1630–1695* (São Paulo: Editora Brasiliense, 1947), 82, 182.

12 R. K. Kent, "Palmares: An African State in Brazil," *Journal of African History* 6, no. 2 (1965): 169. Thirty years later, Robert Nelson Anderson deftly illustrated

the many instances of Kent mistranslating primary sources and omitting evidence that complicated his conclusions. See R. N. Anderson, "Quilombo of Palmares," 545–66.

13 Sidney Mintz and Richard Price, *An Anthropological Approach to the Afro-American Past: A Caribbean Perspective* (Philadelphia: Institute for the Study of Human Issues, 1976).

14 Kent, "Palmares," 175.

15 Nei Lopes, *Enciclopédia brasileira da diáspora africana* (São Paulo: Selo Negro Edições, 2004), 58, 152, 553; emphasis in the original.

16 John Thornton confirms that he has not encountered the name Andalaquituche outside of the "Relação." John Thornton, personal communication, March 23, 2011.

17 See Heintze, "Angolan Vassal Tributes," 57–78.

18 "Cópia da carta ao Soba Cafuchi, que pede o baptismo," February 23, 1693, Caixa 14, Doc. 100, AHU, and "Consulta do Conselho Ultramarino sobre o Soba de Quiçama," March 13, 1694, AHU, Cód. 554, fls. 79–79 v., in *MMA* 14:279–81, 349–50 cited in *MMA* 14:279–81, 349–50.

19 Lopes, *Enciclopédia brasileira*, 113. Cadornega writes, "Saint Benedict of Palermo, Head of the Kingdom of Sicily, where he flourished in virtue and sanctity; and there is no shortage of Authors who say that he was from Ethiopia, that his mother was from this kingdom of Angola from the province of Quisama, that she was captured while young." Cadornega, *História geral das guerras angolanas*, 3:27; João Pereira Bastos, *Angola e Brasil, duas terras lusíadas do Atlântico* (Lourenço Marques: Minerva Central, 1964), 40.

20 Flávio dos Santos Gomes, "Apresentação: Palmares, historiografia e fontes," in *Mocambos de Palmares: Histórias e fontes (séculos XVI–XIX)*, ed. Flávio dos Santos Gomes (Rio de Janeiro: 7Letras, 2010), 9–10. Thornton and Heywood found the early eighteenth-century recopies of the correspondences of the governor of Pernambuco with the king of Portugal from 1654 to roughly 1720—sources unavailable in Brazil—the Arquivo da Universidade de Coimbra (AUC) in 2006, and Thornton cited some in his article in 2008. They have yet to be more widely utilized, however. John K. Thornton, "Les Etats de l'Angola et la formation de Palmares (Bresil)," *Annales de'histoire e sciences sociales* 63, no. 4 (2008): 769–98.

21 Couto was born in Kongo and was likely a native Kikongo speaker, though Bontinck argues that the true author of the catechism was native Kimbundu speaker Dionisio de Faria Baretto.

22 It is somewhat misleading to speak of Kimbundu as a singular language in the mid-seventeenth century, when the creation of Kimbundu as a trade-oriented *lingua franca* was an ongoing process through the nineteenth and even twentieth centuries. See Vieira-Martinez, "Building Kimbundu." These translations were often marked by multiple layers of mutual misunderstandings. See Wyatt Macgaffey,

"Dialogues of the Deaf: Europeans on the Atlantic Coast of Africa," in *Implicit Understandings: Observing, Reporting, and Reflecting on the Encounters between Europeans and Other Peoples in the Early Modern Era*, ed. Stuart Schwartz (New York: Cambridge University Press, 1994).

23 I make use here of the 1661 Capuchin adaptation of the original Jesuit text from 1642. Antonio do Couto and Francisco Paccónio, *Gentilis Angollae fidei mysteriis* (Rome: Congregatio de Propaganda Fide, 1661), 86; emphasis mine.

24 See, for example, Bernardo Maria de Cannecattim, *Diccionario da lingua bunda, ou angolense, explicada na portugueza, e latina* (Lisboa: Impressão Regia, 1804), 221; Maia, *Dicionário complementar*, 154; William H. Sanders and William Edwards Fay, *Vocabulary of the Umbundu Language: Comprising Umbundu-English and English-Umbundu* (Boston: T. Todd, 1885), 10; and Barbosa, *Dicionário cokwe-português*, 615.

25 The literature on the politics of witchcraft in Central Africa is vast. See, for example, Janzen, *Lemba*; Peter Geschiere, *The Modernity of Witchcraft: Politics and the Occult in Postcolonial Africa* (Charlottesville: University Press of Virginia, 1997); and Wyatt MacGaffey, *Kongo Political Culture: The Conceptual Challenge of the Particular* (Bloomington: Indiana University Press, 2000).

26 Cavazzi, *Descrição histórica*, 1:106.

27 See Janzen, *Lemba*. For examples from West Africa, see G. Ugo Nwokeji, *The Slave Trade and Culture in the Bight of Biafra: An African Society in the Atlantic World* (New York: Cambridge University Press, 2010); Sweet, *Domingos Álvares*.

28 Cadornega, *História geral das guerras angolanas*, 3:322.

29 Cavazzi, *Descrição histórica*, 1:106.

30 For a detailed discussion of the commodification of relationships throughout the region, and the role of debt in transforming political and social relationships, see Miller, *Way of Death*.

31 "Ofício do Secretário Geral do Governador de Angola," November 4, 1853, cód. 111, fl. 122v., AHNA, cited in Ferreira, *Cross-Cultural Exchange*, 67.

32 See, for example, the cases cited in João de Castro Maia Veiga Figueiredo, "Feitiçaria na Angola oitocentista: Razões por detrás de uma suposta maior tolerância administrativa face a crenças locais," *Revista de Humanidades* 11, no. 29 (2011): 21–51.

33 Candido, *African Slaving Port*, 228.

34 There are many examples from Angola and throughout West and West Central Africa of the role of judicial processes in enslavement. Ferreira cites a mid-nineteenth-century process in Bié in southern Angola in which "the judge would prepare a poisonous drink with herbs, which both accuser and defendant would drink. They would then perform a ceremonial dance until one of them collapsed due to the effect of the drink. If the plaintiff were the first to collapse, he or she would have to pay 'six slaves, two cows and two goats to the accuser.' If the

defendant collapsed first, 'he would be left to die, since he would not receive an antidote to the poisonous drink. His assets and properties would then be taken away and his relatives would be sold as slaves.'" Ferreira, *Cross-Cultural Exchange*, 198. Perhaps the most well-known example of judicial processes being used to generate captives for sale is the Ibiniukpabi oracle at Arochukwu in the Niger Delta. See Nwokeji, *Slave Trade and Culture*.

35 For a discussion of individuals taking names that marked the conditions of their enslavement in the nineteenth century, see Daniel Domingues da Silva, "The Kimbundu Diaspora to Brazil," *African Diaspora* 8, no. 2 (2015): 213.

36 Thornton, "Les Etats de l'Angola," 770.

37 "Journael van de voyagie," in Carneiro, *O quilombo do Palmares*, 234–37.

38 "Journael van de voyagie," in Carneiro, *O quilombo do Palmares*, 237.

39 R. N. Anderson, "Quilombo of Palmares," 556–57.

40 "Relação das guerras feitas," 306.

41 Sílvia Hunold Lara, "Palmares and Cucaú: Political Dimensions of a Maroon Community in Late Seventeenth-Century Brazil," *12th Annual Gilda Lehrman International Conference* (New Haven, CT: Yale University, 2010).

42 "Bando do sargendo-mor Manuel Lopes chamando à obediência o capitão Zumbi dos Palamres (1680)," cited in Carneiro, *O quilombo dos Palmares*, 247.

43 See, for example, Décio Freitas, *Palmares: A guerra dos escravos* (Porto Alegre, Brazil: Editora Movimento, 1973). For a critique of the historiographical silence on the treaty and for the polemical interpretations of both its negotiation and Zumbi's rebellion, see Lara, "Palmares and Cucaú."

44 For a parallel discussion of discourses dissent around the terms of a treaty within a Jamaican Maroon community, see Krug, "Social Dismemberment, Social (Re) membering," 537–58.

45 "Requerim.to que aos pés de VMg.do humildem.to prostrado fás em seu nome, e em aquelle de todos os officiaes e Soldados do terço de Infantr.a São Paulista de que He M.e de campo Domingos George volho, que actualmte serve a VMag. de na guerra dos Palmares, contra os negros rebelados nas capitanias de Pern.co," cited in Ernesto Ennes, *As guerras nos Palmares (subsidios para a sua história)* (São Paulo: Companhia Editora Nacional, 1938), 325.

46 R. N. Anderson, "Quilombo of Palmares," 559.

47 Thornton, "Les Etats de l'Angola," 774. Thornton's critique of Anderson does not appear in the French version of this article in print, but rather in the English original.

48 Manso, *Dicionário etimológico Bundo-Português*, 2:1712; emphasis in the original.

49 Barbosa, *Dicionário cokwe-português*, 385, 707. Note that both the Kimbundu and Cokwe glosses I have provided here are in class concord with "Angola." It is possible that the Kimbundu and Cokwe terms here reflect two different roots—the Cokwe term relating more directly to the Kimbundu term *nganga*—that, deeper in antiquity, were related. Carolyn Vieira-Martinez, personal communication, August 5, 2012.

Chapter 6. "The Ashes of Revolutionary Fires Burn Hot"

1 See, for example, Miller, *Way of Death*; José C. Curto, *Enslaving Spirits: The Portuguese-Brazilian Alcohol Trade at Luanda and its Hinterland, c. 1550–1830* (Boston: Brill, 2004); Roquinaldo Ferreira, "Atlantic Microhistories: Mobility, Personal Ties, and Slaving in the Black Atlantic World (Angola and Brazil)," in *Cultures of the Lusophone Black Atlantic*, ed. Nancy Priscilla Naro, Dave Treece, and Roger Sansi-Roca (New York: Palgrave Macmillan, 2007); Mariana Candido, "Merchants and the Business of the Slave Trade at Benguela, 1750–1850," *African Economic History*, no. 35 (2007): 1–30; and Jacopo Corrado, *The Creole Elite and the Rise of Angolan Protonationalism: 1870–1920* (Amherst, NY: Cambria Press, 2008); Candido, *African Slaving Port*.

2 Nicolau Abreu de Castelo Branco, Ofícios para o reino, September 4, 1824, Caixa 11, n. 14, f. 19, AHNA; emphasis mine.

3 Compare Castelo Branco's complaints to those of Portuguese governor in Luanda Sousa Chicorro in 1655, as discussed in chapter 3. See Consulta do Conselho Ultramarino, "Exame das cartas do Governador de Angola acerca do estado da Provincia, guerra da Quiçama e do Congo," July 13, 1655, in Brásio, *MMA*, 11:498–99. See also R. Ferreira, *Cross-Cultural Exchange*.

4 Mariana Candido, "Enslaving Frontiers: Slavery, Trade and Identity in Benguela, 1780–1850" (Toronto: York University, 2006), 4, 23; R. Ferreira, *Cross-Cultural Exchange*, 35; Candido, *African Slaving Port*.

5 "Carta do Rei do Congo a Paulo III," February 21, 1535, cited in Brásio, *MMA*, 2:38.

6 See Heintze, "Historical Notes," 411.

7 "Carta régia para o governador geral de Angola," November 23, 1735, cod. 546, fls. 92v-93, AHU; "Carta régia para o governador geral de Angola," November 27, 1746, cod. 546, fl. 153, AHU; "Carta de João Jacques de Magalhães a el rei," August 3, 1747, Caixa 35, Doc. 125, AHU; "Carta de António de Vasconcelhos a el rei," June 12, 1762, Caixa 45, Doc. 44, AHU.

8 Cadornega, *História geral das guerras angolanas*, 3:248–49.

9 "Carta de António Álvares da Cunha a el rei," December 4, 1754, Caixa 39, Doc. 89, AHU. For a general discussion of fugitivity in this period, see R. Ferreira, "Slave Flights and Runaway Communities."

10 See R. Ferreira, *Cross-Cultural Exchange*, Miller, *Way of Death*.

11 Joseph Miller, "Kings, Lists, and History in Kasanje," *History in Africa* 6 (1979): 53.

12 Daniel Domingues da Silva, *The Atlantic Slave Trade from West Central Africa* (New York: Cambridge University Press, 2017), 66.

13 "Memória dos Usos, Ritos e Costumes dos Sobas e mais Povos desta Jurisdição," 1820, lata 347, pasta 30, IHGB, cited in R. Ferreira, *Cross-Cultural Exchange*, 197.

14 Evá Sebestyén, Jan Vansina, and Manoel Correia Leitão, "Angola's Eastern Hinterland in the 1750s: A Text Edition and Translation of Manoel Correia Leitão's 'Voyage' (1755-1756)," *History in Africa* 26 (1999): 339.

15 Cavazzi, *Descrição histórica*, 2:210.

16 Cadornega, *História geral das guerras angolanas*, 1:70.

17 Cavazzi, *Descrição histórica*, 2:210.

18 It is not surprising that over the longue durée I discuss, political powers would wax and wane. In a similar three centuries of Iberian history, for example, no one would expect any type of equivalent political stability. In the case of West Central Africa, the civil wars that ravaged the Kingdom of Kongo for nearly half of the seventeenth century certainly led to a far different political landscape in the eighteenth century. Mariana Candido, too, details the ways in which the Portuguese presence at Kakonda eventually quashed the political power of Soba Kakonda in the nineteenth century. See Candido, *African Slaving Port*, 228. What is unique in the case of Kafuxi Ambari is that in spite of a long, seemingly dormant period, his reputation remained intact well into the late nineteenth and twentieth century, when it again directly animated resistance.

19 Paulo Martins Pinheiro de Lacerda, "Notícias das regiões e povos de Quisama e do Mussulo, 1798," *Annaes Marítimos e Coloniaes* 6, no. 4 (1846): 126.

20 Report of José Ignácio de Sousa Andrade, January 13, 1885, Sala 1L, Caixa 6/790, Doc. 227, AHU; "Apontamento de Antônio José de Seixas," December 13, 1856, papéis de Sá da Bandeira, maço 827, AHU, cited in Ferreira, "Slave Flights and Runaway Communities," 87n77.

21 For an analysis of the ethnographic account as genre, see Jan Vansina, "The Ethnographic Account as a Genre in Central Africa," in *European Sources for Sub-Saharan Africa before 1900: Use and Abuse*, ed. Beatrix Heintze and Adam Jones (Stuttgart: Franz Steiner Verlag Wiesbaden, 1987), 433–44.

22 Livingstone, *Missionary Travels*, 440.

23 Anthropologists have vigorously debated whether or not the Khoisan-speaking people living in the Kalahari desert are remnants of ancient subsistence practices marginalized by "invading" Bantu-speaking agrarian people, or whether the Khoi and San identities were forged in relation to and in reaction against the violence, rupture, theft, and slavery associated with colonialism. See Edwin N. Wilmsen et al., "Paradigmatic History of San-Speaking Peoples and Current Attempts at Revision (and Comments and Replies)," *Current Anthropology* 31, no. 5 (1990): 489–524.

24 See chapters 1 and 3.

25 F. G. H. Price, "A Description of the Quissama Tribe," *Journal of the Anthropological Institute of Great Britain and Ireland* 1 (1872): 190.

26 Bilby, *True-Born Maroons*. Anecdotally, when I was working in Jamaica during the summer of 2004, I happened to arrive in the Maroon village of Accompong on Emancipation Day (August 1). While the rest of the island marked the day with festivals and celebrations, in Accompong, people remarked with disdain that they had nothing to celebrate, as they had emancipated themselves and had not waited for the British to do it.

27 Monteiro even remarks upon the introduction of steamships. J. J. Monteiro, "On the Quissama Tribe of Angola," *Journal of the Anthropological Institute of Great Britain and Ireland* 5 (1876): 198. See also Achim von Oppen and Beatrix Heintze, eds., *Angola on the Move: Transport Routes, Communications, and History* (Frankfurt am Main: Lembeck, 2008).

28 "Deligéncia de Policia a Quissama—tenente Alberto da Silva Pais," September 26, 1911, 2/2/17/4, Calulo, AHM.

29 *História de Angola* (Porto: Afrontamento, 1965), 5.

30 *História de Angola*, 49; emphasis in the original.

31 When referring specifically to the Jamaican Maroons, who have their own political identity, I capitalize the term "Maroons." Otherwise, I use the uncapitalized version, "maroons," to refer to all who fled enslavement.

32 See Krug, "Social Dismemberment, Social Remembering."

33 Bilby, *True-Born Maroons*, 33–34.

34 Dea Drndarska and Ange-Séverin Malanda, *Pepetela et l'écriture du mythe et de l'histoire* (Paris: Harmattan, 2000), 23.

35 Pepetela, *As aventuras de Ngunga* (Lisbon: Edições 70, 1976), 57–58.

36 Heywood, *Njinga of Angola*, 245–57.

37 Dionísio Gonçalves, interview by author, Muxima, July 9, 2010. For a comparison with the Protestant missions the Central Highlands, see Linda Heywood, "Towards an Understanding of Modern Political Ideology in Africa: The Case of the Ovimbundu of Angola," *Journal of Modern African Studies* 36, no. 1 (1998): 139–67; and Didier Péclard, "Religion and Politics in Angola: The Church, the Colonial State and the Emergence of Angolan Nationalism, 1940–1961," *Journal of Religion in Africa* 28, no. 2 (1998): 160–86.

38 See Serafim Quintino's blog, Kudisanza, http://kudisanza.wordpress.com/2010 /05/10/descoberto-tumulo-do-rei-da-kissama/, last accessed April 15, 2018. For more autobiographical details about Quintino and CNAL, see Development Workshop Angola, Youth Ambassadors of Peace and Citizenship, "Youth Participating in Decision Making: Angola Research Paper," June 2007, http:// www.iapss.org/aac/belgrade2009/literature_english/youth_participation_in _decision-making_in_conflict_and_10.pdf.

39 While CNAL has had some limited success in attracting missionary attention, Mariana Candido called my attention to the Angolan discursive genre of speculative tourism, mentioning the museums, resorts, and sites of historical memory scattered throughout the nation intended for tourists who simply do not exist.

40 "Carta de Frederico Augusto Esteves, Capitania Mor da Quissama, ao Chefe da Secretaria Militar do Distrito do Cuanza," August 1, 1916, 2/2/45/7, Muxima, AHM.

41 For a discussion of a similar process in Cuba, for example, see Ada Ferrer, *Insurgent Cuba: Race, Nation, and Revolution, 1868–1898* (Chapel Hill: University of North Carolina Press, 1999). For Puerto Rico, see Francisco A. Scarano, "The

Jíbaro Masquerade and the Subaltern Politics of Creole Identity Formation in Puerto Rico, 1745–1823," *American Historical Review* 101, no. 5 (1996): 1398–431.

42 Greg Tate, *Everything but the Burden: What White People Are Taking from Black Culture* (New York: Broadway Books, 2003).

43 Gilberto Freyre, *Casa grande and senzala: Formação de família brasileira sob o regimen de economía patriarchal* (Rio de Janeiro: Maia and Schmidt, 1933).

44 For an extensive interrogation of lusotropicalism and its impact on politics and culture in contemporary Angola, see Jessica Krug, "The Strange Life of Lusotropicalism in Luanda: On Race, Nationality, Gender, and Sexuality in Angola," in *Black Subjects in Africa and Its Diasporas: Race and Gender in Research and Writing*, ed. Benjamin Talton and Quincy T. Mills (New York: Palgrave Macmillan US, 2011), 109–27.

45 See Obi, *Fighting for Honor.*

46 Matory, *Black Atlantic Religion.*

47 For a recent example of these paradoxical claims, see Gomes, "Apresentação," 7.

48 Jessita Maria Nogueira Moutinho, "A paulistanidade revista: Algumas reflexões sobre um discurso político," *Tempo Social* 3, no. 1–2 (1991): 110.

49 Curiously, from the beginning of the twentieth century until today, a strange bifurcation between scholars who claim that there is an extensive bibliography on Palmares and those who claim that Palmares is little studied. For examples of the former position, see Nina Rodrigues, *Os africanos no Brasil* (São Paulo: Companhia Editora Nacional, 1932); Gérard Police, *Quilombos dos Palmares: Lectures sur un marronnage brésilien* (Matoury Cedex, French Guiana: Ibis Rouge, 2003); Lara, "Como fé, lei, e rei." For the latter position, see Gomes, "Apresentação."

50 The most important works of the initial period include Rodrigues, *Os africanos no Brasil*; Ernesto Ennes, *Os Palmares: Subsídios para a sua história* (Lisbon: Arquivo Histórico Ultramarino, 1937); Carneiro, *O quilombo do Palmares*; Kent, "Palmares," 161–75; Freitas, *Palmares*. For the latter period, see especially Clóvis Moura, *Quilombos, resistência ao escravismo* (São Paulo: Editora Atica, 1987); Péret, *O quilombo de Palmares*; Pedro Paulo A. Funari et al., *The Archaeology of Palmares and Its Contribution to the Understanding of the History of African-America Culture* (Columbia: South Carolina Institute of Archaeology and Anthropology, 1995); João José Reis and Flávio dos Santos Gomes, *Liberdade por um fio: História dos quilombos no Brasil* (São Paulo, Brazil: Companhia das Letras, 1996); Police, *Quilombos dos Palmares*; Flávio dos Santos Gomes, *Palmares: escravidão e liberdade no Atlântico Sul* (São Paulo: Contexto, 2005); Thornton, "Les Etats de l'Angola," 769–98; Flávio dos Santos Gomes, *Mocambos de Palmares: histórias e fontes (séculos XVI–XIX)* (Rio de Janeiro: 7Letras, 2010); Flávio dos Santos Gomes, *De olho em Zumbi dos Palmares: Histórias, símbolos e memória social* (São Paulo: Claro Enigma, 2011).

51 Article 68 of the constitution awkwardly reads, "Aos remanescentes das comunidades dos quilombos que estejam ocupando suas terras é reconhecida a propriedade definitiva, devendo o Estado emitir-lhes os títulos respetivos." Federal Consti-

tution of Brazil, 1988, accessed on Georgetown University's Public Database of the Americas, http://pdba.georgetown.edu/Constitutions/Brazil/brazil05.html #mozTocId178055.

52 An excellent, locally grounded analysis of this process can be found in Jan Hoffman French, *Legalizing Identities: Becoming Black or Indian in Brazil's Northeast* (Chapel Hill: University of North Carolina Press, 2009).

53 Vicente Salles, *A defesa pessoal: A capoeira no Pará*, pamphlet accessed in the Arquivo Público do Estado do Pará. For an excellent trans-Atlantic history of capoeira detailing its origins in southern Angola and its evolution in Brazil, see Obi, *Fighting for Honor*.

54 For a history of the uses and values attached to dendê, see Livio Sansone, "Os objetos da identidade negra: Consumo, mercantilização, globalização e a criação de culturas negras no Brasil," *Mana* 6 (2000): 87–119. According to Matory, "An indirect way of identifying a Candomblé member is to say that he or she is 'in the [red palm] oil [*no azeite*].'" Recall that red palm oil was an important item in the trans-Atlantic trade linking Bahia and Nigeria in the 1930s. Matory, *Black Atlantic Religion*, 336n15.

55 As of early 2010, for example, residents of Bacabal no longer had access to the community's graveyard, as cattle ranchers had occupied and fenced off the area.

Conclusion

1 Dog Murras, "Angola Bwé das Carras." Dog Murras's song, which describes the ways in which people of all nationalities save Angolan benefit from Angola's resources, created tremendous national controversy upon release, including being banned from play on the national radio and censure from the president's daughter in an article whose claims of national unity were clumsy, at best. For a discussion, see Krug, "Strange Life of Lusotropicalism."

2 Khadija Sharife, "Leaks Reveal Extensive Siphoning of $5bn Angolan Sovereign Wealth Fund," last accessed April 16, 2018, https://panamapapers.investigativecenters .org/angola/; Norimitsu Onishi, "Angola's 'Omnipresent' Leader Won't Run Again. But Will He Relinquish Power?," *New York Times*, May 20, 2017.

3 Consulta do Conselho Ultramarino, "Exame das cartas do Governador de Angola acerca do estado da Provincia, guerra da Quiçama e do Congo," July 13, 1655, in Brásio, *MMA*, 11:498–99; Cavazzi, *Descrição histórica*, 1:22; Nicolau Abreu de Castelo Branco, September 4, 1824, Ofícios para o reino, caixa 11, n. 14, f. 19, AHNA.

4 For early seventeenth-century Ndongo, see Thornton, "Legitimacy and Political Power," 29.

5 Cadornega, *História geral das guerras angolanas*, 2:381.

6 Saidiya V. Hartman, *Lose Your Mother: A Journey along the Atlantic Slave Route* (New York: Farrar, Straus and Giroux, 2007), 234.

BIBLIOGRAPHY

Abrahamsen, Rita. "African Studies and the Postcolonial Challenge." *African Affairs* 102, no. 407 (April 1, 2003): 189–210.

Ahmad, Aijaz. "The Politics of Literary Postcoloniality." *Race & Class* 36, no. 3 (January 1, 1995): 1–20.

Albuquerque Felner, Alfredo de. *Angola: Apontamentos sôbre a ocupace início do estabelecimento dos portugueses no Congo, Angola e Benguela: Extraídos de documentos históricos.* Coimbra: Imprensa da Universidade, 1933.

Alencastro, Luiz Felipe de. *O trato dos viventes: Formaçaõ do Brasil no Atlântico Sul.* São Paulo: Companhia das Letras, 2000.

Anderson, Benedict. *Imagined Communities: Reflections on the Origin and Spread of Nationalism.* Rev. ed. London: Verso, 1998.

Anderson, Robert Nelson. "The Quilombo of Palmares: A New Overview of a Maroon State in Seventeenth-Century Brazil." *Journal of Latin American Studies* 28, no. 3 (1996): 545–66.

Arrazola, Roberto. *Palenque: Primer pueblo libre de América.* Cartagena: Ediciones Hernández, 1970.

Attwell, David. *Rewriting Modernity: Studies in Black South African Literary History.* Athens: Ohio University Press, 2006.

Barbosa, Adriano C. *Dicionário cokwe-português.* Coimbra: Universidade de Coimbra, 1989.

Bastos, João Pereira. *Angola e Brasil, duas terras lusíadas do Atlântico.* Lourenço Marques: Tipografia Minerva, 1964.

Battell, Andrew. *The Strange Adventures of Andrew Battell of Leigh, in Angola and the Adjoining Regions.* London: The Hakluyt Society, 1901 [1625].

Berman, Bruce, and John Lonsdale. *Unhappy Valley: Conflict in Kenya and Africa.* 2 vols. Athens: Ohio University Press, 1992.

Bhabha, Homi K., ed. *Nation and Narration.* London: Routledge, 1990.

Bilby, Kenneth. *True-Born Maroons.* Gainesville: University Press of Florida, 2005.

Borrego Plá, María del Carmen. *Cartagena de Indias en el siglo XVI.* Seville: Escuela de Estudios Hispano-Americanos, Consejo Superior de Investigaciones Científicas, 1983.

Brandão, Alfredo. *Viçosa de Alagoas: O municipio e a cidade (notas historicas, geographicas, e archeologicas).* Recife: Imprensa Industrial, 1914.

Brandão, Paes. "Diário da marcha do chefe do Concelho de Libolo, tenente Paes Brandão, a região de Quibala." *Portugal em Africa* 11, no. 123 (1904): 137–41.

Brásio, Antonio, ed. *Monumenta Missionaria Africana: África Occidental.* 10 vols. Lisbon: Agência Geral do Ultramar Divisão de Publicações e Biblioteca, 1962.

Bromlei, Yulián Vladimirovich. *Etnografía teórica.* Moscow: Editorial Nauka, 1986.

Brown, Vincent. *The Reaper's Garden: Death and Power in the World of Atlantic Slavery.* Cambridge, MA: Harvard University Press, 2008.

Brown, Vincent. "Social Death and Political Life in the Study of Slavery." *American Historical Review* 24, no. 5 (2009): 1231–49.

Cadornega, António de Oliveira de. *História geral das guerras angolanas.* 3 vols. Lisbon: Agência Geral do Ultramar, 1972 [1680].

Candido, Mariana. *An African Slaving Port and the Atlantic World: Benguela and Its Hinterland.* New York: Cambridge University Press, 2013.

Candido, Mariana. "Enslaving Frontiers: Slavery, Trade and Identity in Benguela, 1780–1850." Toronto: York University, 2006.

Candido, Mariana. "Jagas e sobas no 'Reino de Benguela': Vassalagem e criação de novas categorias políticas e sociais no contexto da expansão portuguesa na África durante os séculos XVI e XVII." In *África: Histórias Conectadas,* edited by Alexandre Vieira Ribeiro, Alexsander de Almeida Gebara, and Marina Berthet, 41–77. Niterói: Programa de Pós-graduação em História da Universidade Federal Fluminense, 2015.

Candido, Mariana. "Merchants and the Business of the Slave Trade at Benguela, 1750–1850." *African Economic History,* no. 35 (2007): 1–30.

Cannecatim, Bernardo Maria de. *Colleccaõ de observacaõs grammaticas sobre a lingua Bunda ou Angolense e diccionario abreviado da lingua Congueza (aque acresce uma quarta columna que contém os termos da lingua Bunda identicos ou similhantes à lingua Congueza).* Lisbon: Imprensa Nacional, 1859.

Cannecatim, Bernardo Maria de. *Diccionario da lingua bunda, ou angolense, explicada na portugueza, e latina.* Lisbon: Impressão Regia, 1804.

Carneiro, Edison. *O quilombo dos Palmares.* 2nd ed. São Paulo: Companhia Editora Nacional, 1958.

"Catalogo dos governadores de Angola." In *Ensaios sobre a statistica das possessoes portuguezas na Africa occidental e oriental, na Asia occidental, na China e na Oceania escriptos de ordem do Governo de S. M. D. Maria II,* edited by José Joaquim Lopès de Lima, 3:88–135. Lisbon: Imprensa Nacional, 1784.

Cavazzi, Giovanni Antonio. *Descrição histórica dos três reinos do Congo, Matamba, e Angola.* 3 vols. Lisbon: Junta de Investigações do Ultramar, 1965 [1665].

Cedulario indiano. Edited by Diego de Encinas and Alfonso García Gallo. Madrid: Ediciones Cultura Hispánica, 1946.

Chakrabarty, Dipesh. *Provincializing Europe: Postcolonial Thought and Historical Difference.* Princeton: Princeton University Press, 2000.

Childs, Greg. "Insanity, the Historian, and the Slave Catcher: 'Capturing' Black Voices." In *Black Perspectives*, African American Intellectual History Society, February 15, 2015.

Cipolla, Carlo M. *Fighting the Plague in Seventeenth-Century Italy.* Madison: University of Wisconsin Press, 1981.

Comaroff, John L., and Jean Comaroff. *Christianity, Of Revelation and Revolution: Colonialism, and Consciousness in South Africa.* Volume 1. Chicago: University of Chicago Press, 1991.

Cooper, Frederick. *Colonialism in Question: Theory, Knowledge, History.* Berkeley: University of California Press, 2005.

Cooper, Frederick. "Conflict and Connection: Rethinking Colonial African History." *American Historical Review* 99, no. 5 (1994): 1516–45.

Corrado, Jacopo. *The Creole Elite and the Rise of Angolan Protonationalism, 1870–1920.* Amherst, NY: Cambria Press, 2008.

Costa, Emilia Viotti da. "The Portuguese-African Slave Trade: A Lesson in Colonialism." *Latin American Perspectives* 12 (1985): 41–61.

Couto, Antonio do, and Francisco Paccónio. *Gentilis Angollae fidei mysteriis.* Rome: Congregatio de Propaganda Fide, 1661.

Crais, Clifton, and Pamela Scully. *Sara Baartman and the Hottentot Venus: A Ghost Story and a Biography.* Reprint, Princeton, NJ: Princeton University Press, 2010.

Curto, José C. *Enslaving Spirits: The Portuguese-Brazilian Alcohol Trade at Luanda and Its Hinterland, c. 1550–1830.* Boston: Brill, 2004.

Dallas, Robert Charles. *The History of the Maroons: From Their Origin to the Establishment of Their Chief Tribe at Sierra Leone.* 2 vols. New York: Cambridge University Press, 2010.

Dapper, Olfert. *Description de L'Afrique . . . avec des cartes and des figures en taille-douce . . . traduite du Flamand [A Translation of "Naukeurige beschrijvinge der Afrikaensche gewesten van Egypten" and "Naukeurige beschrijvinge der Afrikaensche eilanden" by Two Separate Translators].* Amsterdam: Wolfgang, 1686.

Da Silva, Daniel B. Domingues. *The Atlantic Slave Trade from West Central Africa.* New York: Cambridge University Press, 2017.

Da Silva, Daniel B. Domingues. "The Atlantic Slave Trade from Angola: A Port-by-Port Estimate of Slaves Embarked, 1701–1867." *The International Journal of African Historical Studies* 46, no. 1 (2013): 105–22.

Da Silva, Daniel B. Domingues. "The Kimbundu Diaspora to Brazil." *African Diaspora* 8, no. 2 (2015): 200–219.

Dias, Jill R. "Famine and Disease in the History of Angola c. 1830–1930." *Journal of African History* 22 (1981): 349–78.

Documents Concerning English Voyages to the Spanish Main, 1569–1580. Edited by Irene Aloha Wright. London: Hakluyt Society, 1932.

Dog Murras. "Angola Bwé das Carras."

Drndarska, Dea, and Ange-Séverin Malanda. *Pepetela et l'écriture du mythe et de l'histoire*. Paris: Harmattan, 2000.

du Jarric, Pierre. *Histoire des choses plvs memorables advenves tant ez Indes Orientales, que autres païs de la descouuerte des Portugais, en l'establissement et progrez de la foy chrestienne, et catholique: et principalement de ce que les religieux de la Compagnie de Iesvs y ont faict, et enduré pour la mesme fin; depuis qu'ils y sont entrez jusques à l'an 1600*. 3 vols. Vol. 2, Bordeaux: S. Milanges, 1614.

Eltis, David. *Atlas of the Transatlantic Slave Trade*. Edited by David Richardson. New Haven, CT: Yale University Press, 2010.

Ennes, Ernesto. *As guerras nos Palmares (subsidios para a sua história)*. São Paulo: Companhia Editora Nacional, 1938.

Ennes, Ernesto. *Os Palmares: Subsídios para a sua história*. Lisbon: Arquivo Histórico Ultramarino, 1937.

Eppinger, Mark, Patricia L. Worsham, Mikeljon P. Nikolich, David R. Riley, Yinong Sebastian, Sherry Mou, Mark Achtman, Luther E. Lindler, and Jacques Ravel. "Genome Sequence of the Deep-Rooted *Yersinia pestis* Strain Angola Reveals New Insights into the Evolution and Pangenome of the Plague Bacterium." *Journal of Bacteriology* 192, no. 6 (March 15, 2010): 1685–99.

Fabian, Johannes. *Remembering the Present: Painting and Popular History in Zaire*. Berkeley: University of California Press, 1996.

Fabian, Johannes, and Matti Bunzl. *Time and the Other: How Anthropology Makes Its Object*. New York: Columbia University Press, 2002.

Feierman, Steven. "Change in African Therapeutic Systems." *Social Science and Medicine* 13, no. 4 (1979): 277–84.

Feierman, Steven. *Peasant Intellectuals: Anthropology and History in Tanzania*. Madison: University of Wisconsin Press, 1990.

Ferreira, Aurora da Fonseca. *A Kisama em Angola do século XVI ao início do século XX: Autonomia, ocupação e resistência*. Luanda: Kilombelombe, 2012.

Ferreira, Aurora da Fonseca. "La Kisama (en Angola) du XVIe au début du XXe siècle." PhD diss., École des hautes études en sciences sociales, 2000.

Ferreira, Roquinaldo. "Atlantic Microhistories: Mobility, Personal Ties, and Slaving in the Black Atlantic World (Angola and Brazil)." In *Cultures of the Lusophone Black Atlantic*, edited by Nancy Priscilla Naro, Dave Treece, and Roger Sansi-Roca, 99–128. New York: Palgrave Macmillan, 2007.

Ferreira, Roquinaldo. *Atlantic Microhistory: Slaving, Transatlantic Networks, and Cultural Exchange in Angola (ca. 1700–ca. 1830)*. New York: Cambridge University Press, 2011.

Ferreira, Roquinaldo. *Cross-Cultural Exchange in the Atlantic World: Angola and Brazil during the Era of the Slave Trade*. New York: Cambridge University Press, 2012.

Ferreira, Roquinaldo. "Dos sertões ao Atlântico: Tráfico ilegal de escravos e comércio lícito em Angola, 1830–1860." Master's thesis, Universidade Federal do Rio de Janeiro, 1996.

Ferreira, Roquinaldo. "Slave Flights and Runaway Communities in Angola (17th–19th Centuries)." *Revista Anos 90* 21, no. 40 (2015): 65–90.

Ferreira, Roquinaldo. "The Supply and Development of Horses in Angolan Warfare (17th and 18th Centuries)." In *Angola on the Move: Transport Routes, Communications, and History*, edited by Beatrix Heintze and Achim Von Oppen, 41–51.. Frankfurt: Lembeck, 2008.

Ferrer, Ada. *Insurgent Cuba: Race, Nation, and Revolution, 1868–1898*. Chapel Hill: University of North Carolina Press, 1999.

Figueiredo, João de Castro Maia Veiga. "Feitiçaria na Angola oitocentista: Razões por detrás de uma suposta maior tolerância administrativa face a crenças locais." *Revista de Humanidades* 11, no. 29 (2011): 21–51.

Finch, Aisha K. *Rethinking Slave Rebellion in Cuba: La Escalera and the Insurgencies of 1841–1844*. Chapel Hill: University of North Carolina Press, 2015.

Fonseca, João Severiano da. *Origem de alguns nomes patronímicos da provincia das Alagoas*. Maceió: Revista do IAGA, 1876.

Fonseca, João Severiano da. *Viagem ao redor do Brasil, 1875–1878*. Rio de Janeiro: Typ. de Pinheiro, 1880.

Freitas, Décio. *Palmares: A guerra dos escravos*. Porto Alegre: Editora Movimento, 1973.

Freitas, Décio. *República de Palmares: Pesquisa e comentários em documentos históricos do século XVII*. Maceió: Edufal: Ideário Comunicação e Cultura, 2004.

French, Jan Hoffman. *Legalizing Identities: Becoming Black or Indian in Brazil's Northeast*. Chapel Hill: University of North Carolina Press, 2009.

Freudenthal, Aida, and Selma Pantoja. *Livro dos baculamentos: Que os sobas deste reino de Angola pagam a sua majestade, 1630*. Luanda: Arquivo Nacional de Angola, Ministério da Cultura, 2013.

Freyre, Gilberto. *Casa grande and senzala: Formação de familia brasileira sob o regimen de economia patriarchal*. Rio de Janeiro: Maia and Schmidt, 1933.

Fuentes, Marisa J. *Dispossessed Lives: Enslaved Women, Violence, and the Archive*. Philadelphia: University of Pennsylvania Press, 2016.

Funari, Pedro Paulo A., Stanley A. South, J. Silveira Mario, and Facundo Gómez Romero. *The Archaeology of Palmares and Its Contribution to the Understanding of the History of African-America Culture*. Columbia: South Carolina Institute of Archaeology and Anthropology, 1995.

Funari, Pedro Paulo, and Aline Vieira de Carvalho. *Palmares, ontem e hoje*. Rio de Janeiro: Zahar, 2005.

Geschiere, Peter. *The Modernity of Witchcraft: Politics and the Occult in Postcolonial Africa*. Charlottesville: University Press of Virginia, 1997.

Gomes, Flávio dos Santos. "Apresentação: Palmares, historiografia e fontes." In *Mo-cambos de Palmares: Histórias e fontes (séculos XVI–XIX)*, edited by Flávio dos Santos Gomes, 119–30. Rio de Janeiro: 7Letras, 2010.

Gomes, Flávio dos Santos. *De olho em Zumbi dos Palmares: Histórias, símbolos e memória social.* São Paulo: Claro Enigma, 2011.

Gomes, Flávio dos Santos. *Mocambos de Palmares: Histórias e fontes (séculos XVI–XIX).* Rio de Janeiro: 7Letras, 2010.

Gomes, Flávio dos Santos. *Palmares: Escravidão e liberdade no Atlântico Sul.* São Paulo: Contexto, 2005.

Gómez, Pablo F. *The Experiential Caribbean: Creating Knowledge and Healing in the Early Modern Atlantic.* Chapel Hill: University of North Carolina Press, 2017.

Green, Toby. *The Rise of the Trans-Atlantic Slave Trade in Western Africa, 1300–1589.* New York: Cambridge University Press, 2014.

Hair, Paul E. H. "Milho, Meixoeira and Other Foodstuffs of the Sofala Garrison, 1505–1525 (Milho, meixoeira et autres aliments de la garnison de Sofala, 1505–1525)." *Cahiers d'études africaines* 17, no. 66/67 (1977): 353–63.

Hartman, Saidiya V. *Lose Your Mother: A Journey along the Atlantic Slave Route.* New York: Farrar, Straus and Giroux, 2007.

Hartman, Saidiya. "Venus in Two Acts." *Small Axe* 12, no. 2 (2008): 1–14.

Hawthorne, Walter. *Planting Rice and Harvesting Slaves: Transformations along the Guinea-Bissau Coast, 1400–1900.* Portsmouth, NH: Heinemann, 2003.

Heintze, Beatrix. "The Angolan Vassal Tributes of the 17th Century." *Revista de História Económica e Social* 6 (1980): 57–78.

Heintze, Beatrix. *Asilo ameaçado: Oportunidades e consequências da fuga de escravos em Angola no século XVII.* Luanda: Museu Nacional da Escravatura, 1995.

Heintze, Beatrix. "Beiträge zur Geschichte und Kultur der Kisama (Angola)." *Paideuma* 16 (1970): 159–86.

Heintze, Beatrix. "The Extraordinary Journey of the Jaga through the Centuries: Critical Approaches to Precolonial Angolan Historical Sources." *History in Africa* 34 (2007): 67–101.

Heintze, Beatrix, ed. *Fontes para a história de Angola do século XVII.* 2 vols. Stuttgart: Franz Steiner Verlag Wiesbaden, 1988.

Heintze, Beatrix. "Historical Notes on the Kisama of Angola." *Journal of African History* 13, no. 3 (1972): 407–18.

Heywood, Linda M. *Njinga of Angola: Africa's Warrior Queen.* Cambridge, MA: Harvard University Press, 2017.

Heywood, Linda M. "Slavery and Its Transformations in the Kingdom of Kongo: 1491–1800." *Journal of African History* 50 (2009): 1–22.

Heywood, Linda M. "Towards an Understanding of Modern Political Ideology in Africa: The Case of the Ovimbundu of Angola." *Journal of Modern African Studies* 36, no. 1 (1998): 139–67.

Heywood, Linda, and John Thornton. *Central Africans, Atlantic Creoles, and the Making of the Foundation of the Americas, 1585–1660*. New York: Cambridge University Press, 2007.

História de Angola. Porto: Afrontamento, 1965.

Horton, A. E. *A Dictionary of Luvale*. El Monte, CA: Lithographed by Rahn Bros. 1953.

Hunt, Nancy Rose. "An Acoustic Register, Tenacious Images, and Congolese Scenes of Rape and Repetition." *Cultural Anthropology* 23, no. 2 (2008): 220–53.

Indios y negros en Panamá en los siglos XVI y XVII: Selecciones de los documentos del Archivo General de Indias. Edited by Carol F. Jopling. South Woodstock, VT: Plumsock Mesoamerican Studies, 1994.

Jadin, Louis. *L'ancien Congo et l'Angola, 1639–1655: D'après les archives romaines, portugaises, néerlandaises et espagnoles*. 3 vols. Brussels: Institut Historique Belge de Rome, 1975.

Janzen, John. *Lemba, 1650–1930: A Drum of Affliction in Africa and the New World*. New York: Garland, 1982.

Janzen, John, and Steven Feierman. *The Social Basis of Health and Healing in Africa*. Berkeley: University of California Press, 1992.

Jones, Adam. "Decompiling Dapper: A Preliminary Search for Evidence." *History in Africa* 17 (1990): 171–209.

Jordão, Levy Maria. *História do Congo: Obra posthuma do Visconde de Paiva Manso, socio effectivo da Academia real das sciencias de Lisboa*. Lisbon: Academia Real das Sciencias, 1877.

Kent, R. K. "Palmares: An African State in Brazil." *Journal of African History* 6, no. 2 (1965): 161–75.

Kodesh, Neil. *Beyond the Royal Gaze: Clanship and Public Healing in Buganda*. Charlottesville: University of Virginia Press, 2010.

Kodesh, Neil. "History from the Healer's Shrine: Genre, Historical Imagination, and Early Ganda History." *Comparative Studies in Society and History* 49, no. 3 (2007): 527–52.

Krug, Jessica. "'Amadou Diallo, Reggae Music Knows Your Name': Popular Music, Historical Memory, and Black Identity in New York City in the Wake of Amadou Diallo's Murder." In *Remembering Africa: Memory, Public History, and Representations of the Past: Africa and Its Diasporas*, edited by Audra Diptee and David Vincent Trotman, 291–308. Trenton, NJ: Africa World Press, 2012.

Krug, Jessica. "Social Dismemberment, Social (Re)membering: Obeah Idioms, Kromanti Identities and the Trans-Atlantic Politics of Memory, c. 1675–Present." *Slavery & Abolition* 35, no. 4 (2014): 537–58.

Krug, Jessica. "The Strange Life of Lusotropicalism in Luanda: On Race, Nationality, Gender, and Sexuality in Angola." In *Black Subjects in Africa and Its Diasporas: Race and Gender in Research and Writing*, edited by Benjamin Talton and Quincy T. Mills, 109–27. New York: Palgrave Macmillan US, 2011.

Lacerda, Paulo Martins Pinheiro de. "Notícias das regiões e povos de Quisama e do Mussulo, 1798." *Annaes Marítimos e Coloniaes* 6, no. 4 (1846): 119–33.

Landers, Jane. "Leadership and Authority in Maroon Settlements in Spanish America and Brazil." In *Africa and the Americas: Interconnections during the Slave Trade*, edited by José Curto and Renée Soulodre-La France, 173–84. Trenton, NJ: Africa World Press, 2005.

Lane, Kris E. *Pillaging the Empire: Piracy in the Americas, 1500–1750*. Armonk, NY: M. E. Sharpe, 1998.

Lara, Sílvia Hunold. "Como fé, lei, e rei: Um sobado africano em Pernambuco no século XVII." In *Mocambos de Palmares: Histórias e fontes (séculos XVI–XIX)*, edited by Flávio dos Santos Gomes, 106–29. Rio de Janeiro: 7Letras, 2010.

Lara, Sílvia Hunold. "Marronnage et pouvoir colonial: Palmares, Cucaú et les frontières de la liberté au Pernambouc à la fin du XVIIe siècle." *Annales: Histoire, Sciences Sociales* 62, no. 3 (2007): 639–62.

Lara, Sílvia Hunold. "Palmares and Cucaú: Political Dimensions of a Maroon Community in Late Seventeenth-Century Brazil." *12th Annual Gilda Lehrman International Conference*. New Haven, CT: Yale University, 2010.

Law, Robin. *Ouidah: The Social History of a West African Slaving "Port," 1727–1892*. Athens: Ohio University Press, 2004.

Lawrance, Benjamin N. *Amistad's Orphans: An Atlantic Story of Children, Slavery, and Smuggling*. New Haven, CT: Yale University Press, 2014.

Lima de Sousa, Maria Fátima, Vatomene Kukanda, and Joane Lima Santiago. "A posição lexical do Songo dentro do Gruop H20 (Kimbundu *strictu sensu*, Sama, Bolo, e Songo)." *Papia* 21, no. 2 (2011): 303–14.

Livingstone, David. *Missionary Travels and Researches in South Africa: Including a Sketch of Sixteen Years' Residence in the Interior of Africa*. New York: Harper and Brothers, 1858.

Lofkrantz, Jennifer. "Protecting Freeborn Muslims: The Sokoto Caliphate's Attempts to Prevent Illegal Enslavement and Its Acceptance of the Strategy of Ransoming." *Slavery and Abolition* 32, no. 1 (2011): 109–27.

Lopes, Nei. *Enciclopédia brasileira da diáspora africana*. São Paulo: Selo Negro Edições, 2004.

Lopès de Lima, José Joaquim. *Ensaios sobre a statistica das possessoes portuguezas na Africa occidental e oriental, na Asia occidental, na China, e na Oceania escriptos de ordem do governo de S. M. D. Maria II*. 3 vols. Vol. 3, Lisbon: Imprensa Nacional, 1844.

Macgaffey, Wyatt. "Changing Representations in Central African History." *Journal of African History* 46, no. 2 (2005): 189–207.

Macgaffey, Wyatt. "Dialogues of the Deaf: Europeans on the Atlantic Coast of Africa." In *Implicit Understandings: Observing, Reporting, and Reflecting on the Encounters between Europeans and Other Peoples in the Early Modern Era*, edited by Stuart Schwartz, 249–67. New York: Cambridge University Press, 1994.

Macgaffey, Wyatt. *Kongo Political Culture: The Conceptual Challenge of the Particular.* Bloomington: Indiana University Press, 2000.

Maia, António da Silva. *Dicionário complementar: Português-Kimbundu-Kikongo.* Cucujães: Tipografia das Missões, 1961.

Maisch, John M. "On Some Panama Drugs." *American Journal of Pharmacy* 61, no. 18 (1869): 230–38.

Maldonado, Miguel Ayres, and Jozé de Castilho Pinto Pinto. "Descripção que faz o Capitão Miguel Ayres Maldonado e o Capitão Jozé de Castilho Pinto e seus compaheiros dos trabalhos e fadigas das suas vidas, que tiveram nas conquistas da capitania do Rio de Janeiro e São Vicente, com a gentilidade e com os piratas n'esta costa." *Revista Trimensal do Instituo Histórico e Geographico Brazileiro* 56 (1893): 345–400.

Manso, João Albino Alves. *Dicionário etimológico Bundo-Português: Ilustrado com muitos milhares de exemplos, entre os quais 2.000 provérbios indígenas.* Lisbon: Tipografia Silvas, 1951.

Matory, James Lorand. *Black Atlantic Religion: Tradition, Transnationalism, and Matriarchy in the Afro-Brazilian Candomblé.* Princeton, NJ: Princeton University Press, 2005.

Matory, James Lorand. *Sex and the Empire That Is No More: Gender and the Politics of Metaphor in Oyo Yoruba Religion.* Minneapolis: University of Minnesota Press, 1994.

May Restrepo, Luz Adriana. "Botanica y medicina africanas en la Nueva Granada, siglo XVII." *Historia crítica* 19 (2000): 27–47.

McCann, James. *Maize and Grace: Africa's Encounter with a New World Crop, 1500–2000.* Cambridge, MA: Harvard University Press, 2005.

McKnight, Kathryn. "Confronted Rituals: Spanish Colonial and Angolan 'Maroon' Executions in Cartagena de Indias (1634)." *Journal of Colonialism and Colonial History* 5 (2004): 1–23.

McKnight, Kathryn, and Leo Garofalo. *Afro-Latino Voices: Narratives from the Early Modern Ibero-Atlantic World, 1550–1812.* Indianapolis: Hackett, 2009.

Métraux, Alfred. "The Concept of Soul in Haitian Vodu." *Southwestern Journal of Anthropology* 2, no. 1 (1946): 84–92.

Miller, Joseph. "The Imbangala and the Chronology of Early Central African History." *Journal of African History* 13 (1972): 549–74.

Miller, Joseph. "Imbangala Lineage Slavery." In *Slavery in Africa: Historical and Anthropological Perspectives*, edited by Suzanne Miers and Igor Kopytoff, 205–33. Madison: University of Wisconsin Press, 1977.

Miller, Joseph. *Kings and Kinsmen: Early Mbundu States in Angola.* Oxford: Clarendon Press, 1976.

Miller, Joseph. "Kings, Lists, and History in Kasanje." *History in Africa* 6 (1979): 51–96.

Miller, Joseph. "A Note on Kasanze and the Portuguese." *Canadian Journal of African Studies / Revue canadienne des études africaines* 6, no. 1 (1972): 43–56.

Miller, Joseph. "Requiem for the 'Jaga.'" *Cahiers d'Études africaines* 13 (1973): 121–49.

Miller, Joseph. "The Significance of Drought, Disease and Famine in the Agricul-turally Marginal Zones of West-Central Africa." *Journal of African History* 23 (1982): 17–61.

Miller, Joseph. *Way of Death: Merchant Capitalism and the Angolan Slave Trade, 1730–1830.* Madison: University of Wisconsin Press, 1988.

Mintz, Sidney, and Richard Price. *An Anthropological Approach to the Afro-American Past: A Caribbean Perspective.* Philadelphia: Institute for the Study of Human Issues, 1976.

Monteiro, J. J. *Angola and the River Congo.* 2 vols. London: Cass, 1968 [1875].

Monteiro, J. J. "On the Quissama Tribe of Angola." *Journal of the Anthropological Institute of Great Britain and Ireland* 5 (1876): 198–201.

Moura, Clóvis. *Quilombos, resistência ao escravismo.* São Paulo: Editora Atica, 1987.

Moutinho, Jessita Maria Nogueira. "A paulistanidade revista: Algumas reflexões sobre um discurso político." *Tempo Social* 3, no. 1–2 (1991): 109–17.

Nas. *Illmatic.* New York: Columbia Records, 1994.

Navarrete, María Cristina. "Cimarrones y palenques en las provincias al norte del Nuevo Reino de Grenada, siglo XVII." *Fronteras de la historia* 6 (2001): 97–122.

Nwokeji, G. Ugo. *The Slave Trade and Culture in the Bight of Biafra: An African Society in the Atlantic World.* New York: Cambridge University Press, 2010.

Obi, T. J. Desch. *Fighting for Honor: The History of African Martial Art Traditions in the Atlantic World.* Columbia: University of South Carolina Press, 2008.

Obi, T. J. Desch. "The Jogo de Capoeira and the Fallacy of 'Creole' Cultural Forms." *African and Black Diaspora: An International Journal* 5, no. 2 (2012): 211–28.

Obi, T. J. Desch. "'Koup Tet': A Machete-Wielding View of the Haitian Revolu-tion." In *Activating the Past: History and Memory in the Black Atlantic World*, edited by Andrew Apter and Lauren Derby, 245–66. Newcastle upon Tyne, UK: Cambridge Scholars, 2010.

Oliva Melgar, José María, and Carlos Martínez Shaw. *Sistema atlántico español: Siglos XVII–XIX.* Madrid: Marcial Pons, Ediciones de Historia, 2005.

Oliveira, Vanessa S. "The Gendered Dimension of Trade: Female Traders in Nineteenth-Century Luanda." *Portuguese Studies Review* 23, no. 2 (2015): 93–121.

One9. *Time Is Illmatic*, 2014.

Onishi, Norimitsu. "Angola's "Omnipresent' Leader Won't Run Again. But Will He Relinquish Power?" *New York Times*, May 20, 2017.

Oppen, Achim von, and Beatrix Heintze, eds. *Angola on the Move: Transport Routes, Communications, and History.* Frankfurt am Main: Lembeck, 2008.

Palmié, Stephan. *Wizards and Scientists: Explorations in Afro-Cuban Modernity and Tradition.* Durham, NC: Duke University Press, 2002.

Parés, Luis Nicolau. *A formação do candomblé: História e ritual da nação jeje na Bahia.* Campinas, Sao Paulo: Editora Unicamp, 2006.

Parker, David, and Christian Karner. "Reputational Geographies and Urban Social Cohesion." *Ethnic and Racial Studies* 33, no. 8 (2010): 1451–70.

Péclard, Didier. "Religion and Politics in Angola: The Church, the Colonial State and the Emergence of Angolan Nationalism, 1940–1961." *Journal of Religion in Africa* 28, no. 2 (1998): 160–86.

Pepetela. *As aventuras de Ngunga*. Lisbon: Edições 70, 1976.

Péret, Benjamin. *O quilombo de Palmares: Crónica da "república dos escravos," Brasil, 1640–1695*. Lisbon: Fenda Edições, 1988.

Pérez, Jesús Guanche. "Contribución al estudio del poblamiento africano en Cuba." *África: Revista do centro de estudos africanos* 18–19 (1996): 119–38.

Pike, Ruth. "Black Rebels: The Cimarrons of Sixteenth-Century Panama." *Americas* 64, no. 2 (2007): 243–66.

Pike, Ruth. "Sevillian Society in the Sixteenth Century: Slaves and Freedmen." *Hispanic American Historical Review* 47, no. 3 (1967): 344–59.

Police, Gérard. *Quilombos dos Palmares: Lectures sur un marronnage brésilien*. Matoury Cedex, French Guiana: Ibis Rouge, 2003.

Portelli, Alessandro. *The Death of Luigi Trastulli, and Other Stories: Form and Meaning in Oral History*. Albany: State University of New York Press, 2001.

Price, F. G. H. "A Description of the Quissama Tribe." *Journal of the Anthropological Institute of Great Britain and Ireland* 1 (1872): 185–93.

Prins, Gwyn. "But What Was the Disease? The Present State of Health and Healing in African Studies." *Past & Present*, no. 124 (1989): 159–79.

Putnam, Lara. "To Study the Fragments/Whole: Microhistory and the Atlantic World." *Journal of Social History* 39, no. 3 (2006): 615–30.

Ranger, T. O., and Richard P. Werbner. *Postcolonial Identities in Africa*. Atlantic Highlands, NJ: Zed Books, 1996.

Reis, João José. *Domingos Sodré, um sacerdote africano: Escravidão, liberdade, e candomblé na Bahia do século XIX*. São Paulo: Companhia das Letras, 2008.

Reis, João José, and Flávio dos Santos Gomes. *Liberdade por um fio: História dos quilombos no Brasil*. São Paulo, Brazil: Companhia das Letras, 1996.

"Relação das guerras feitas aos Palmares de Pernambuco no tempo do governador dom Pedro de Almeida de 1675 a 1678 (M. S. offerecido pelo Exm. Sr. Conselheiro Drummond)." *Revista do Instituto Histórico e Geográfico Brasileiro* 22 (1859 [1678]): 303–29.

Rodrigues, Nina. *Os africanos no Brasil*. São Paulo: Companhia Editora Nacional, 1932.

Salles, Vicente. *A defesa pessoal: A capoeira no Pará*. Pamphlet accessed in the Arquivo Público do Estado do Pará.

Sanders, William H., and William Edwards Fay. *Vocabulary of the Umbundu Language: Comprising Umbundu-English and English-Umbundu*. Boston: T. Todd, 1885.

Sandoval, Alonso de. *De instauranda aethiopum salute: El mundo de la esclavitud negra en America*. Bogota: Biblioteca de la Presidencia de Colombia, 1956 [1627].

Sansone, Livio. "Os objetos da identidade negra: Consumo, mercantilização, globalização e a criação de culturas negras no Brasil." *Mana* 6 (2000): 87–119.

Scarano, Francisco A. "The Jíbaro Masquerade and the Subaltern Politics of Creole Identity Formation in Puerto Rico, 1745–1823." *American Historical Review* 101, no. 5 (1996): 1398–431.

Schultz, Kara D. "'The Kingdom of Angola Is not Very Far from Here': The South Atlantic Slave Port of Buenos Aires, 1585–1640." *Slavery & Abolition* 36, no. 3 (2015): 424–44.

Scott, David. *Conscripts of Modernity: The Tragedy of Colonial Enlightenment*. Durham, NC: Duke University Press, 2005.

Scott, James C. *The Art of Not Being Governed: An Anarchist History of Upland Southeast Asia*. New Haven, CT: Yale University Press, 2009.

Scott, Rebecca J. *Freedom Papers: An Atlantic Odyssey in the Age of Emancipation*. Edited by Jean M. Hébrard. Cambridge, MA: Harvard University Press, 2012.

Sebestyén, Evá, Jan Vansina, and Manoel Correia Leitão. "Angola's Eastern Hinterland in the 1750s: A Text Edition and Translation of Manoel Correia Leitão's 'Voyage' (1755–1756)." *History in Africa* 26 (1999): 299–364.

Seibert, Gerhard. "Tenreiro, Amador e os Angolares ou a reinvenção da história da Ilha de São Tomé." *Revista de Estudos AntiUtilitaristas e PosColoniais* 2, no. 2 (March 25, 2013): 21–39.

Sharife, Khadija. "Leaks Reveal Extensive Siphoning of $5bn Angolan Sovereign Wealth Fund." Last accessed April 16, 2018. https://panamapapers .investigativecenters.org/angola/.

Shetler, Jan Bender. *Imagining Serengeti: A History of Landscape Memory in Tanzania from Earliest Times to the Present*. Athens: Ohio University Press, 2007.

Shohat, Ella. "Notes on the 'Post-Colonial.'" *Social Text*, no. 31/32 (1992): 99–113.

Sidbury, James, and Jorge Cañizares-Esguerra. "Mapping Ethnogenesis in the Early Modern Atlantic." *William and Mary Quarterly* 68, no. 2 (2011): 181–208.

Soares, Mariza de Carvalho. *Devotos da cor: Identidade étnica, religiosidade e escravidão no Rio de Janeiro, século XVIII*. Rio de Janeiro: Civilização Brasileira, 2000.

Soares, Mariza de Carvalho. "A 'nação' que se tem e a 'terra' de onde se vem: Categorias de inserção social de africanos no Império português, século XVIII." *Estudos Afro-Asiáticos* 26, no. 2 (2004): 303–30.

Spyrou, Maria A., Rezeda I. Tukhbatova, Michal Feldman, Joanna Drath, Sacha Kacki, Julia Beltrán de Heredia, Susanne Arnold, et al. "Historical Y. *pestis* Genomes Reveal the European Black Death as the Source of Ancient and Modern Plague Pandemics." *Cell Host & Microbe* 19, no. 6 (June 8, 2016): 874–81.

Staller, Jared. "Rivalry and Allegory: Reflections on Andrew Battell's Jaga Materials Printed by Samuel Purchas from 1613 to 1625." *History in Africa* 43 (2016): 7–28.

Stoler, Ann Laura. *Along the Archival Grain: Thinking through Colonial Ontologies*. Princeton, NJ: Princeton University Press, 2008.

Sweet, James H. *Domingos Álvares, African Healing, and the Intellectual History of the Atlantic World*. Chapel Hill: University of North Carolina Press, 2011.

Sweet, James H. "Mistaken Identities? Olaudah Equiano, Domingos Álvares, and the Methodological Challenges of Studying the African Diaspora." *American Historical Review* 114, no. 2 (2009): 279–306.

Sweet, James H. "The Quiet Violence of Ethnogenesis." *William and Mary Quarterly* 68, no. 2 (2011): 209–14.

Sweet, James H. *Recreating Africa: Culture, Kinship, and Religion in the African-Portuguese World, 1441–1770*. Chapel Hill: University of North Carolina Press, 2003.

Tardieu, Jean-Pierre. *Cimarrones de Panamá: La forja de una identidad afroamericana en el siglo XVI*. Madrid: Iberoamericana, 2009.

Tate, Greg. *Everything but the Burden: What White People Are Taking from Black Culture*. New York: Broadway Books, 2003.

Taussig, Michael. *Mimesis and Alterity: A Particular History of the Senses*. New York: Routledge, 1993.

Thornton, John. "Angola e as origens de Palmares." In *Mocambos de Palmares: Histórias e fontes (séculos XVI–XIX)*, edited by Flávio dos Santos Gomes. Rio de Janeiro: 7Letras, 2010.

Thornton, John. "The Art of War in Angola, 1575–1680." *Comparative Studies in Society and History* 30 (1988): 360–78.

Thornton, John. "Les Etats de l'Angola et la formation de Palmares (Bresil)." *Annales de'histoire e sciences sociales* 63, no. 4 (2008): 769–98.

Thornton, John. "Legitimacy and Political Power: Queen Njinga, 1624–1663." *Journal of African History* 32 (1991): 25–40.

Thornton, John. "The Origins and Early History of the Kingdom of Kongo, c. 1350–1550." *International Journal of African Historical Studies* 34, no. 1 (2001): 89–120.

Thornton, John. "A Resurrection for the Jaga." *Cahiers d'études africaines* 18 (1978): 223–31.

Trouillot, Michel-Rolph. *Silencing the Past: Power and the Production of History*. Boston: Beacon Press, 1995.

Vansina, Jan. "Ambaca Society and the Slave Trade c. 1760–1845." *Journal of African History* 46, no. 1 (2005): 1–27.

Vansina, Jan. "The Ethnographic Account as a Genre in Central Africa." In *European Sources for Sub-Saharan Africa before 1900: Use and Abuse*, edited by Beatrix Heintze and Adam Jones, 433–44. Stuttgart: Franz Steiner Verlag Wiesbaden, 1987.

Vansina, Jan. "Histoire du manioc en Afrique centrale avant 1850." *Paideuma* 43 (1997): 255–79.

Vansina, Jan. *How Societies Are Born: Governance in West Central Africa before 1600*. Charlottesville: University of Virginia Press, 2004.

Vansina, Jan. *Kingdoms of the Savanna*. Madison: University of Wisconsin Press, 2011.

Vansina, Jan. "More on the Invasions of Kongo and Angola by the Jaga and the Lunda." *Journal of African History* 7 (1966): 421–29.

Vansina, Jan. *Paths in the Rainforests: Toward a History of Political Tradition in Equatorial Africa*. Madison: University of Wisconsin Press, 1990.

Vieira-Martinez, Carolyn. "Building Kimbundu: Language Community Reconsidered in West Central Africa, c. 1500–1750." PhD diss., University of California–Los Angeles, 2006.

Vila Vilar, Enriqueta. "Cimarronaje en Panamá y Cartagena: El costo de una guerrila en el siglo XVII." *Cahiers du monde hispanique et luso-brésilien* 49 (1987): 77–92.

Vila Vilar, Enrique. "The Large-Scale Introduction of Africans into Veracruz and Cartagena." In *Comparative Perspectives on Slavery in New World Plantation Societies*, edited by Vera D. Rubin and Arthur Tuden, 267–80. New York: New York Academy of Sciences, 1977.

Voyages: The Trans-Atlantic Slave Trade Database. www.slavevoyages.org, last accessed April 13, 2018.

Warner-Lewis, Maureen. "African Continuities in the Rastafari Belief System." *Caribbean Quarterly* 39, no. 3–4 (1993): 108–23.

Wheat, David. *Atlantic Africa and the Spanish Caribbean, 1570–1640*. Chapel Hill: Published for the Omohundro Institute of Early American History and Culture, Williamsburg, Virginia, by the University of North Carolina Press, 2016.

Wheat, David. "The First Great Waves: African Provenance Zones for the Transatlantic Slave Trade to Cartagena de Indias, 1570–1640." *Journal of African History* 52, no. 1 (2011): 1–22.

Wheat, David. "Mediterranean Slavery, New World Transformations: Galley Slaves in the Spanish Caribbean, 1578–1635." *Slavery & Abolition* 31, no. 3 (2010): 327–44.

White, Luise. "Hodgepodge Historiography: Documents, Itineraries, and the Absence of Archives." *History in Africa* 42, no. 1: 309–18 (2015): 309–18.

White, Luise. *Speaking with Vampires: Rumor and History in Colonial Africa*. Berkeley: University of California Press, 2009.

Wilmsen, Edwin N., James R. Denbow, M. G. Bicchieri, Lewis R. Binford, Robert Gordon, Mathias Guenther, Richard B. Lee, et al. "Paradigmatic History of San-Speaking Peoples and Current Attempts at Revision (and Comments and Replies)." *Current Anthropology* 31, no. 5 (1990): 489–524.

Wilson-Fall, Wendy. *Memories of Madagascar and Slavery in the Black Atlantic*. Athens: Ohio University Press, 2015.

Witte, Ludo de. *The Assassination of Lumumba*. New York: Verso, 2001.

Wolf, Eric R. *Europe and the People without History*. Berkeley: University of California Press, 1983.

Young, Jason. *Rituals of Resistance: African Atlantic Religion in Kongo and the Low-country South in the Era of Slavery.* Baton Rouge: Louisiana State University Press, 2007.

Zimmerman, Andrew. "Guinea Sam Nightingale and Magic Marx: Conjure and Communism in Civil War Missouri." Forthcoming.

INDEX